Management Scholarship and Organisational Change

T0362333

Change is a crucial and inescapable process for many organisations. It remains a constant challenge for managers and many change management initiatives fail. Burns and Stalker's seminal text on managing change, *The Management of Innovation*, has often been used as a basis for research in mainstream management journals and has been represented as an important theory in popular and long-established management text-books. The issues raised in that book are still being grappled with by academics and practitioners today.

Miriam Green provides a critical analysis of the mainstream construction of knowledge on change management through an examination of representations of that text. The main thesis of her book is that this literature, though valuable, does not provide a full picture. Its objectivist approach ignores the role of other factors raised in the original study. These factors include the effects of power, politics, resistance and employee influence on the outcomes of managerial change strategies and on other organisational processes, with important consequences for the understanding of change initiatives by both academics and practitioners. This is part of an ongoing debate in management studies and more widely in the social sciences about theoretical approaches and research methods.

The originality of this book lies in its in-depth comparison of an entire monograph on organisations facing technological and commercial change, with an equally in-depth analysis of the ways this work has been represented and used as a basis for teaching and research. It highlights the limitations of the exclusive use of one approach to explain the complications arising from organisational change. It challenges the scientific justification offered for that approach and supports arguments for more inclusive and sustainable scholarship, of greater relevance to academics, managers and other organisational stakeholders.

Miriam Green was for many years a Senior Lecturer at London Metropolitan University and is currently teaching at Icon College of Technology and Management. She completed a PhD in Organisation Studies, on which this book is based, and has also written journal articles and book chapters in this field. Her current research interests include critiques of neo-liberalism and postmodernism.

Finance, Governance and Sustainability: Challenges to Theory and Practice Series

Series Editor:
Professor Güler Aras, Yildiz Technical University, Turkey;
Georgetown University, Washington DC, USA

Focusing on the studies of academicians, researchers, entrepreneurs, policy makers and government officers, this international series aims to contribute to the progress in matters of finance, good governance and sustainability. These multidisciplinary books combine strong conceptual analysis with a wide range of empirical data and a wealth of case materials. They will be of interest to those working in a multitude of fields, across finance, governance, corporate behaviour, regulations, ethics and sustainability.

Cosmopolitan Business Ethics
Towards a Global Ethos of Management
Jacob Dahl Rendtorff

Sustainability Accounting and Integrated Reporting
Edited by Charl de Villiers and Warren Maroun

Women on Corporate Boards
An International Perspective
Edited by Maria Aluchna and Güler Aras

Stakeholder Engagement and Sustainability Reporting
Marco Bellucci and Giacomo Manetti

Management Scholarship and Organisational Change
Representing Burns and Stalker
Miriam Green

For more information about this series, please visit www.routledge.com/ Finance-Governance-and-Sustainability/book-series/FINGOVSUST

Management Scholarship and Organisational Change

Representing Burns and Stalker

Miriam Green

Routledge
Taylor & Francis Group

LONDON AND NEW YORK

First published 2019 by Routledge

2 Park Square, Milton Park, Abingdon, Oxfordshire OX14 4RN
52 Vanderbilt Avenue, New York, NY 10017

Routledge is an imprint of the Taylor & Francis Group, an informa business

First issued in paperback 2020

British Library Cataloguing-in-Publication Data
A catalogue record for this book is available from the British Library

Library of Congress Cataloging-in-Publication Data
Names: Green, Miriam, author.
Title: Management scholarship and organisational change : representing Burns and Stalker / Miriam Green.
Description: Abingdon, Oxon ; New York, NY : Routledge, 2019. | Series: Finance, governance and sustainability: challenges to theory and practice series
Subjects: LCSH: Organizational change–Study and teaching (Higher) | Management–Study and teaching (Higher) | Burns, Tom, 1913- Management of innovation.
Classification: LCC HD58.8 .G7243 2019 | DDC 658.4/063–dc23
LC record available at https://lccn.loc.gov/2018041736

ISBN: 978-1-138-69838-3 (hbk)
ISBN: 978-0-367-66263-9 (pbk)

Typeset in Bembo
by Integra Software Services Pvt. Ltd.

To Vic, Liz, Cat, Simon and Ben

Contents

Foreword

It is a sad fact that as we age we have a tendency to forget things and as time passes our memories of things can tend to become distorted. It is for this reason that we have a tendency to excuse ourselves for memory lapses and blame it on old age – a reason, or excuse, which is accepted by everyone. In actual fact events happen and their memories are built into our memory through integration with those memories which are already there. It is for this reason that we can all have different memories of the same event which we all experienced, as our previous experiences and memories cause differing parts of the common experience to be highlighted and integrated with our existing memories. Of course there is also the existence of false memories which are about the recollection of events which have never actually happened. Each one of us has experienced all of these as it is just a part of everyday life which we must accept.

In a separate context, we are all familiar with the arguments of Roland Barthes in his "Death of the Author" paper of 1967 that the reputation of the author is irrelevant to what is being argued. In a similar vein Derrida has argued that once something has been written, the intentions of the author become irrelevant and it is only the interpretations extracted by the reader which have any importance. And similarly we have all had the experience of something which we have said or written being misinterpreted by the listener or reader. Or rather they have interpreted our words within their own context and experiences.

Bearing all this in mind it is perhaps surprising that we ever agree upon anything, but it is generally accepted that we share a common body of knowledge and understanding. Indeed social life would be very difficult without this. Indeed life would be virtually impossible without this shared understanding as would the existence of knowledge which we can impart to our students through our teaching and writing and to our peers through our research and writing. Indeed, the need to fit our work within the existing canon is paramount, and even the post-structuralists do not really argue otherwise. This is symptomised in the difficulty of a new paradigm becoming recognised and accepted. Consider for example the difficulties and ridicule which James Lovelock experienced when he first proposed his Gaia hypothesis. Similarly, once a new paradigm has been accepted, it becomes universal and almost unchallengeable – at least until the next new paradigm comes along, gets ridiculed and eventually accepted. All this of course is expounded by Kuhn.

It is generally accepted within the discourse of teaching in higher education that modern learning theory is founded in the student-centred learning paradigm initiated by Carl Rogers (1951), and that the teaching strategies used in higher education are based upon this paradigm. It has been argued however that there is an unquestioning acceptance within this discourse that the subject matters being taught are appropriate for the needs of students. Consequently, the only topic for debate within the discourse are the mechanisms for transferring the knowledge contained within these subjects from the holders of that knowledge (the academics in higher education) to the persons desirous of receiving that knowledge (the students). It has also been argued that the subject matter which is involved in the process of knowledge transfer needs also to be an integral part of the discourse and that this consideration is of particular relevance within the business school community of higher education. It has been further argued that in this arena the development of the subject matter taught is in danger of becoming irrelevant to the needs of the customers purported to be served (i.e. present and future business managers) and hence, at best marginalised and at worst excluded, from the discourse of education.

It is generally accepted that we all share an understanding of what management knowledge is and what should be taught. The language of the dominant discourse within the business school environment is concerned with the teaching of management, or business, as a subject which is conveniently subdivided into different specialist areas for practicalities of teaching. Conveniently this divides the subject area into suitable areas for research by individual academics within institutions and enables the development of specialist expertise. At the same time the sublanguage of the discourse is founded upon an acceptance of the free market as a mediating mechanism and hence an acceptance of classical liberal theory. Implicit within classical liberal theory is the freedom of an individual to pursue his/her own ends, and this matches the ethos of academic freedom completely. Also implicit within classical liberalism however, is the tendency of communities to atomise into lonely individuals and it is argued that this is taking place within the domain of business schools as individuals and groups diverge and develop their own subject specialisms. This has led to the fragmentation of management as a subject into a number of discrete disciplines which increasingly have little connection, or even perceived relevance, to each other. Within the paradigm of modernity, within which this view of higher education operates, acceptance of this is unquestioning and each discipline continues to distance itself from other disciplines within the business school environment, continues to fragment into subdisciplines (which eventually become new disciplines in their own right), and continues to legitimate each as a discrete discipline without regard to the legitimation of other parts of the business environment. This has also been argued to be the case in social sciences generally.

The enlightenment values of modernity therefore require serious academic disciplines within the management metadiscipline to legitimate themselves by adopting a scientific philosophy. Management as an area of study, and the individual disciplines which have developed within the generic subject area of management, are relative newcomers to academe and so, of necessity, have a greater preoccupation with legitimation than have more established disciplines. This legitimation is sought partly by developing a body of theory which is specific and unique to the discipline itself and partly by reference to, and building upon, the theory of older disciplines, which have greater perceived legitimacy. Thus the management disciplines seek to ground themselves within the disciplines of social science, which in turn seek to ground themselves within the disciplines of science, which seek to ground themselves upon ascertained fact as manifest empirically.

As these disciplines within the management metadiscipline become more established, and hence more secure in themselves, there is a tendency among the academics who teach and research in these areas to consider each discipline as a separate and discrete discipline in its own right which is no longer subsumed within any older and more established discipline (in this case the management discipline). There is also a natural tendency for the members of the community within the discipline to ignore the origins of the discipline and forget the roots of legitimation for their discipline. Instead legitimation entirely from within the discipline itself becomes desirable and eventually possible, thereby establishing to the satisfaction of the academics within the discipline that the discipline is discrete and not part of any greater discipline. Once this stage is reached the process of fragmentation and development of new disciplines can begin anew.

Thus one of the features of the current higher education environment, as far as management teaching is concerned, is the polarisation of teaching and research into increasingly local disciplines and subdisciplines while at the same time extending the boundary of the metadiscipline of management to increased knowledge domains in the pursuit of relevance and legitimation. For individual academics this polarisation is reflected in the increasingly local focus of their teaching and research as their individual subject areas narrow down and increasingly seek legitimation from within their own knowledge domain. Thus increased localisation is the direction of polarisation for individual academics whereas for business schools as a whole the polarity is towards increased globalisation as the schools compete with each other for resources, customers and recognition through the vaunting of their universal specialisms and relevance.

The localisation of focus for academics as far as teaching is concerned can be seen to be manifest in the increasing number of disciplines studied, researched and taught in business schools, together with the increasing separation of these disciplines from each other. Increasingly these disciplines are taught as discrete subjects, with little or no overlap between them, and with little perceived relationship and relevance of one to another. At the same time however the courses taught in business schools are constructed from components made up of segments of these discrete disciplines and the discourse, adopting the modernist metanarrative of the whole uniting the parts, assumes that this form of aggregation provides a learning vehicle for students which is implicitly useful and relevant to these students and the organisations which will eventually employ the successful outputs (i.e. graduates) of the business school courses. There is little questioning of this relevance within the discourse even though an examination of the market place demonstrates that this is not the case.

While this academic discourse continues to develop through an increasing array of specialisms the world of management continues to change, and change in a different manner to this increasing specialisation. For organisational management the postmodern era is manifest not so much in the local/global polarisation of business schools but rather in the space – time compression. This is particularly evident in organisations through the increased technologies and information architectures which have become prevalent in the recent past. These technologies have had the effect of facilitating the organisational reorganisations which have taken place under the label of downsizing which have had the effect of the removal of vast numbers of middle management and subject specialists from within the structures of organisations. The result of this is fewer managers within organisations but more significantly those who remain are no longer specialists in particular areas but rather increasingly require very broad knowledge and skills from throughout the domain of management learning. Thus while business schools, and the academics within, continue to seek legitimation from within their own community through increasingly self-referential discourse and specialisation, the world of their customers is increasingly requiring generalisation rather than specialisation. Academics therefore are in serious danger of marginalising themselves through their desire to legitimate their knowledge through the development of theory integral to each particular discipline and are therefore in the process of seeking legitimacy for the increasing irrelevance of their knowledge domains by means of this process of specialising while their market is generalising.

The question of what counts as knowledge can therefore be seen to be important within the discourse. Equally it can be seen to be in dispute and each of us may well have our own understanding of it and of the place of any particular fragment within the discourse. The canon is of course so large that we cannot be familiar with all of it as we have most certainly never studied all of it as well as having our own individual preferences. And additionally, we have all integrated the parts we know into our own individual bodies of previous knowledge and experience. Thus we should not be content – even with some of the basic building blocks or with our understanding of the management discipline and its components. With this in mind, this book is timely in its re-examination of some aspects of the discourse.

Professor David Crowther, UK

Acknowledgements

I would like to express my thanks first to those who encouraged me in the writing of my doctoral thesis on which this book is based. My special thanks to Professor David Crowther, my primary supervisor, who over a very long time, proved to be a staunch and unfailing guide.

I have many people to thank from London Metropolitan University, among them Frances Tomlinson, Faruk Merali, Donald Nordberg, Christina Schwabenland, Margaret Grieco, Adrian Merton, Bob Morgan, Yochanan Altman, Lez Rayman-Bacchus and David Clark. David Andrew was team teaching with me in the session when some students raised a problem with our case study. This proved to be the germ for the research for my thesis, and later for this book. I thank him for his perception that this was worth pursuing and the accounting students for having questioned the research methodology in that journal article. I also want to thank Professor Nurun Nabi and the staff at Icon College of Technology and Management for their interest and support.

I have had fruitful collaboration through the Social Responsibility Research Network and the Social Responsibility Journal in the useful and enjoyable conferences it has organised and the collaborative research with some of its members. Similarly, Philosophy of Management conferences and the journal *Philosophy of Management* have been a great source of support, education and delight. Encouragement to pursue this study also came from Management Accounting Research Group and Management Control Association meetings.

I am grateful to the late Derek and Natalie Pugh, who were always interested in my work, and for their valuable suggestions, not least for Professor Pugh's advice on how to prepare for and negotiate a doctoral *Viva Voce*.

And now directly to this book. As well as my thanks to the continued interest by many of those mentioned above, my special thanks to Professor Guler Aras for accepting my monograph for her book series. And my thanks again to Professor David Crowther for his continuing interest in my work, and for his writing the foreword to this book.

I would like to express my enormous gratitude to Kristina Abbotts, the Editor, Business and Economics at Routledge Taylor & Francis Group, for her excellent and prompt advice and her tremendous support through the minefield of publishers' requirements. I also want to thank her staff, Christiana

Mandizha, Laura Hussey, Matthew Ranscombe and Elanor Best for their help in the preparation for the book's publication. My thanks also to Sasikumar Selvaraj, Senior Project Manager, for his clear instructions and prompt and helpful responses to all my questions.

I am grateful to Springer for permission to reuse material from my articles published in *Philosophy of Management*: "Are management texts produced by authors or by readers? Representations of a Contingency Theory" (2005) vol. 5, no. 1, pp. 85–96; "Analysis of a text and its representations: univocal truth or a situation of undecidability" (2009) vol. 7, no, 3, pp. 27–42; and "Can deconstructing paradigms be used as a method for deconstructing texts" (2012) vol. 11, no. 2, pp. 85–113. My thanks to Hermine Vloemans, Oda Siqveland, Amy Larocque and Jessica LaFata at Springer for their help in arranging the copyright permission.

I would like to thank Emerald Publishing for permission to reuse material from my articles published in *Social Responsibility Journal*: "The embedding of knowledge in the academy: 'tolerance' irresponsibility or other imperatives?" (2009) vol. 5, no. 2, pp. 165–177; and "Objectivism in organization/management knowledge: an example of Bourdieu's 'mutilation'?" (2012) vol. 8, no.4, pp. 495–510; and also for permission to reuse material from my chapter "Organisational governance and accountability: do we have anything to learn from studying African traditional societies?" (2016), in *Accountability and Social Responsibility: International Perspectives*, edited by D. Crowther and L.M. Lauesen, pp. 75–100. I am grateful to Lauren Flintoft and Brynn Callahan for helping me obtain this permission.

I am grateful to Edward Elgar for permission to reuse material from my chapter "Research methods in organization, management and management accounting: an evaluation of quantitative and qualitative approaches" (2017) in the *Handbook of Research Methods in Corporate Social Responsibility*, edited by D. Crowther and L.M. Lauesen, pp. 76–93. My thanks to Amy Ellis for facilitating this.

My thanks also to Routledge for granting permission to reuse material from my chapter "Behaviour in academe: an investigation into the sustainability of mainstream scholarship in management studies" (2017) in *Corporate Behavior and Sustainability: Doing well by being good*, edited by G. Aras and C. Ingley, pp. 42–63. I want to thank Kristina Abbotts again for directing me to the relevant office for copyright permission, and Michelle Dickson for arranging the permission.

Finally, my family. My daughters, Liz and Cat, have been supportive, patient and proud of me, and I would also like to thank their partners Simon and Ben for their interest both in my doctoral research and in the writing of this book. When I initially asked my husband, Vic, how he felt about my undertaking a PhD, his reply was that he didn't think it would make much difference to our lives. I hope he didn't later think he had been much mistaken. He didn't show any sign of this, nor did he waver at the prospect of my writing this book. I thank him for his encouragement, faith in me and for making me think. A huge thanks to them all.

1   Introduction

Introduction[1]

The focus of this book is an analysis of the ways in which change management has been represented and researched in mainstream academic literature. These representations and research applications have been and remain a strong influence on scholars in the organisation, management and management accounting fields. This construction of knowledge by scholars writing on the management of change is examined through the detailed analysis of a seminal book on change management by highly regarded 'contingency' theorists, accompanied by an equally detailed comparison of mainstream representations of that original text.

The book on which this study is based is Burns and Stalker's *The Management of Innovation*, first published in 1961, with second and third editions in 1966 and 1994.[2] That book raised issues regarding the implementation of change, still being grappled with by academics and more widely by practitioners, as evidenced in more practical texts, such as those published by the Harvard Business Review, and by professional institutions such as the Chartered Institute of Personnel and Development. *The Management of Innovation* has been used extensively in research and teaching in the management and management accounting fields throughout the second half of the twentieth and into the twenty-first century. Chapman (1997:198) described *The Management of Innovation* as 'Perhaps the most influential and long lasting source of ideas in the contingency area'. In 2016 it was described by Otley as having constituted 'ground breaking work' (Otley 2016:50) and is still seen as a classic in the field (Barley 2016).

Rationale

The significance of this study lies in its claim that while orthodox scholarship has been widely and usefully concerned with the management of change, such representations, fully legitimated in the academy in the UK and US, are contestable, with importance consequences for the understanding of change initiatives by scholars and professional practitioners. The construction of mainstream[3] scholars' representations and research applications of works such as Burns and Stalker's, it is argued here, puts into question much of what has been regarded in dominant scholarship as being adequate for understanding successful change. Because these representations have long been accepted by the academy as legitimate knowledge on change management, this raises important epistemological[4] and practical issues of concern to academics, students, professional managers, management consultants and not least employees at various levels in their organisations.

The main contention in this book is over the almost exclusive recourse to one single ontological,[5] epistemological and methodological[6] paradigm adopted in mainstream scholarship. The consequences of this are that the meanings in Burns and Stalker's original text have been limited to an emphasis on formal organisational systems and structures to an extent, it is argued here, that much of the substance – to do with distortions, resistance, dysfunctions and even failures of management strategies - is lost. Problems for managers implementing change raised in *The Management of Innovation* have been minimised if not entirely omitted.

The critique in this book is based on the absences (Bhaskar 2008) of subjectivist aspects of organisational processes – the influence that members at all levels in organisations can have on the direction and success of managerial strategies and their implementation. One positive outcome of the publication of this book would be to influence researchers and other scholars to broaden the parameters for what is accepted as legitimate knowledge and to consider alternative, more holistic research methodologies. It should highlight factors likely to result in the success or failure of managerial policies, rather than the 'abstracted empiricism' (Burrell and Morgan 1979:104–106) or 'idealized worlds' (Panozzo 1997:459) so often seen to be on offer in academic books and journals. It should provide tools to critique various theoretical and methodological approaches. It might also encourage students to be critical of the smooth and glib models and solutions with respect to organisational change so often presented in more popular books on management.

What is novel about this book is that its research is done through the exploration and analysis of an entire monograph. A close examination of mainstream representations and research applications of that monograph details the similarities and differences between it and many of its interpretations, demonstrating the need to raise questions as to what counts as valid knowledge in the academy and what counts as the stuff of successful management. The rationale for the book stretches beyond the interpretation of one academic monograph, as much orthodox scholarship has relied on similar approaches, widening the implications for management scholarship and practice.

Background to contingency theory

The second half of the twentieth century saw changes and challenges to organisations in the UK and the US. These included increased global competition alongside a decline in protected markets and rapid technological development, with its effects on production, product innovation and information processing. The need arose for flexible organisation systems and management styles that would respond to the rapid changes in market demand and competition from Europe and the Far East (Ashton et al. 1995). Contemporary organisation theories on the design and running of successful organisations, be they classical or scientific management, human relations or a mixture of both, were thought to be unfit to cope with these developments. These theories had assumed largely closed systems which did not take external factors into account. They had advocated one best way, applicable to all organisations in all situations (Burrell and Morgan 1979).

Various 'contingency theories' were developed out of those early managerial ideas in the 1950s and 1960s. Major theorists included Woodward (1958, 1965), Burns and Stalker (1961, 1966, 1994) and Lawrence and Lorsch (1967a, 1967b). Their writings were aimed at helping organisations cope with different organisational environments, structures and technologies. They took concepts from mechanistic classical and scientific management theories and from humanist or psychological human relations and motivation theories, and changed them from being rigidly prescriptive with universalist recipes, to ideas where organisations had to match their systems, structures and leadership styles to particular contingencies. They recommended that these elements be adapted according to developments in the external environment, as circumstances dictated (Burrell and Morgan 1979).

These theorists offered various explanations as to what kind of organisation system would be effective in different environments, linking organisation structure with a variety of variables. Woodward claimed that the relationship between organisation structure and type of production technology was the most important. She found that successful organisation structures varied in their degree of hierarchy depending on whether the technology was large or small batch, or process technology (Woodward 1958). The Aston School, considered to have produced the most coherent body of empirical research between 1976 and 1981 (Otley 1995), pointed to the various contingencies of size, production technology and external environment as factors influencing the structures of organisations (Pugh et al. 2007). Lawrence and Lorsch developed a theory which maintained that in different economic and market conditions different parts of organisations would be subject to different rates of environmental change. There therefore needed to be differentiation in the internal structures of the various organisational subsystems. But there also needed to be integration for those tasks requiring interdepartmental co-ordination (Lawrence and Lorsch 1967a, 1967b).

Contingency theory has been an important theory in the organisation/management and management accounting fields and is considered to have had a 'long and distinguished role' in management and particularly management accounting research (Hall 2016:73). According to a survey of research papers in the two decades of the life of one prominent management accounting journal (*Management Accounting Research*) (*MAR*) contingency theory was used in 7% of the articles in the first decade (1990–2000) and in 13% in 2000–2010 (Scapens and Bromwich 2010). Cadez and Guildiing went so far as to describe contingency theory as having become 'the dominant paradigm in management accounting research' (Cadez and Guilding 2008:840).

Burns and Stalker's contingency theory

Burns and Stalker's work on contingency theory is among the best known. Their ideas have been central to organisation and management theory from the 1960s and into the twenty-first century, and are still referred to in textbooks and used as a model for research. Burns himself noted that the end of the 1950s marked the end of post-war physical reconstruction, followed by political renovation, economic expansion and technological innovation (Burns 1994). What was now required was a theory which addressed the need for organisational flexibility in these new environmental circumstances (Burrell and Morgan 1979; Ashton et al. 1995).

Burns and Stalker's research involved a study of twenty English and Scottish companies setting up new technologies for electronics development work. Their book dealt with an evaluation of successful as opposed to unsuccessful companies in environments of rapid technological and commercial change. As part of their analysis Burns and Stalker developed a continuum for two 'ideal types' in organisations – an 'organic' system appropriate for the contingencies of rapid change in technology and the market, and a 'mechanistic' one more appropriate in stable environmental conditions (Burns and Stalker 1961:119–120).

Their research was about the properties and effects of mechanistic (hierarchical) and organic (flexible) organisation systems in environmental conditions of both stability and change. The more volatile the market preference and probably therefore the technology required to deliver it, the more effective an organic structure would be – a structure with a looser definition of roles, more decentralised decision-making and more leeway for expertise over formal authority. This would enable innovative and timely responses to task uncertainties (Burns and Stalker 1961). These ideas are the ones most usually presented by mainstream scholars, with market or technological change being the independent variable selected – Burns and Stalker's first of three variables.

A large part of Burns and Stalker's book, however, also included the difficulties in implementing change from mechanistic to organic structures. The second variable introduced by Burns and Stalker – employee commitment – was about the power, politics and resistance strategies engaged in by employees in different parts of their organisations. These were manifested in departmental rivalries and conflicts, the influence of informal groups and the pull of previous bureaucratic systems. Burns and Stalker's third variable was concerned with the capacities of the companies' senior executives and the problems they faced in delivering organisational change. Burns and Stalker's analysis showed that all these factors were potentially inimical to successful change, and had played a large part in hindering the implementation of change strategies, sometimes to the point of rendering them dysfunctional (Burns and Stalker 1961; Burns 1966).

Management[7] of change

Change is currently a crucial and inescapable process for many organisations. An understanding of what makes for successful or unsuccessful change outcomes is vital both for scholars and practitioners. It has been widely acknowledged that successful change is difficult to achieve and that there are as many, if not more, failures as successes. Kotter studied management change initiatives to cope with new market environments in over one hundred companies, including large organisations. He concluded that:

> A few of these corporate change efforts have been very successful. A few have been utter failures. Most fall somewhere in between, with a distinct tilt toward the lower end of the scale.
>
> (Kotter 2011:1)

Other research has shown similar results. Garvin and Roberto (2011) pointed to the predictability and inadequacies of many managers' change strategies:

> [Managers] revamp the organization's strategy, then round up the usual set of suspects – people, pay and processes ... They then wait patiently for performance to improve, only to be bitterly disappointed.
>
> (Garvin and Roberto 2011:17)

Previous successes by high-ranking managers have also not proved a guarantee for success. Heifetz and Linsky wrote about such 'top executives ... who ... have crashed and burned' because of

> the high-stake risks you face whenever you try to lead an organization through difficult but necessary changes.
>
> (Heifetz and Linsky 2011:99)

With regard to these efforts and those of leaders who 'walk the talk', aim to change organisational culture and employees' attitudes, and make decision-making more participative,

> studies show that in most organizations, two out of three transformation initiatives fail. The more things change, the more they stay the same.
>
> (Sirkin et al. 2011:155)

Critiques of mainstream scholarship

Reasons for failures in successful organisational change might also be laid at the feet of academics who might be expected to have the knowledge to be able to advise on the successful management of change. It is one of the main arguments in this book, supported by scholars in the management and management accounting fields, that much mainstream scholarship may not be able to produce the necessary knowledge as it is often not close enough to the realities and practicalities of organisations.

Criticisms of mainstream management scholarship over the decades have been to do with the ways organisations are conceived; what has been assumed to make for successful change; the exclusive use of certain theoretical approaches to the exclusion of others; the questionable matching of organisational issues to academic disciplinary boundaries; inappropriate research methods and the ignoring of organisational processes driven by human factors influenced by power, politics and self-interest. The presumption generally has been that organisational success can be achieved through formal, objective factors such as appropriate organisation structures and systems, attainable through appropriate management strategies.

An important book on the research and practice of management, initially published in 1989 and still considered relevant to problems both in management scholarship and practice, has been revived twenty-four years later.[8] Two of the authors, Cooper and Fox, contest the idea that organisations epitomise a unitarist entity where 'unity, identity, permanence, foundation, structure' prevail 'over "anti-organization" processes such as dissonance, disparity, change' (Cooper and Fox 2013:247). Dickson et al. similarly support the idea that most management studies use a framework based on the assumption of a coherent, rational process, rather than the more complex picture of organisations driven by a more 'messy' process including conflicts and informal activities and grouping (Dickson et al. 2013:141). And Frug (1984) has criticised organisation theorists for legitimating formal structures to the exclusion of informal ones. He sees the 'central problem of bureaucracy' as a failure to reconcile the relationship between objectivity with subjectivity, as informal processes are 'intrinsically inseparable' from formal ones (Frug 1984, cited in Cooper and Fox 2013:258).

Even when more practical managerial issues germane to actual organisational problems and outcomes are researched, there are still difficulties with the analysis of organisational processes, as these cannot be categorised into the neat divisions between disciplines and subjects prevalent in the academy:

> In real life, these problems are multi-faceted and do not come with the convenient labels used in business schools such as organizational behaviour or financial management or marketing. Most real-life problems have aspects of all these involved in them and the manager has to comprehend the interaction between the different issues involved in any single real-life problem.
>
> (Mansfield 2013:3–4)

Argyris agrees with the proposition that management, to be both a credible academic discipline and a useful, relevant guide to management practice, must integrate knowledge from the various functional areas such as marketing, finance and accounting, along with broader disciplines such as psychology, sociology and economics. According to him, this is far from being realised in actuality. Scholars in different disciplines have different standards and if anything, discourage integrative measures, even at the expense of these particular standards showing inconsistencies. Argyris uses Kuhn's (1970) concept of the boundaries erected and norms established in an academic community as defensive mechanisms against the standards of other disciplines and in defiance of empirical reality, bolstered by a lack of empirical research (Argyris 2013).

This lack of attention to what is actually happening on the ground is taken further by Argyris. He emphasises the 'substance of practice' which management scholars must focus on to provide the knowledge that people under the 'pressures and constraints of everyday life' must have in order to implement their strategies effectively. And conversely, management activity should be subjected to stringent testing by scholars in order to ensure that its strategies are effective and produce only consequences that are intended (Argyris 2013:8).

Hendry, writing specifically about innovation, has pointed to the importance many writers have given to political issues arising in organisations, as indeed were highlighted by Burns and Stalker in *The Management of Innovation*. These include the political nature of decision-making; political activity resulting in the encouragement or blocking of change and the potential conflict between rival interest groups – all of which managers have to be aware of and deal with. Hendry acknowledges that this has often been ignored in mainstream academic research (Hendry 2013). Some critics have pointed to scholarship itself being political, and working in the interests of one group – managers. Puxty (1993) for example argued that the knowledge produced has served to enhance managerial effectiveness and problem-solving skills.

In sum, according to Pettigrew, researchers should avoid neat, rational, linear theories of change with the assumptions of ordered actions and organisational participants acting neutrally, if not altruistically, in pursuing organisational goals. Instead, they should look for the

> complex, haphazard and often contradictory ways that change emerges and to construct a model that allows for an appreciation of conflicting rationalities, objectives and behaviours.
>
> (Pettigrew 2013:24)

He sees in the role of academic scholarship a challenge to

> connect up the content, contexts and processes of change over time to explain the differential achievement of change objectives.
>
> (Pettigrew 2013:24)

Critiques of mainstream research methodologies

Issue is taken also with the methodologies used in much mainstream academic research. Again the focus there has been on objective factors such as formal structure, to the exclusion of human subjectivities and their influence on organisational processes – research methods and techniques not always in themselves sufficient to produce knowledge that deals with actual organisational problems, processes and management practices.

Research techniques have standardly involved 'positivist'[9] methods such as devising a survey with closed questions where a Lickert-type scale with answers plotted on a range is employed. The questions asked about change management have often been about the tightness or flexibility of the organisation's systems. The organisational members surveyed are usually senior managers, and sometimes only one manager per organisation. Organisational members lower down the hierarchy are not usually included in this research. More varied, qualitative scholarship involving in-depth research methods such as semi-structured interviews is also generally not pursued.

Pettigrew makes the point that research is a craft process and that the application of a formal set of techniques and rules, which has often been the accepted procedure, is not sufficient to produce broad and deep research on the management of change. Hitherto, much change research had been 'acontextual, ahistorical, and aprocessual' (Pettigrew 2013:28). But the fact is that a more historical focus to understand current problems and prepare for long-term planning has not always been practically possible for researchers because of the difficulties of longer term access to organisations, and the pressures to be research-productive.[10]

There are of course examples where research techniques have been varied and more inclusive of employees at different levels in their organisations, such as Dickson's et al. study. In their work on interfirm collaboration for innovation they used a method of case study research where for each case study there were semi-structured interviews at different levels of the firm which served 'to highlight both the consistencies and inconsistencies between the various actors, and so provide a richer and more realistic story' (Dickson et al. 2013:143).

Another example of the use of a more intensive methodology was in research done by Hendry et al. (2013), who studied ten companies' strategies in skills acquisition. They conducted an average of 40 interviews; spent periods of real-time observation; looked at company documents and reports. In another ten firms they conducted fewer interviews, but with employees across the board from directors, training managers to shop stewards and shop floor employees (Hendry et al. 2013). Such research is likely to produce a wider coverage of employee attitudes and could complement research based solely or largely on psychometric scale-based questionnaires for senior managers.

Spur to this study

In the course of teaching organisational aspects of management accounting to management accounting students as part of their degree in Accounting and Finance, case studies were used in order to help the students develop their understanding of organisational processes. These case studies were often selected from *Accounting, Organizations and Society* (*AOS*), a journal focussed on research at the interface between management accounting and organisational issues. Its role, according to the editorial in its first issue, was 'to actively encourage new approaches and perspectives' with advances in social accounting 'alongside behavioural studies of how accounting information is actually used' (Hopwood 1976:3–4).

One of the case studies used in the class was a research paper by Simons (1987). His research was based on Burns and Stalker's ideas, which he tested by applying their thesis to organisations either facing technological and market change or being in stable environments. Simons' research methodology involved carrying out semi-structured interviews with senior managers in order to select appropriate organisations for his study and questions for his survey, which was intended to analyse the differences in controls between the two kinds of organisation. This sought to test Burns and Stalker's 'model' of looser controls in organisations facing rapid change than in those in stable situations.

Simons took great care to develop scale questions for the control system attributes through checking against the information he received from senior managers, using previously validated research and information from colleagues, senior managers and financial officers in a set of companies not included in the study. The questionnaire he developed was designed to focus on different aspects of the companies' accounting control systems. It was then sent to CEOs and senior managers reporting to CEOs (Simons 1987). This was careful and painstaking research and was a common interpretation in the dominant literature of Burns and Stalker's book and a common methodology used in research applications of their ideas.

Simons' paper was however queried by some of the students because of what they saw to be limitations in the research methodology. What concerned them was whether, when considering control systems throughout an organisation, the research would not have been stronger if data had been obtained from employees at more levels in the organisations studied than exclusively from those at senior management level. Senior managers might not have had all the necessary information about their organisations' control systems. In the light of this query, an investigation into *The Management of Innovation* was undertaken in order to see how Simons' research methods compared with Burns and Stalker's, whether they were consistent with those used by Burns and Stalker, or indicated by them to be appropriate.

The introductory chapter of the first edition of *The Management of Innovation* (1961) and the preface to the second edition (1966) immediately showed substantial differences between Burns and Stalker's methodology and Simons'. Burns and Stalker had not restricted themselves to seeking information from senior managers. After interviewing the heads of the firms studied, they conducted a series of interviews with 'as large a number of persons as possible in managerial and supervisory positions' (Burns and Stalker 1961:13). And instead of relying mainly on questionnaires as had Simons, Burns and Stalker conducted interviews; sat in on meetings and discussions; listened to casual remarks, lengthy expositions and mealtime conversations; and observed everyday routines in offices, research laboratories and workshops factories (Burns and Stalker 1961).

The subject matter too appeared to be broader in *The Management of Innovation*. In Simons' article, and, as became evident in many others' research papers, the object of inquiry focussed on the types of formal organisational structures and systems in organisations. Simons' research was aimed at seeing whether there was a match between those systems and their environments, testing Burns and Stalker's ideas that different organisational environments required particular organisational structures to ensure successful outcomes.

But Burns and Stalker's research, in addition to being an examination of the structures of organisations, also used space and argument in their book on other, less objective, factors, which those authors saw as crucial in determining the success or otherwise of the change strategies in the organisations they were studying. They were interested in seeing how management controlled and coordinated the operations of a working community. They sought opportunities to study 'how people dealt with each other'. Such dealings included sectional conflicts, people's insecurities about their power and status in changing circumstances, the consequent formations of cliques, engagement with organisational politics and resistance to managerial change strategies (Burns and Stalker 1961:14). Because these more subjective factors involving attitudes, intentions and actions of employees at various organisational levels were often absent in mainstream interpretations of Burns and Stalker's findings, this raised further questions about whether the meanings in Burns and Stalker's book had been adequately presented or whether they were limited, with some of the substance lost.

As the research progressed, it became clear that what had been foregrounded in interpretations of *The Management of Innovation*, was part of a more general pattern of objectivist[11] scholarship with preferences given to formal organisation structures and systems as factors considered crucial for organisational change (Green 2005). Epistemological questions arose regarding these interpretations and research applications which for long had been accepted and legitimated in the academy. An initial question was how far the knowledge produced in Burns and Stalker's original text was similar to and different from interpretations of their work.

Because there were differences in representations of Burns and Stalker's book in the academic literature, it added interest to the question of what has been and is still accepted as valid knowledge, and what has been ignored. This study was undertaken with the primary question being what counts as knowledge in the organisation/management field, with particular reference to representations of Burns and Stalker. Both Burns and Stalker as contingency theorists and Simons as a management accounting researcher were substantial figures in their fields. The apparent discrepancies in the knowledge produced from *The Management of Innovation* led first to research for a PhD thesis and then to this book, in which the focus has been extended to include implications for more practical management issues.

Dialectical[12] contradictions

The focus in this book is on objectivist or functionalist[13] scholarship and the ramifications resulting from these objectivist approaches. The implications of the almost exclusive recourse to a single theoretical position and the dialectical oppositions constructed with regard to subjectivist[14] approaches have been analysed by various social theorists. The main point of contention is over what this leaves out or 'absents' (Bhaskar 2008). Derrida's rejection of binary oppositions (Derrida 2002a, 2002b, 2002c); Bourdieu's (1990) claim that oppositions between subjectivism and objectivism are invalid, dangerous and politically supportive of dominant social and political structures; and Bhaskar's totalising critique of partial 'disemancipatory' ontologies (2008:11) have been referred to at various points in the book. A critique of exclusively objectivist research runs throughout this book, studied from different perspectives. Objectivist scholarship *per se* is not what is being critiqued. Its epistemological validity is not in question. What is under scrutiny is its exclusive use.

There are, of course, political underpinnings to the way knowledge has been produced and legitimated. The pressures both from within academe and from outside are examined as are the ideological bases of the knowledge produced, and more subtly, the parameters within which such knowledge has been framed. This is a recurring theme in the book, explaining the choices for what has counted as valid organisational knowledge, including to whom power and prerogative to institute organisational change strategies have been accorded. In the introduction to a critical handbook on management, a critique is similarly offered of knowledge produced 'for' management rather than 'of' management (Alvesson et al. 2009:4).

Analytical framework

A Hegelian dialectical methodology, an investigation of a topic from a number of different perspectives as a circular rather than a linear process, is used to examine the contradictions constructed between objectivist and subjectivist approaches (Bhaskar 1998). The advantage of a methodology where the topic is viewed from different angles is that it enables a deeper exploration and understanding of the issues, perhaps with more confidence in the findings if they support each other from the different perspectives studied. The analysis shows that the issues explored are deeply embedded in mainstream management scholarship generally, with consequences for both scholarship and practice. The reasons for the persistence of preferences for objectivist over subjectivist approaches, despite stringent criticisms from within the field are examined. Connections are made between this imperviousness and political, economic and ideological pressures.

Contents of the book

The book is divided into two sections. In the first (Chapters 2–5) problems of deriving meanings from texts are discussed. *The Management of Innovation* and its representations are compared. A detailed analysis of the similarities and differences between the original monograph and its representations is undertaken from different perspectives, with particular emphasis on the differences in the approaches to human agency, and the implications of this for scholarship and practice.

In the second part of the book (Chapters 6–8) reasons for the continuance over many decades of these representations in the face of sustained criticism on methodological grounds from eminent scholars, themselves often located within the academic mainstream, are explored. Examples are also given of scholarship that goes against this trend – scholarship that is multi-paradigmatic and often subjectivist, taking account of the knowledge and intentions of people in organisations at many more levels. Comparisons are made between these objectivist and subjectivist types of knowledge, and questions are raised about the prospects for these different approaches continuing separately, and or with these oppositions eliminated in favour of a more holistic approach, arguably with greater practical as well as epistemological value.

Chapter 1: introduction

Chapter 1 outlines the spur to this research, raising epistemological questions as to what has been legitimated as knowledge, through an initial discussion of the differences between Burns and Stalker's text and its mainstream representations. This is held to be particularly relevant to practical issues and problems concerning change management. The analytical framework, based on a dialectic constructed between different scholarly approaches, is outlined. A critical realist ontology is used, which regards structure and human agency as close and interdependent, unlike the dialectical oppositions constructed between them in much mainstream scholarship. It seeks to question such oppositions and the absences in representations of Burns and Stalker's research of its subjectivist findings. A resolution through a more practical, totalising and emancipatory approach is suggested.

Chapter 2: meanings of texts

Problems of determining meanings in texts are discussed, using the writings of Barthes (1977a), Derrida (2002a) and Eco (1992a, 1992b). Examples are given of other texts in the organisation/management field and in other disciplines where interpretations have been contested – Kurt Lewin's management theories, Adam Smith's economics, and the ideas of the philosophers Karl Popper and Ludwig Wittgenstein. A comparison is then made between *The Management of Innovation* and its interpretations in popular, widely used textbooks.

Chapter 3: representations of texts

Chapter 3 raises epistemological issues to do with representation. Problems with respondents' data had been discussed several decades earlier by social anthropologists (e.g. Vansina 1965), and with researchers' handling of the data (e.g. Sarbin and Kitsuse 1994; Bourdieu 1998). Mainstream representations of Burns and Stalker's text are analysed, this time in academic journals, showing the dialectical oppositions constructed between rational, structural change strategies and the effects of human agency on organisational change. Critiques by scholars of this exclusive focus on structural issues are highlighted, as is the persistence of such scholarship despite these critiques. Alternative research in the journal literature is discussed.

Chapter 4: textual analysis

Following Derrida's (1981, 2002a) recommendations for a minute *explication de texte* and Eco's (1992a, 1992b) reliance on *intentio operis*, a textual analysis of Burns and Stalker's work is used as a basis for further comparisons with the selected textbooks, particularly in terms of the binary oppositions between structural and human factors constructed in dominant approaches. Comparisons between *The Management of Innovation* and the textbook representations are then developed through a critical discourse analysis (Fairclough and Hardy 1997). The analysis is extended to show the paucity of relying solely or mainly on structural factors when compared with the work of more practically oriented management scholars such as Rosabeth Moss Kanter (1977, 1983, 2009). Issues raised by her include the importance of bringing organisational members on board with regard to change programmes and the multi-faceted requirements placed on senior executives for achieving successful organisational innovation.

Chapter 5: paradigm commensurabilities

Chapter 5 comprises a final comparison through an investigation of the ontological, epistemological and methodological similarities and differences between *The Management of Innovation* and its research applications. Burrell and Morgan's (1979) work on sociological paradigms is used as the framework for this analysis. Derrida's (1988, 2002a) views on binary oppositions and supplementarity are used further to highlight differences with Burns and Stalker's approach, particularly in respect of the latter's synthesis between formal and informal structures, and between human agency, organisational processes and structures. This completes the comparison of the two kinds of text from several perspectives, and its significance for an understanding of organisation processes and management practice.

Chapter 6: the academy

Chapter 6 is primarily about the academy, as the place where mainstream scholarship is grounded. The types of knowledge published in the influential *Administrative Science Quarterly (ASQ)* journal are investigated, and other influences on scholarship are analysed including less common ones such as US–Soviet rivalry over the successful launching of the Sputnik in 1957. Deeper epistemological explanations are located in the ambiguities in journal editors' requirements, and in their different interpretations of key fundamental concepts, particularly in relation to what constitutes science and scientific method. These form the basis for the following chapter.

Chapter 7: science vs scientificity

The dialectical oppositions constructed between objectivist knowledge and the exclusion of other, mainly subjectivist, approaches are considered in terms of categorisations of science and positivism. Different definitions and interpretations of key terms such as science are used to explain further what has counted as legitimate knowledge and what has been rejected. Broader views of science put forward by Kuhn (1970), Hanson (1972) and Feyerabend (1993) are discussed in terms of their implications for the dialectical oppositions mentioned above. The analysis is extended to theorists writing about the social sciences generally, including Mannheim (1952), Habermas (1972) and Bourdieu (1990). The definitions of these terms are then connected with other dialectical constructions of scholarship in organisation/management studies, principally the commensurability/incommensurability debate, all of which have influenced what has counted as legitimate knowledge, and may have influenced understandings of organisational processes and the knowledge considered relevant for organisational practice.

Chapter 8: dialectical oppositions

Chapter 8 is the last chapter concerned with the continued legitimation and persistence of mainstream objectivist scholarship in the face of strong critiques from within the management fields and from outside. Examples of management accounting research, using both objectivist and more pluralist methods are examined, with questions posed about the kind of knowledge gained from each approach, the scientific nature of the research and the commensurability or otherwise of the different paradigmatic approaches.

Chapter 9: conclusions

The conclusion re-iterates the view that the dominant knowledge in this field has been framed mainly in terms of dialectical oppositions and that the objectivist paradigm, while in itself a valid approach, can provide only a partial, often structuralist, managerialist view if used to the exclusion of other approaches. The analysis in the book is intended to highlight the ways the influence on organisational change strategies of people other than managers risks being obscured, and the possibility of more inclusive and practically useful knowledge obviated. Difficulties in linking this mainstream academic scholarship with the knowledge acquired and employed by professional practitioners are outlined. The question is then posed about the possibility of more complementary, holistic, and emancipatory scholarship becoming more widespread – to scholars and students; to a wider constituency in organisations including senior executives, managers and other practitioners as well as employees at all levels; and possibly to a wider audience.

Notes

1 This chapter is based on published papers by Green (2005, 2009). The author would like to thank Springer for copyright permission.

2 Unless otherwise stated only the 1961 edition of Burns and Stalker's book will be cited in future. The later editions are exactly the same, apart from the prefaces in the 1966 and 1994 editions by Burns, which will also be referred to in support of the arguments put forward in the book.

3 'Mainstream' for research papers is defined as papers published in academic journals that can have a high ranking in journal lists and also influence and status, primarily in the UK and the US. Mainstream textbooks are those running into several editions and widely used in universities. The ones used in this book were published in both the UK and the US.

4 Epistemology has been defined as the 'nature of the relationship between the knower ... and what can be known', or what counts as knowledge (Guba and Lincoln 1998:201).

5 Ontology has been defined as the 'form and nature of reality, and therefore what is there that can be known about it' (Guba and Lincoln 1998:201).

6 Methodology has been defined as how researchers find what they believe can be known (Guba and Lincoln 1998).

7 'Organisation' and 'management' studies have been linked throughout this book as they can be said to be similar or closely related, depending on the context. Puxty and Chua (1989) among others have, on the other hand, argued that they are distinct in that organisation theory is more concerned with sociological questions, and management theory with more practical ones. However for some, e.g. Salancik (1975) and Clegg and Dunkerley (1980) the distinction has always been murky, particularly in textbooks. Stern and Barley (1996) argued that initial differences between sociological and administrative approaches had narrowed by the late 1950s. The influence of business schools by the 1980s was another influence on their becoming closer in approach. By the mid-1990s Stern and Barley (1996) were of the opinion that organisation studies were broadening again. See Chapter 6 *passim*.

8 Authors in that book, *Frontiers of Management: Research and Practice* edited by Roger Mansfield, have, among others, been used to support the critique suggested here of mainstream management scholarship and its relationship to the knowledge it has produced about management practice, not least regarding the exclusiveness of that knowledge and its significant absences concerning the intentions and actions of people at different levels in organisations and the resulting problems facing management.

9 Positivism is often associated with its extreme version, logical positivism, which was about knowledge having to be scientific through a raw empiricism, verifiable by experience, with the use of 'hard' methods and quantitative methodologies alone (Halfpenny 2001).
10 This is discussed in more detail in Chapter 6.
11 Objectivism is a belief that ontologically there is an objective reality uninfluenced by human agency and that this reality is knowable. The researcher, who should be an objective observer unable to influence the object of study, has the task of discovering and portraying this external reality. People are passive subjects and do not influence their reality, in this instance their organisations. Such research has been thought to be neutral and morally value-free. This is an approach, which claims to explain the natural order, seen as interlocking objective elements arranged logically and according to rules, which can ultimately be discovered (Chua 1986:606). Quantitative, statistically based methodologies are often used. See e.g. Modell (2009). Another term often used is 'functionalist'.
12 Dialectic has been defined variously: by Morgan (1990:28) as an 'attempt to counterpose the insights generated from competing perspectives'; Bhaskar has described it as 'essentially to do with the absenting of constraints on absenting absences … This presupposes … the critique of ontological monovalence' (Bhaskar 2008:xxxii).
13 Functionalism has been defined as objectivist, empirical and highly oriented to conceptions of organisations focussed on managerial problems and priorities (Burrell and Morgan 1979).
14 Subjectivist approaches are those which scholars use in attempting to understand social processes and the social world from the points of view of the actors involved (Burrell and Morgan 1979).

References

Alvesson, M., Bridgman, T., and Willmott, H. (2009). Introduction. In: M. Alvesson, T. Bridgman and H. Willmott, eds., *The Oxford Handbook of Critical Management Studies*. Oxford: Oxford University Press, pp. 1–28.

Argyris, C. (2013). The Discipline of Management and Academic Defensive Routines. In: R. Mansfield, ed., *Frontiers of Management: Research and Practice*. London: Routledge Revivals, pp. 8–20.

Ashton, D., Hopper, T., and Scapens, R.W. (1995). The Changing Nature of Issues in Management Accounting. In: D. Ashton, T. Hopper and R.W. Scapens, eds., *Issues in Management Accounting*. 2nd ed. London: Prentice Hall, pp. 1–20.

Barley, S.R. (2016). 60th Anniversary Essay: Ruminations on How We Became a Mystery House and How We Might Get Out. *Administrative Science Quarterly*, 61 (1), pp. 1–8.

Barthes, R. (1977a). *Image Music Text*. Trans S. Heath. London: Harper Collins.

Bhaskar, R. (1998). General Introduction. In: M. Archer, R. Bhaskar, A. Collier, T. Lawson, and A. Norrie, eds., *Critical Realism: Essential Readings*. London: Routledge, pp. ix–xxiv.

Bhaskar, R. (2008). *Dialectic: The Pulse of Freedom*. London: Routledge.

Bourdieu, P. (1990). *The Logic of Practice*. Trans. R. Nice. Stanford, CA: Stanford University Press.

Bourdieu, P. (1998). *Practical Reason: On the Theory of Action*. Cambridge: Polity Press.

Burns, T. (1966). Preface to the Second Edition. In: T. Burns and G.M. Stalker, eds., *The Management of Innovation*. 2nd ed. London: Tavistock Publications, pp. vii–xxii.

Burns, T. (1994). Preface to the Third Edition. In: T. Burns, and G.M. Stalker, *The Management of Innovation*. 3rd ed. Oxford: Oxford University Press, pp. vii–xx.

Burns, T. and Stalker, G.M. (1961). *The Management of Innovation*. London: Tavistock Publications.

Burns, T. and Stalker, G.M. (1966). *The Management of Innovation*. 2nd ed. London: Tavistock Publications.

Burns, T. and Stalker, G.M. (1994). *The Management of Innovation*. 3rd ed. Oxford: Oxford University Press.

Burrell, G. and Morgan, G. (1979). *Sociological Paradigms and Organisational Analysis: Elements of the Sociology of Corporate Life*. Aldershot: Ashgate.

Cadez, S. and Guilding, C. (2008). An Exploratory Investigation of an Integrated Contingency Model of Strategic Management Accounting. *Accounting, Organizations and Society*, 33 (7–8), pp. 836–863.

Chapman, C.S. (1997). Reflections on a Contingent View of Accounting. *Accounting, Organizations and Society*, 22 (2), pp. 189–205.

Chua, W.F. (1986). Radical Developments in Accounting Thought. *The Accounting Review*, LXI (4), October, pp. 601–632.

Clegg, S.R. and Dunkerley, D. (1980). *Organization, Class and Control*. London: Routledge & Kegan Paul.

Cooper, R. and Fox, S. (2013). Two Modes of Organization? In: R. Mansfield, ed., *Frontiers of Management: Research and Practice*. London: Routledge Revivals, pp. 247–261.

Derrida, J. (1981). *Dissemination*. Trans. B. Johnson. London: Athlone Press.

Derrida, J. (1988). *Limited Inc*. Trans. S Weber. Evanston, IL: Northwestern University Press.

Derrida, J. (2002a). Implications: Interview with Henri Ronse. In: Derrida, J., *Positions*. Trans. A. Bass. 2nd ed. London: Continuum, pp. 1–14.

Derrida, J. (2002b). Semiology and Grammatology: Interview with Julia Kristeva. In: J. Derrida, *Positions*. Trans. A. Bass. 2nd ed. London: Continuum, pp. 17–36.

Derrida, J. (2002c). Positions: Interview with Jean-Louis Houdebine and Guy Scarpetta. In: J. Derrida, *Positions*. Trans. A. Bass. 2nd ed. London: Continuum, pp. 37–96.

Dickson, K., Lawton Smith, H. and Smith, S. (2013). Interfirm Collaboration and Innovation: Strategic Alliances or Reluctant Partnerships? In: R. Mansfield, ed., *Frontiers of Management: Research and Practice*. London: Routledge Revivals, pp. 140–160.

Eco, U. (1992a). Interpretation and History. In: S. Collini, ed., *Interpretation and Over-interpretation: Umberto Eco with Richard Rorty, Jonathan Culler and Christine Brooke-Rose*. Cambridge: Cambridge University Press, pp. 23–44.

Eco, U. (1992b). Overinterpreting Texts. In: S. Collini, ed., *Interpretation and Over-interpretation: Umberto Eco with Richard Rorty, Jonathan Culler and Christine Brooke-Rose*. Cambridge: Cambridge University Press, pp. 45–66.

Fairclough, N. and Hardy, G. (1997). Management Learning as Discourse. In: J. Burgoyne and M. Reynolds, eds., *Management Learning: Integrating Perspectives in Theory and Practice*. London: Sage, pp. 144–160.

Feyerabend, P. (1993). *Against Method*. 3rd ed. London: Verso.

Frug, G.E. (1984). The Ideology of Bureaucracy in American Law. *Harvard Law Review*, 97, pp. 1276–1388.

Garvin, D.A. and Roberto, M.A. (2011). A Change through Persuasion. In: *HBR's 10 Must Reads: On Change Management*. Boston, MA: Business Review Press, pp. 17–33.

Green, M. (2005). Are Management Texts Produced by Authors or by Readers? Representations of a Contingency Theory. *Philosophy of Management*, 5 (1), pp. 85–96.

Green, M. (2009). Analysis of a Text and Its Representations: Univocal Truth or a Situation of Undecidability?. *Philosophy of Management*, 7 (3), pp. 27–42.

Guba, E.G. and Lincoln, Y.S. (1998). Competing Paradigms in Qualitative Research. In: N.K. Denzin and Y.S. Lincoln, eds., *The Landscape of Qualitative Research: Theories and Issues*. Thousand Oaks, CA: Sage, pp. 195–220.

Habermas, J. (1972). *Knowledge and Human Interests*. Trans. J.J. Shapiro. London: Heinemann.

Hall, M. (2016). Realising the Richness of Psychology Theory in Contingency-based Management Accounting Research. *Management Accounting Research*, 31, pp. 63–74.

Halfpenny, P. (2001). Positivism in the Twentieth Century. In: G. Ritzer and B. Smart. eds., *Handbook of Social Theory*. London: Sage, pp. 371–385.

Hanson, N.R. (1972). *Patterns of Discovery: An Inquiry into the Conceptual Foundations of Science*. Cambridge: At the University Press.

Heifetz, R.A. and Linsky, M.A. (2011). Survival Guide for Leaders. In: *HBR's 10 Must Reads: On Change Management*. Boston, MA: Business Review Press, pp. 99–118.

Hendry, C., Pettigrew, A., and Sparrow, P. (2013). Linking Strategic Change, Competitive Performance and Human Resource Management: Results of a UK Empirical Study. In: R. Mansfield, ed., *Frontiers of Management: Research and Practice*. London: Routledge Revivals, pp. 195–220.

Hendry, J. (2013). Technology, Marketing, and Culture: The Politics of New Product Development Practice. In: R. Mansfield, ed., *Frontiers of Management: Research and Practice*. London: Routledge Revivals, pp. 96–126.

Hopwood, A.G. (1976). Editorial: The Path Ahead. *Accounting, Organizations and Society*, 1 (1), pp. 1–4.

Kanter, R.M. (1977). *Rosabeth Moss Kanter on the Frontiers of Management*. Boston, Mass: Harvard Business Review Press.

Kanter R.M. (1983). *The Change Masters: Corporate Entrepreneurs at Work*. London: Unwin Paperbacks.

Kanter, R.M. (2009). *Supercorp: How Vanguard Companies Create Innovation, Profits, Growth and Social Good*. London: Profile Books.

Kotter, J.P. (2011). Leading Change: Why Transformation Efforts Fail. In: *HBR's 10 Must Reads: On Change Management*. Boston, MA: Business Review Press, pp. 1–16.

Kuhn, T.S. (1970). *The Structure of Scientific Revolutions*. 2nd ed. Chicago, IL: Chicago University Press.

Lawrence, P.R. and Lorsch, J.W. (1967a). *Organization and Environment: Managing Differentiation and Integration*. Boston, MA: Harvard Business School Press.

Lawrence, P.R. and Lorsch, J.W. (1967b). Differentiation and Integration in Complex Organizations. *Administrative Science Quarterly*, 12 (1), June, pp. 1–47.

Mannheim, K. (1952). *Essays on the Sociology of Knowledge*. London: Routledge & Kegan Paul.

Mansfield, R. (2013). Management Research and the Development of Management Practice. In: R. Mansfield, ed., *Frontiers of Management: Research and Practice*. London: Routledge Revivals, pp. 3–7.

Modell, S. (2009). In Defence of Triangulation: A Critical Realist Approach to Mixed Methods Research in Management Accounting. *Management Accounting Research*, 20 (3), pp. 208–221.

Morgan, G. (1990). Paradigm Diversity in Organizational Research. In: J. Hassard and D. Pym, eds., *The Theory and Philosophy of Organizations: Critical Issues and New Perspectives*. London: Routledge, pp. 13–29.

Otley, D. (1995). Management Control, Organisational Design and Accounting Information Systems. In: D. Ashton, T. Hopper and R.W. Scapens, eds., *Issues in Management Accounting*. 2nd ed. London: Prentice Hall, pp. 45–64.

Otley, D. (2016). The Contingency Theory of Management Accounting and Control: 1980–2014. *Management Accounting Research*, 31, pp. 45–62.

Panozzo, F. (1997). The Making of the Good Academic Accountant. *Accounting, Organizations and Society*, 22 (5), pp. 447–480.

Pettigrew, A.M. (2013). Longitudinal Methods to Study Change: Theory and Practice. In: R. Mansfield, ed., *Frontiers of Management: Research and Practice*. London: Routledge Revivals, pp. 21–49.

Pugh, D.S. and Hickson, D.J. (2007). *Writers on Organizations*. 6th ed. London: Penguin Books.

Puxty, A.G. (1993). *The Social and Organizational Context of Management Accounting*. London: Academic Press.

Puxty, A.G. and Chua, W.F. (1989). Ideology, Rationality and the Management Control Process. In: W.F. Chua, T. Lowe and T. Puxty, eds., *Critical Perspectives in Management Control*. Houndmills: The Macmillan Press, pp. 115–139.

Salancik, G.R. (1975). Book Review of Management: A Contingency Approach by D. Hellriegel and J.W. Slocum. *Administrative Science Quarterly*, 20 (2), pp. 311–313.

Sarbin, T.R. and Kitsuse, J.I. (1994). A Prologue to Constructing the Social. In: T.R. Sarbin and J.I. Kitsuse, eds., *Constructing the Social*. London: Sage, pp. 1–18.

Scapens, R.W. and Bromwich, M. (2010). Management Accounting Research: 20 Years On. *Management Accounting Research*, 21 (4), pp. 278–284.

Simons, R. (1987). Accounting Control Systems and Business Strategy: An Empirical Analysis. *Accounting Organizations and Society*, 12 (4), pp. 357–374.

Sirkin, H.L., Keenan, P., and Jackson, A. (2011). The Hard Side of Change Management Persuasion. In: *HBR's 10 Must Reads: On Change Management*. Boston, MA: Business Review Press, pp. 155–176.

Stern, R.N. and Barley, S.R. (1996). Organizations and Social Systems: Organization Theory's Neglected Mandate. *Administrative Science Quarterly*, 41 (1), pp. 146–162.

Vansina, J.M. (1965). *Oral Tradition: A Study in Historical Methodology*. Trans. H.M. Wright. London: Routledge & Kegan Paul.

Woodward, J. (1958). *Management and Technology*. Department of Scientific and Industrial Research. The Problems of Progress in Industry No 3. London: Her Majesty's Stationary Office.

Woodward, J. (1965). *Industrial Organization: Theory and Practice*. New York, NY: Oxford University Press.

2 Meanings of texts

Introduction[1]

There are differences between mainstream interpretations of Burns and Stalker's text and the text itself. This has significant implications for both scholarship and practice. In an initial evaluation of these representations of Burns and Stalker's book, the main difference identified was a narrowing of the original content to a focus on formal structural aspects of organisations undergoing change. In keeping with this version of an essentially functionalist approach, concepts like formal structure and environment have been treated as ontologically real and not as in some other approaches as uncertain, ambiguous, and subject to non-managerial influences such as informal structures and vulnerabilities to human agency (e.g. Burns 1966; Willmott 1993; Cooper and Fox 2013; Dickson et al. 2013).

Absented from these interpretations are factors that can impinge on the implementation and functionality of change strategies. These are to do mainly with human intentions and actions – the capacities of senior executives to effect change and employees' potential to influence the direction of such change. *The Management of Innovation* itself included analyses of threats to successful change by employees looking out for their own interests, leading to resistance, to dysfunctionality and to outright failure. Burns and Stalker found evidence of difficulties in the successful achievement of structural change in the English and particularly the Scottish companies (Burns and Stalker 1961).

Because the interpretations in this book of both the original text and many of its representations might be seen as merely another mediated interpretation in competition with those by mainstream scholars, it was decided to examine issues surrounding meanings in texts. Problems in arriving at definitive meanings of texts are considered through ideas from Barthes (1977), Derrida (1977, 2002a) and Eco (1992a, 1992b). A way forward to analyse texts is suggested, which here is briefly applied to Burns and Stalker's book in preparation for lengthier analyses later on.

Deciding on meanings of texts is problematic and not exclusive to interpretations of Burns and Stalker or indeed to scholarship generally. The works of Kurt Lewin, Adam Smith, Karl Popper and Ludwig Wittgenstein, it has been argued, have been represented in ways that are significantly different from the original texts. Short comparisons of Burns and Stalker's text are then made with its interpretations in three, popular management textbooks widely disseminated in management curricula. A minority interpretation of *The Management of Innovation* which includes more of the issues raised by Burns and Stalker is also presented.

Interpretations of texts

Kurt Lewin

Issues similar to those in interpretations of Burns and Stalker's book have been raised about other theorists' work such as Kurt Lewin's. According to Cooke, politics underpinned the way Lewin's work was presented. A great deal of the work was omitted from the managerial literature, and what was represented was simplified with *lacunae* that were politically and practically significant (Cooke 1999).

The famous experiment Lewin engaged in in the 1930s with Lippit and White regarding democratic, autocratic and *laissez-faire* styles of leadership was deeply political, and intended by Lewin to help effect social change on behalf of the disadvantaged (Cooke 1999). This angle has been ignored and his research used instead as a guide to management leadership. Cooke affirmed the tendency of management scholarship to be about discourses presenting a managerialist version of theory – a point made later in relation to interpretations of Burns and Stalker's book.

Lewin's belief in the application of theory and his opposition to *laissez-faire* leadership has been linked to his desire for political change (Cooke 1999). It can also be connected to his concern for intrapersonal, interpersonal and group dynamics during change initiatives in organisations. Lewin's concepts of reflective feedback on group processes in order to enhance change management were intended by him to deal with the high interethnic conflict present in the US at a time of racial segregation, denial of the vote to Afro-Americans and racist lynchings. Cooke pointed out that this has generally not been included in the literature. Instead Lewin has been depicted as the founding father of change management and group dynamics theory from a managerialist stance (Cooke 1999).

Adam Smith

Examples from other fields include, most notably, Adam Smith's work. Some have claimed that dominant interpretations are limited to, if not suggestive of, the opposite of what had been intended by Smith. Interpretations of Smith have been partial and self-serving. The idea in *The Wealth of Nations* of 'let the market alone' was promoted as an argument against humanitarian legislation by the new industrialists whom Smith had warned against:

> Our merchants and master-manufacturers complain much of the bad effects of high wages … They say nothing concerning the bad effects of high profits. They are silent with regard to the pernicious effects of their own gains.
>
> (Smith 2007:81)

Smith had strongly advocated government regulation rather than 'untrammelled' free market competition (Collison 2003:864).

Interpretations of *The Wealth of Nations* have focused on the freedom of trade, ignoring Smith's critique of various political and religious institutions which he castigated for their injustices. Rothschild, among others, has emphasised Smith's concerns and anger in respect of the poverty engendered by low wages for labourers, which Smith described as an oppression of the poor by the rich. Quotes from his writings demonstrate this. The poor labourer, according to Smith

> supports the whole frame of society; [but is] himself possessed of a very small share.
>
> (Smith 1982:341)

and

> Laws and government may be considered ... in every case as a combination of the rich to oppress the poor, and preserve to themselves the inequality of the goods which would otherwise be soon destroyed by the attacks of the poor...
>
> (Smith 1982:208)

Hence Smith's approval of government interference in measures to reduce poverty such as wage regulation and progressive taxes on carriages in order that 'the indolence and vanity of the rich is made to contribute in a very easy manner to the relief of the poor' (Smith 1976:725 cited in Rothschild 2001:69).

Interpretations of the 'invisible hand' as the cornerstone of Smith's thinking, and as an encouragement for the system and the market to be free to work invisibly and to promote self-interest, are problematic. Rothschild claims that Smith did not attach much importance to the phrase, and used the expression ironically, as an attack on people who believed in the invisible actions of gods, demons, witches, genii and fairies – which fitted in with Smith's views on religion (Rothschild 2001). In the more important field of political economy, Smith saw disadvantages in allowing merchants to employ their capital freely, as they were rapacious, seeking to gain advantage over their countrymen sometimes through manipulating the system and state regulations. In addition, the populace was blind to the invisible hand and thus could not be the best judge of its own interests (Rothschild 2001).

Karl Popper and Ludwig Wittgenstein

It has been claimed that philosophers like Wittgenstein and Popper have been interpreted in ways that are contentious. In his popularised journey through modern western philosophy, Magee pointed out that logical positivists wrongly interpreted Popper's falsifiability thesis as supporting their own claims to truth.

Instead Popper was simply demarcating what he considered to be scientific from non-scientific statements (Green 2005b). Popper in fact saw religion, myth and metaphysical beliefs as important, alternative ways of seeing the world (Magee 1998).

Similarly, logical positivists assumed that Wittgenstein's *Tractatus* was based on logical positivist ideas (Green 2005b). However Magee is of the opinion that Wittgenstein, while being in agreement with the logical positivists that certain utterances could only be valid according to whether or not they fulfilled scientific rules of verification, himself believed that such utterances encompassed the comparatively unimportant areas of factual discourse and logic, and not the more important questions of ethics, morals, values, and meanings of life and death (Magee 1998).

Interpretations of Burns and Stalker's book

Interpretations of *The Management of Innovation* in textbooks and academic journals have been broadly of two kinds. Most have concentrated on the ideal types of mechanistic and organic structures and on the characteristics attributed by Burns and Stalker to each of these systems. The interpretations have been about organisations needing to have their structures and systems adapted to an organic rather than to a mechanistic system in times of change.

Textbooks have been used in this book as one of the two main sources of data to demonstrate mainstream representations of Burns and Stalker's work, the other being academic journals. This chapter analyses textbook interpretations; the following deals with representations of *The Management of Innovation* in journal articles. Though related, the two are different enterprises, and it was felt they would be better handled separately.

Mainstream textbooks used as examples are Daft (2001), Robbins (2003) and Mullins (2005). The first two are US textbooks, the last, British. They have been used as they are popular, have run into several editions and have been adopted internationally. Textbooks are important as they have a large role in framing and legitimating the boundaries and content of a subject. Stambaugh and Trank (2010) have emphasised that they present a view of a discipline with the content and boundaries standardised and widely disseminated.

In the seventh edition of his textbook *Organization Theory and Design*, Daft portrayed Burns and Stalker's ideas as providing a choice between two alternative structures:

> When the external environment was stable, the internal organization was characterized by rules, procedures, and a clear hierarchy of authority... In rapidly changing environments, the internal organization was much looser, free-flowing, and adaptive. Rules and regulations often were not written down or, if written down, were ignored...

> As environmental uncertainty increases, organizations tend to become more organic, which means decentralizing authority and responsibility to lower levels ... Thus, the organization is more fluid and is able to adapt continually to changes in the external environment.
>
> (Daft 2001:144–145)

Robbins, after describing the characteristics of mechanistic and organic systems, noted that

> An organization's structure is a means to help management achieve its objectives ... structure should follow strategy. If management makes a significant change in its organization's strategy, the structure will need to be modified to accommodate and support this change.
>
> (Robbins 2003:440)

There was no suggestion in either of these textbooks that human attitudes, actions and interests needed to be taken into account if such change was to be supported, as, it will be shown, had been discussed at length by Burns and Stalker.

Mullins (2005) stated that according to Burns and Stalker, both mechanistic and organic systems represented a rational form of organisation which could be:

> created and maintained explicitly and deliberately to make full use of the human resources in the most efficient manner according to the circumstances ...
>
> (Mullins 2005:642)

Here too there was no discussion of the many difficulties raised by Burns and Stalker in achieving these aims. All three authors then set out tables summarising only[2] Burns and Stalker's mechanistic and organic 'forms'. These are examples of mimeticism, common to both textbooks and to researchers using Burns and Stalker's ideas (Green 2005b).[3] For further observations about the scope and subject matter of textbooks, see Green (2012b).

Alternative interpretations of Burns and Stalker's book

There were minority textbook interpretations of *The Management of Innovation* indicating that some saw more in the book than recommendations for a fit between organisational form and environment. One of these was by Pugh et al., in which they stated as early as 1964 that Burns and Stalker had found that it was not at all easy to achieve organic systems, particularly if the organisation was being changed from a mechanistic one:

> The almost complete failure of the traditional Scottish firms to absorb electronics research and development engineers into their organizations

leads Burns to doubt whether a mechanistic firm can consciously change
to an organismic one.

(Pugh et al. 1964:16)

This is a substantially different interpretation of Burns and Stalker's work.
Although it remains within a discourse about structure, it highlights the
difficulties in achieving change from a mechanistic to an organic system.
That short paragraph introduces the problem of human agency, in the shape
of the new cadres of engineers. These had been acknowledged by Burns and
Stalker to be important in influencing the outcomes of structural change,
and were analysed by them at some length. These findings are relevant for
management practice, and their absence, as is demonstrated throughout the
book, risks doing a disservice to managers, other practitioners and employees, as well as to scholars and students.

The first set of interpretations has been privileged over the last in terms of
what has become accepted knowledge about *The Management of Innovation*.
Daft's (2001), Robbins' (2003) and Mullins' (2005) foci on structural aspects
are present in many organisation and management textbooks. Many researchers
have also concentrated on Burns and Stalker's model of mechanistic and
organic systems when testing their theory against organisational practice, as
discussed in the next chapter. Simons' (1987) paper is analysed in later chapters
as a more detailed example of research using Burns and Stalker's ideas as a basis
for investigating organisations in stable and volatile environments.

Meanings of texts

These different interpretations raise issues about where the meanings of texts lie.
Given that the interpretation in this book is yet another, subjective interpretation, questions arise as to whether both sets of readings of Burns and Stalker's
monograph are valid or whether one is more legitimate. This is important as the
establishment of what counts as justifiable knowledge arising from Burns and
Stalker's text has both epistemological and practical implications for the understanding and practice of the management of change in organisations.

The textbook interpretations of *The Management of Innovation* are necessarily
much shorter versions of a book stretching to 262 pages. Kuhn, writing about
representations of the history of science, acknowledged that the representation of
theory must necessarily be a summary and perforce a simplification. Scientists
often did not apply a full theory to their research, but instead abstracted from it a
narrower set of 'rules' for their empirical work (Kuhn 1970:43). However, this
was unsatisfactory for Kuhn, as the narrower set of rules left out important
developments in the history of science, particularly the non-linearity, randomness,
complexity and conflictual nature of scientific theories, especially where new
paradigms contradicted older ones (Kuhn 1970).

Here the problem is similar – a narrower interpretation with complexity,
conflict and potential problems written out. This is particularly true of

mainstream interpretations and may be true to an extent of Pugh's et al. representation on account of its brevity. One could explain these different representations on the grounds that there are, for many reasons, going to be different interpretations of any text, and leave it at that. More foolhardy, perhaps, in the light of post-structuralist[4] strictures on the possibilities of arriving at definitive meanings of texts, is an attempt to establish the meanings in the original book, and then to evaluate its interpretations.

Poststructuralists on the meanings of texts

Questions about the meanings of texts have been raised by many theorists (Green 2009, 2012b). Some have framed these in terms of meanings lying alternatively with the author, the reader, the text itself or some combination of these, and have suggested criteria for adjudicating on the validity of diverse interpretations. In order to evaluate interpretations of texts with some confidence, post-structuralist and other theorists, principally Barthes (1977), Derrida (1977, 2002a) and Eco (1992a, 1992b) are used to highlight problems in defining meanings in texts, and then as bases for establishing, if not definitive, at least defensible meanings of texts.

Barthes and Derrida among others have strongly denied the notion of an *a priori* subject situated outside a context (Barthes 1977; Derrida 1977). Their ideas have encouraged the questioning of meanings of texts, particularly their authors' intentions, and have opened up the possibility of there being different valid interpretations. Barthes and Derrida in particular emphasised the essential undecidability of a text − for many, often different reasons, but also with strong arguments recurring for both (Derrida 1976; Barthes 1977).

Barthes' death of the author

The most extreme of these views is Barthes'. Like Derrida he wrote about the deferred meaning of the signified:

> The Text … practises the infinite deferment of the signified, is dilatory; its field is that of the signifier [word] and the signifier must not be conceived of as the 'first stage of meaning', its material vestibule, but in complete opposition to this, as its *deferred action.*
>
> (Barthes 1977:158) (emphasis in the original)

Barthes extends the idea of limitless possibilities for interpretation in order to attack the use of authors' intentions as a guide to the meaning of texts:

> To give a text an Author is to impose a limit on the text, to furnish it with a final signified [meaning], to close the writing …
>
> (Barthes 1977:147)

A text does not stand as a discrete creation in its own right. The author brings with her a formed ontology and epistemology with all the cultural, ideological and normative bases on which these rest. The text therefore does not have a single 'theological' meaning but is made up of 'a tissue of quotations' from other texts and 'the innumerable centres of culture'. An author can never be original, but can only pick and reject from 'this immense dictionary'. Who then is speaking in the text? Is it the author or is it something like 'man' or universal wisdom? Barthes answers by saying that it is always impossible to know, as writing consists of all these indiscernible voices (Barthes 1977:146).

Readers do not come to a text with a blank slate either. They too have been immersed in a particular culture with its own literature. Their reading of the text is influenced by their own 'immense dictionary' in addition to the author's. Barthes in numerous analyses comes down in favour of the reader as the producer of the text. This has led to his famous or notorious proclamation of the 'death of the author':

> a text is made of multiple writings, drawn from many cultures ... but there is one place where this multiplicity is focused and that place is the reader, not, as was said hitherto, the author. The reader is the space on which all the quotations that make up a writing are inscribed without any of them being lost; a text's unity lies not in its origin but in its destination ... the birth of the reader must be at the cost of the death of the author.
>
> (Barthes 1977:148)

However Barthes does not dispose entirely with the author. In the same volume he softens his position:

> Text ... can be read without the guarantee of its father ... It is not that the Author may not 'come back' in the Text, in his text, but he then does so as a 'guest'.
>
> (Barthes 1977:161)

Barthes' awarding of authority to the reader as the 'producer of the text' is also tempered in other writings. According to Keuneman, when Barthes writes about the 'critic', for whom one can presumably substitute 'reader', he is said to take a more rigorous view of the interpretation of texts:

> Barthes considers the criticism does still operate within a set of constraints ... The specific limiting constraints are first, everything in a work is intelligible, and critical discourse must be able to account for all of it ... this question is answered by an act of choice on the part of the critic, who must himself decide that a meaningful pattern has emerged.
>
> (Keuneman 1987:xviii)

Notwithstanding these *caveats*, Barthes' favouring the interpretive powers of the reader could support a justification for mainstream foci on formal structures with regard to Burns and Stalker's book.

Derrida's *différance*

Derrida too supports the concept of the undecidability of texts and the impossibility of arriving at finite meanings for them. Derrida's concept of *différance* contains the argument that texts offer infinite possibilities for interpretation, because the meaning of a text may extend beyond the limits of our knowledge at any one time. *Différance*, according to Derrida, is the movement that consists in 'deferring ... delegation, reprieve, referral, detour, postponement, reserving' (Derrida 2002a:8).

Derrida's concept of *différance* bears similarities with Barthes' claim that words always exist in relation to other words and accordingly their meanings change as these other words and the contexts in which they are used change. The meaning of any word is derived from a process of ceaseless differing from and deferral to other words, and thus the analysis of a text offers unending possibilities for interpretation (Derrida 2002a).

> In the extent to which what is called 'meaning' ... is already ... constituted by a tissue of differences, in the extent to which there is already a *text*, a network of textual referrals to *other* texts, a textual transformation in which each allegedly 'simple term' is marked by the trace of another term, the presumed interiority of meaning is already worked upon by its own exteriority.
>
> (Derrida 2002b:33) (emphasis in the original)

Although Derrida, like Barthes, thinks that there is no underlying, final decipherable meaning in a text, he has more confidence than Barthes in the author's intentions as an indicator of a text's meaning. He gives more credence to the role of the author, accepting the validity of the author's consciousness and intentions as a creator of meaning in the texts, others being the situatedness and historical context of the text and the text itself (Norris 1987).

After denying the author's existence in *Of Grammatology* (1997), Derrida counters this in an interview with Houdebine and Scarpetta, where he asserts: 'I have never said that there is not a 'subject of writing' (Derrida 2002c:88). Derrida for the most part accepts the validity of the author's consciousness and intentions as one of the sources of meaning in texts. He does however pose questions around the author's intentions. While not disregarding them, he also imputes significance and meanings to the text not intended by the author:

> the category of intention will not disappear; it will have its place, but from that place it will no longer be able to govern the entire scene and system of utterance.
>
> (Derrida 1988:18)

Derrida welcomes close analysis of his own writings. When referring to his work *Glas*, he states:

> Perhaps it is better – in any case it interests me more – to speak of what is not there and what should have been there in what I have written.
>
> (Derrida 1995a:6)

Consistent with his views of others' writings, Derrida is careful to disclaim his own authorship and intentions once he himself has published a text[5]:

> Au fond, ce n'est pas moi qui signe, dès que c'est lancé sur le marché littéraire, ça ne vient plus de moi, ça ne s'adresse pas à toi, la trace m'échappe, elle tombe dans le monde… le risque de perversion, de corruption, de dérive est en même temps la seule chance de m'addresser à l'autre.
>
> (Derrida 2005:26)[6]

Derrida's supplementarity

Derrida's notion of the 'logic of supplementarity'[7] is a further way of analysing texts, as it disprivileges obvious meanings by overturning hierarchy in oppositions and questioning univocal definitions of meaning. Derrida describes the supplement as another name for *différance* (Derrida 1977:150). His oppositions to binary distinctions in texts, which, he claims, are fundamental to western thought, can be seen as a move against the construction of a dialectic in knowledge.[8] Derrida invites the reader to see where binary distinctions break down and where the 'supplementary' or oppositional idea can be claimed to be the dominant one:

> To do justice to this necessity is to recognize that in a classical philosophical opposition we are not dealing with the peaceful coexistence of a *vis-à-vis*, but rather with a violent hierarchy. One of the two terms governs the other … or has the upper hand. To deconstruct the opposition, first of all, is to overturn the hierarchy at a given moment. To overlook this phase of overturning is to forget the conflictual and subordinating structure of opposition.
>
> (Derrida 2002c:41) (emphasis in the original)

Derrida's concept of binary distinctions and supplementarity has a political dimension. According to Smith, Derrida's whole concept of deconstruction is based on the notion of alterity – giving 'the other' space and significance – often ignored in philosophical texts (Smith 2005). *Différance* is to do with such recognition – an element able to be signified only if it is related to something 'other than itself' (Derrida 1973:142). Derrida's notion of the logic of supplementarity is a further development of the notion of alterity because of its role in overturning conventional meanings and oppositional hierarchies in texts. An analogous point is later made about Burns and Stalker's interpretation of the relationship between formal and informal structures, an interpretation at odds with subsequent representations of their book.

In order to meet difficulties of interpretation Derrida favours a 'patient and minutely philological explication de texte', as shown in his detailed and meticulous critique of Plato's *Phaedrus* (Miller 1976:336). Norris supports this view, arguing that according to Derrida,

> ... we should always be willing to adjust or revise our logic in response to whatever anomalies might turn up in the course of empirical investigation ... any break with a priori concepts or guiding intuitions must come as the result of a rigorous and detailed textual analysis rather than provide a kind of coping strategy designed to ensure in advance that such problems simply cannot arise.
>
> (Norris 2002:xlvi)

Eco's limits of interpretation

Like Barthes and Derrida, Eco acknowledges the 'unlimited semiosis' in texts, mirrored by language which is 'incapable of finding any transcendental meaning' (Eco 1992a:39). The arbitrariness of the signifier as outlined by Derrida results in instability in the text, which becomes open-ended, 'where the interpreter can discover infinite interconnections' (Eco 1992a:39). As with Derrida, Eco acknowledges that once in the public domain, his writings are out of his control, regardless of whether or not he agrees with their interpretations (Eco 1992a, 1992b).

But Eco too imposes limits on interpretation. Although texts can have many meanings it does not mean that every meaning is acceptable (Eco 1992a). He is uneasy at some deconstructionists' licence given to readers in 'producing' meanings of texts (Collini 1992:8). Eco imposes limitations on the range of admissible interpretations through distinguishing between the intentions of the author, the reader and the text – *intentio auctoris, intentio lectoris* and *intentio operis* (Eco 1992a:25). The text is reducible neither to the intentions of the author, which might be difficult to uncover, nor to unlimited interpretations by the reader. For Eco, as for Derrida, the *intentio operis* plays an important role as a source of meaning.

However problematic the signifiers and however wide the range of interpretations, it is the text which has to be returned to:

> If there is something to be interpreted, the interpretation must speak of something which must be found somewhere, and in some way respected.
>
> (Eco 1992a:43)

Eco, affirms the primacy of the text, *intentio operis*, in arguing that textual coherence overrides both the author, *intentio auctoris*, and the interpreter or reader, *intentio lectoris* (Eco 1992b). Interpretations of the text are acceptable only if they are checked against the rest of the text, if they fit in with the text 'as a coherent whole' and if they are not challenged by other parts of the same text (Eco 1994:59, citing Augustine, De Doctrina Christiana). Coherence with the text constitutes an interpretation which is supported by the rest of the text, is logically connected with it and provides 'better' or more valid justifications for that interpretation (Eco 1992d:150–151). His emphasis is similar to Derrida's focus on a minute *explication de texte*.

Applications to Burns and Stalker's text

Derrida's deconstruction

There must be more to being able to arrive at conclusions about the meaning of a text than to adopt Barthes' extreme view about the death of the author and his even more extreme suggestion of privileging the reader as a 'producer' of the text. In that case, there would be nothing to discuss as every writer could produce the text she wanted without further argument.

Derrida does not make it easy to follow his methods of deconstruction. He emphasises that deconstruction is speculative and cannot be used to arrive at definite conclusions about the meanings of texts (Norris 1987). He strongly refutes any suggestion that his ideas on analysing texts can be made into a methodology. Deconstruction is not:

> a specialized set of discursive procedures, still less the rules of a new hermeneutic method that works on texts ... It is ... a way of taking a position ... concerning the political and institutional structures that make possible and govern our practices .... Deconstruction is neither a methodological reform that should reassure the organization in place nor a flourish of ... irresponsible-making destruction ...
>
> (Derrida 1982 cited in Culler 1982:156)

Norris claims that Derrida regards deconstruction as neither a 'method', a 'technique or a type of 'critique' (Norris 1987:18). Norris, however, questions these denials. According to him there is some sort of method to Derrida's deconstruction. Most typically Derrida's deconstructive approaches consist of:

> the dismantling of conceptual oppositions, the taking apart of hierarchical systems of thought which can then be *reinscribed* within a different order of textual signification.
>
> (Norris 1987:19) (emphasis in the original)

Derrida's rejection of binary oppositions is used to examine Burns and Stalker's discussions of formal and informal systems and processes. The notion of supplementarity is used to examine the effects of hierarchies and institutional structures and their vulnerabilities to informal groupings. In many of its representations the separation between formal and informal structures, and the omission of human initiatives in creating informal structures might be interpreted as a strong, perhaps 'violent' opposition 'created' between formal and informal systems.

Questions of politics and alterity are relevant to interpretations of *The Management of Innovation* when actions by employees which could (and did) result in failures in managerially driven change strategies are absented from much mainstream discussion. Instead of giving them space and significance, managers are implicitly or explicitly given an exclusive warrant to determine and implement organisational change. As discussed in the next chapter, the same principle applies to researchers using only senior managers as their source of data, and ignoring the possibility of acquiring useful and different information from those in subordinate positions.

Eco's intentio operis

Eco's emphasis on *intentio operis*, particularly the aspects relating to textual coherence, is used to strengthen the analysis here of the meaning of Burns and Stalker's book. Eco develops this concept with certain stipulations relevant to evaluations of Burns and Stalker's work and the possible interpretations deducible from it. The first condition is that the text should not be able to be explained more economically (Eco 1992b). On this point mainstream interpreters of Burns and Stalker could claim that their interpretations are valid as the few pages detailing the structural characteristics for successful organisational change constitute the essence of the book, thereby legitimating their focus on structure.

They may be on weaker ground with Eco's other stipulations. He wanted a single or limited 'class of possible causes' (Eco 1992b:49). If one uses the concept of 'cause' as accounts or explanations Burns and Stalker gave for failures, as well as successes of organisational change strategies, this would fit with the judgement that they were important to Burns and Stalker, as demonstrated by the time and space spent on these in their book. The possibilities of failure, let alone the reasons for it were absent in orthodox interpretations. The dysfunctional aspects of change were not considered and therefore not accounted for. Beyond recommendations for structural change, successful outcomes and explanations for them were not discussed.

Eco's third condition for a valid interpretation – that it fits with the other evidence in the text – is the strongest argument here. Eco stipulates that to explore all possible meanings in a text an interpreter has first to 'take for granted a zero-degree meaning' – the one 'authorized by the dullest and simplest of the existing dictionaries' (Eco 1994:36). Despite unavoidable drift from a textual production to its subsequent interpretations, 'the text qua text still represents a comfortable presence' (Eco 1992c:88).

The case here for a wider interpretation of Burns and Stalker's ideas is that most of their book is about the problems arising from attempts to change mechanistic to organic structures. A further argument lies in the three independent variables stipulated by Burns and Stalker. These did not constitute only the idea always present in mainstream interpretations – the fit between the organisation's structure and its environment. The other variables, which took up several chapters of the book, were about employee commitment and the chief executive's capabilities.

Conclusion

This chapter has been about complexities of meanings and interpretations of texts. Contrasting interpretations in textbooks with Burns and Stalker's book have been presented. The evidence points to a dialectical relationship between the dominant scholarship focused on formal structure, and alternative interpretations concerned with human agency, power, politics, conflict and potential failures in management change strategies.

Attempts to establish meanings of text are problematic given concepts such as 'death of the author' (Barthes 1977); and *différance* and supplementarity (Derrida 1977). A further difficulty lies in the different possible points of entry to understanding a text, be they through the author's or reader's intentions or the work itself (Eco 1992b). In the following chapters a minute *explication de texte*, as suggested by Derrida, and an analysis based on the text (*intentio operis*) as Eco recommended, is undertaken with regard to *The Management of Innovation* and the ways it has been represented in the literature.

Notes

1 This chapter is based on published papers by Green (2005a, 2009, 2012a) (Springer) and (2012b) Emerald. The author would like to thank Springer and Emerald for copyright permission.
2 'Only', because much more can be said about Burns and Stalker's book.
3 *The Management of Innovation* in these textbooks were essentially not different from these.
4 Barthes is sometimes described as a 'structuralist' and sometimes as a 'poststructuralist' theorist. Burke's (1998) definitions are followed.
5 See also Green (2017).
6 'Ultimately, it isn't my mark which will remain; as soon as it is launched onto the literary scene, it no longer comes from me. It doesn't relate to you; my trace slips away and falls into the world ... At the risk of corruption, distortion and diversion, it is, nevertheless, my only chance of speaking to others'.
7 Derrida's concept of supplementarity is analysed in more detail in Chapter 5.
8 Derrida was influenced by Hegelian dialectics, comparing Hegel's concept of *aufhebung* (or resolution) with his analysis of *différance* (Derrida 2002c).

References

Barthes, R. (1977). *Image Music Text*. Trans S. Heath. London: HarperCollins.
Burke, J.M. (1998). *The Death and Return of the Author: Criticism and Subjectivity in Barthes, Foucault and Derrida*. Edinburgh: Edinburgh University Press.

Burns, T. (1966). Preface to the Second Edition. In: T. Burns and G.M. Stalker, eds., *The Management of Innovation*. 2nd ed. London: Tavistock Publications, pp. vii–xxii.

Burns, T. and Stalker, G.M. (1961). *The Management of Innovation*. London: Tavistock Publications.

Collini, S. (1992). Introduction: Interpretation Terminable and Interminable. In: S. Collini, ed., *Interpretation and Overinterpretation: Umberto Eco with Richard Rorty, Jonathan Culler and Christine Brooke-Rose*. Cambridge: Cambridge University Press, pp. 1–22.

Collison, D.J. (2003). Corporate Propaganda: Its Implications for Accounting and Accountability. *Accounting, Auditing and Accountability Journal*, 16 (5), pp. 853–886.

Cooke, B. (1999). Writing the Left Out of Management Theory: The Historiography of the Management of Change. *Organization*, 6 (1), pp. 81–106.

Cooper, R. and Fox, S. (2013). Two Modes of Organization? In: R. Mansfield, ed., *Frontiers of Management: Research and Practice*. London: Routledge Revivals, pp. 247–261.

Culler, J. (1982). *On Deconstruction: Theory and Criticism after Structuralism*. Ithaca, NY: Cornell University Press.

Daft, R.L. (2001). *Organization Theory and Design*. 7th ed. Cincinnati, OH: South-Western College Publishing.

Derrida, J. (1973). *Speech and Phenomena*. Trans. D.B. Allison. Evanston, IL: Northwestern University Press.

Derrida, J. (1976). *Of Grammatology*. Trans. G.C. Spivak. Baltimore, MD: The John Hopkins University Press.

Derrida, J. (1977). *Limited Inc*. Trans. S. Weber and J. Mehlman. Evanston, IL: Northwestern University Press.

Derrida, J. (1988). *Limited Inc*. Trans. S. Weber. Evanston, IL: Northwestern University Press.

Derrida, J. (1995a). Between Brackets I. In: E. Weber, ed., *Points ... Interviews 1974–1994*. Trans. P. Kamuf et al. Stanford, CA: Stanford University Press, pp. 5–29.

Derrida, J. (2002a). Implications: Interview with Henri Ronse. In: J. Derrida, ed., *Positions*. Trans. A. Bass. 2nd ed. London: Continuum, pp. 1–14.

Derrida, J. (2002b). Semiology and Grammatology: Interview with Julia Kristeva. In: J. Derrida, *Positions*. Trans. A. Bass. 2nd ed. London: Continuum, pp. 17–36.

Derrida, J. (2002c). Positions: Interview with Jean-Louis Houdebine and Guy Scarpetta. In: J. Derrida, *Positions*. Trans. A. Bass. 2nd ed. London: Continuum, pp. 37–96.

Derrida, J. (2005). *Sur Parole: Instantanés*. La Tour d'Aigues : Éditions de l'aube.

Dickson, K., Lawton Smith, H. and Smith, S. (2013). Interfirm Collaboration and Innovation: Strategic Alliances or Reluctant Partnerships? In: R. Mansfield, ed., *Frontiers of Management: Research and Practice*. London: Routledge Revivals, pp. 140–160.

Eco, U. (1992a). Interpretation and History. In: S. Collini, ed., *Interpretation and Overinterpretation: Umberto Eco with Richard Rorty, Jonathan Culler and Christine Brooke-Rose*. Cambridge: Cambridge University Press, pp. 23–44.

Eco, U. (1992b). Overinterpreting Texts. In: S. Collini, ed., *Interpretation and Overinterpretation: Umberto Eco with Richard Rorty, Jonathan Culler and Christine Brooke-Rose*. Cambridge: Cambridge University Press, pp. 45–66.

Eco, U. (1992c). Between Author and Text. In: S. Collini, ed., *Interpretation and Overinterpretation: Umberto Eco with Richard Rorty, Jonathan Culler and Christine Brooke-Rose*. Cambridge: Cambridge University Press, pp. 67–88.

Eco, U. (1992d). Reply. In: S. Collini, ed., *Interpretation and Overinterpretation: Umberto Eco with Richard Rorty, Jonathan Culler and Christine Brooke-Rose*. Cambridge: Cambridge University Press, pp. 139–151.

Eco, U. (1994). *The Limits of Interpretation.* Bloomington and Indianapolis, IN: Indiana University Press.

Green, M. (2005a). Are Management Texts Produced by Authors or by Readers? Representations of a Contingency Theory. *Philosophy of Management,* 5 (1), pp. 85–96.

Green, M. (2005b). The Representation of a Contingency Theory in Organization and Management Studies: Knowledge Management in the Academy. *The Icfaian Journal of Management Research,* 4 (1), pp. 62–73.

Green, M. (2009). Analysis of a Text and Its Representations: Univocal Truth or a Situation of Undecidability? *Philosophy of Management,* 7 (3), pp. 27–42.

Green, M. (2012a). Can Deconstructing Paradigms be Used as a Method for Deconstructing Texts? *Philosophy of Management,* 11 (2), pp. 85–113.

Green, M. (2012b). Objectivism in Organization/Management Knowledge: An Example of Bourdieu's "Mutilation"? *Social Responsibility Journal,* 8 (4), pp. 495–510.

Green, M. (2017). Behaviour in Academe: An Investigation into the Sustainability of Mainstream Scholarship in Management Studies. In: G. Aras and C. Ingley, eds., *Corporate Behavior and Sustainability: Doing Well by Being Good.* Finance, Governance and Sustainability: Challenges to Theory and Practice Series. London: Routledge.

Keuneman, K.P. (1987). Preface to English-Language Edition. In: R. Barthes, ed., *Criticism and Truth.* Trans. K.P. Keuneman. London: Continuum.

Kuhn, T.S. (1970). *The Structure of Scientific Revolutions.* 2nd ed. Chicago, IL: Chicago University Press.

Magee, B. (1998). *Confessions of a Philosopher: A Journey through Western Philosophy.* London: Phoenix.

Miller, J.H. (1976). Stevens' Rock and Criticism as Cure II. *Georgia Review,* 30 (2), pp. 330–348.

Mullins, L.J. (2005). *Management and Organisational Behaviour.* 7th ed. Harlow: Prentice Hall.

Norris, C. (1987). *Derrida.* London: Fontana Press.

Norris, C. (2002). Derrida's *Positions,* Thirty Years on: Introduction to the Second English Language Edition. In: J. Derrida, ed., *Positions.* Trans. A. Bass. 2nd ed. London: Continuum, pp. ix–liv.

Pugh, D.S., Hickson, D.J., and Hinings, C.R. (1964). *Writers on Organizations: An Introduction.* London: Hutchinson.

Robbins, S.P. (2003). *Organizational Behavior.* 10th ed. Upper Saddle River, NJ: Pearson Education.

Rothschild, E. (2001). *Economic Sentiments: Adam Smith, Condorcet, and the Enlightenment.* Cambridge, MA: Harvard University Press.

Simons, R. (1987). Accounting Control Systems and Business Strategy: An Empirical Analysis. *Accounting Organizations and Society,* 12 (4), pp. 357–374.

Smith, A. (1982). *Lectures on Jurisprudence* (R.L. Meek, D.D. Raphael and R.G. Stein, eds.), Glasgow Edition of Works, vol. 5 (1762–1766). Indianapolis: Liberty Fund.

Smith, A. (2007). *An Inquiry into the Nature and Causes of the Wealth of Nations* (S.M. Soares, ed., Book I Chapter IX, Amsterdam: Libri.

Smith, J.K.A. (2005). *Jacques Derrida: Live Theory.* New York: Continuum Books.

Stambaugh, J.E. and Trank, C.Q. (2010). Not so Simple: Integrating New Research into Textbooks. *Academy of Management Learning and Education,* 9 (4), pp. 663–681.

Willmott, H. (1993). Breaking the Paradigm Mentality. *Organization Studies,* 14 (5), pp. 681–719.

3   Representations of texts

Introduction[1]

Representation of texts is a related issue but separate from meanings in texts. Representations of texts are influenced by the characteristics of the data and by the context, situatedness (Sarbin and Kitsuse 1994) or *habitus*[2] (Bourdieu 1998) of the researchers responsible for the representations. In this chapter comparisons are made of *The Management of Innovation*, this time with some of its mainstream representations and research applications in academic journal articles. Research published in any field plays a significant role in establishing and legitimating what counts as valid knowledge, and the terms in which it is constructed and framed. Though related to textbooks, journal articles, because they are focussed on research, are different in the type of scholarship, depth of analysis, purpose and production.

Representation

It was shown in the previous chapter that determining meanings of texts is fraught with difficulties, and according to poststructuralists is seen as being open to the winds. Eco (1992) had argued that the important elements in deciding on meanings of texts were whether priority was given to the author, the reader or to the text itself. This has been seen as a way forward, but there are difficulties with the related problem of representation (Green 2005). Derrida was aware that as soon as his work was out in the world it would no longer be in his control and risked being changed and represented differently from his original intention (Derrida 2005). Substantive problems can arise. These can include distortion, diversion and corruption. In this chapter issues are raised about the collection and representation of data. The analysis then moves on to representations, specifically of texts. This raises questions as to whose prerogative it is to establish their meanings – the author, the reader or recourse to the text itself.

The material or testimony

Critiques of representations of researchers' findings in the social sciences emerged at least as early as the early twentieth century in the form of political, cultural and methodological issues regarding social anthropologists with respect to their ethnographic data. These critiques were framed in the context of colonialism. Problems with their research lay both with the material collected and with the researcher. The former included the reliability of traditional material such as historical or hagiographic legends, especially when collected as second-hand or hearsay; ignorance of the way the material was originally transmitted; and the reliability of the original sources. Legends could be intermingled with seemingly historical accounts of events purported to have happened. A chain of transmission could legitimate later or earlier versions of the tradition, and various extraneous factors such as the political context, the power of the state, the good of the community and personal ambition could influence the data presented (Vansina 1965). These problems are also present in the transmission of texts. One issue raised in representations of Burns and Stalker's text has been the mimeticism in textbook representations over the decades – all producing very similar interpretations of *The Management of Innovation* and all ignoring the problems raised regarding human agency.

Researchers and interpreters

Just as respondents' testimonies were liable to be subject to various extraneous factors, so too were researchers' representations, because of their educational, social and ideological backgrounds and the contexts in which they were working. A problem for the specific *habitus* of social anthropologists studying native people under colonial rule was the broad political reality within which their writings were grounded. The heyday of social anthropological research in 'distant' places occurred during colonialism, and one of the criticisms of this work is that it was politically favourable to colonial interests (Alvesson and Skoldberg 2000). Any claims confident that representations by social anthropologists working in this environment could provide objective portrayals of uncontested external realities have been subjected to critical scrutiny by writers from various alternative perspectives – from hermeneutic, through critical to poststructuralist theorists (Alvesson and Skoldberg 2000).

Representation then, rather than being a straightforward recording of results, has raised methodological and political problems, such as the author's voice taking priority over, or silencing altogether, the voices of others. Bourdieu's concept of *habitus* is echoed in postmodern concerns: 'how a certain established style totalizes understanding, creating authority and legitimacy for a certain attempt at providing the truth' (Alvesson and Skoldberg 2000:169). Bourdieu, discussing works by social anthropologists about ritual in the former colonised countries, describes them as

> guilty, as least as regards their objective intention and their social effects, of a particularly scandalous form of ethnocentrism which, ... tending to justify the colonial order, described practices which could only be seen as unjustifiable.
>
> (Bourdieu 1990:2–3)

Rather than being exclusively the problem of social anthropologists such issues are common: the researchers' 'situatedness' – their world views, values and academic training and pressures; the particular paradigm and context in which they are working, all influencing their methodologies and the type of knowledge produced (Sarbin and Kitsuse 1994:11). Bourdieu was against the notion that knowledge and hence representations were passive recordings of objective reality. They were constructed through the *habitus*:

> systems of durable, transposable dispositions, structured structures predisposed to function as structuring structures, that is, as principles which generate and organize practices and representations that can be objectively adapted to their outcomes without presupposing a conscious aiming at end or an express mastery of the operations necessary to attain them.
>
> (Bourdieu 1990:53)

People's *habitus*, and their 'structuring structures' are relevant in all areas of life through their political values, their ethical judgements their cultural preferences and, according to critical theorists, the pressures from dominant interests (Green 2005). This results from their 'economic' and 'cultural' capital or their material, social and political positions in society (Bourdieu 1998:6). Differences in possession of these kinds of capital are used as weapons to fight their corner in the social space, and affect all areas of life even to the point of functioning as distinctive symbolic systems with their own languages (Bourdieu 1998:5).

Bourdieu was quick not to blame social anthropologists for their colonial context (Green 2016). As with respondents, scholars were subject to similar constraints because of their situatedness or *habitus*:

> Those who nowadays set themselves up as judges and distribute praise and blame among the sociologists and ethnologists of the colonial past would be better occupied in trying to understand what it was that prevented the most lucid and best intentioned of those they condemn from understanding things which are now self-evident ... in what is unthinkable at a given time, there is not only everything that cannot be thought of for lack of the ethical or political dispositions which tend to bring it into consideration, but also everything that cannot be thought for lack of instruments of thought such as problematics, concepts, methods and techniques ...
>
> (Bourdieu 1990:5)

Representations of texts

One might be tempted to claim that representations of written texts are simpler. But there are difficulties similar to those with respondents' testimonies, such as the mimetic reproductions of representations of Burns and Stalker's book extending over such a long period (Green 2009a). The chain of transmission in mainstream interpretations of *The Management of Innovation* has not differed over a period of more than fifty years, with the same foci and absences continued into this century.

'Representation' is used partly in the sense of copying external reality, in this case a text, and what is written in it, as Eco's emphasis on the importance of the *intentio operis* acknowledged. What constitutes reality can be contentious (Green 2005). Bourdieu's structuring structures or principles which generate and organise practices are relevant, as is Chia's view that acts of representation are attempts to control and manipulate 'the remote, the obdurate and the intractable' (1996:102). These acts constitute processes to do with 'forming, framing and delimiting' (Chia 1996:213).

An issue about structuring structures raised by Argyris concerns the abstraction of knowledge and its correspondingly increasing inapplicability to practical organisational life. Argyris gives the example of Lewin, Lippit and White's work on leadership, discussed in the previous chapter. As scholars followed up research, they sought to narrow the subject to more rigorous generalisations which became less and less enactable in management practice (Argyris 2013).

Representations of *The Management of Innovation*

Representations of *The Management of Innovation* have been formed, framed and delimited in particular ways in the journal literature as they have in textbooks (Green 2009a). A picture of mainstream journal literature on contingency theory and representations of Burns and Stalker's book is given below. Strong differences in representations are shown, based on very different interpretations of the text. As with the textbooks, these mainly represent two different types of scholarship, with different knowledge produced in each, again raising the question as to what does count as knowledge, how is it evaluated and legitimated, and what are its consequences for management scholarship and practice.

Organisation/management journals

Papers in academic journals were investigated to see how academic scholars have interpreted, represented and applied Burns and Stalker's ideas. The research was carried out through electronic keyword searches in journals as far back as material was found – usually from the 1960s or 1970s. Journals that seemed most likely to have articles referring to contingency theories were also searched manually from the early 1960s. Key journals looked at were the *Administrative Science Quarterly (ASQ), Human Relations (HR)* and *Accounting, Organizations and Society (AOS)*.

Early representations of Burns and Stalker's work include Lawrence and Lorsch's, two other well-known contingency theorists. They published an article and a book in 1967, soon after the second edition of *The Management of Innovation*. They presented Burns and Stalker's ideas as focussed on their two kinds of structure. In the article in the *ASQ*, in which they presented their own contingency theory, Lawrence and Lorsch discussed Burns and Stalker's ideas:

Organizations in the stable industry tended to be what the authors called 'mechanistic'. There was more reliance on formal rules and procedures. Decisions were reached at higher levels of the organization ... effective organizations in the more dynamic industry were typically more 'organic' ... less attention was paid to formal procedures; more decisions were reached at the middle levels of the organization.

(Lawrence and Lorsch 1967b:15)

This constitutes the formulaic outline of Burns and Stalker's theory in which change was not problematised. One difficulty Lawrence and Lorsch did acknowledge in their paper was that Burns and Stalker had found integrative devices, central to Lawrence and Lorsch's own research, not easy to achieve:

Burns and Stalker reported that such devices observed in their study were not effective.

(Lawrence and Lorsch 1967b:12)

Ironically, Lawrence and Lorsch's own work was represented similarly to Burns and Stalker's, in an unproblematised interpretation, where what was discussed was the differentiation and integration these theorists found in high-performing companies. The difficulties they foregrounded, mainly conflict, were underplayed in one of the same textbooks used as an example of interpretations of *The Management of Innovation* in the previous chapter (Green 2012).

Other writers in the management field also presented Burns and Stalker's ideas as conceptually straightforward (Green 2009a). Hellriegel and Slocum, for example, writing in *Business Horizons*, stated that:

The major finding of the British [Burns and Stalker's] study was that, for firms operating in a changing environment, those with a characteristically organic management system were more successful than firms with a mechanistic one.

(Hellriegel and Slocum 1973:64)

Millar wrote in *HR* about the fit of organisation structures to different situations. He gave a more circumspect interpretation:

The best body of hard evidence rests with the Burns and Stalker study (1961) and the Joan Woodward study ... [which] lent confirmation to the Burns and Stalker hypothesis that organizational structures should correspond with their technological environment. The idea that some 'matching' of structure and technology would correlate with organizational effectiveness was seized on with considerable enthusiasm. At first glance it appears to eliminate 'messy value assumptions' and permit controlled testing and applicability.

(Millar 1978:887–888)

Lewin and Volberda (2003) have followed these interpretations into the twenty-first century. They grouped Burns and Stalker (1961), Woodward (1965) and Lawrence and Lorsch (1967a, 1967b) together, describing their contingency theories as ones that

> consider environmental conditions as a direct cause of variation in organizational forms. Management's task is to achieve 'good fits' with the environment.
>
> (Lewin and Volberda 2003:574)

Management accounting journals

Many of the representations of *The Management of Innovation* were in management accounting journals like *AOS*, which dealt with the interface between management accounting and organisation processes. This journal occupies a central position in management accounting scholarship in the UK, in particular because of its original aim of straddling both management accounting and organisational issues (Hopwood 1976). Many of the research papers analysed in this book have come from that journal because of the eminent scholars publishing in that journal and the many articles based on Burns and Stalker's ideas published there.

Management accounting researchers using contingency theories based their work on value-free, non-subjective structural factors, often using positivist approaches.[3] Examples include Bruns and Waterhouse (1975), who produced empirical studies aimed at establishing the connection between the extent of budgetary control, the degree of centralisation of the organisation structure and the level of environmental uncertainty. Gordon and Miller (1976) took organisation structure, the environment and the decision-making style as the main contingent variables and linked them to management policy and accounting information systems. Waterhouse and Tiessen (1978) focussed on two contextual variables, technology and environment in relation to organisational subunits. They examined how these variables impacted on structure and related organisational control processes. The vast majority of research papers using ideas from Burns and Stalker's contingency theory were similar to these, emphasising formal structural factors to the exclusion of the subjective issues mentioned by Burns and Stalker.

Although there were shifts in management scholarship, mainstream management research has generally continued on a path favouring structural over subjective and political factors. Many mainstream management accounting researchers have practised the same dialectic as was shown in the textbooks, concentrating on the formal aspects of change and excluding informal processes and the influence on change strategies by people lower down their organisational hierarchies. This has played an important part in the framing of research questions and methodologies regarding organisational change. Such research methods have often been based on an epistemology in which structural factors and formal processes alone are considered, and knowledge about organisational change assumed to reside exclusively with organisations' senior executives, usually the only people selected as respondents.

Many of the empirical studies about relationships between environmental contingencies, control systems and organisational strategies were carried out through the construction of questions relating to formal structures and processes. They were often based on Likert-type scales, involving large surveys. These

> have come to be seen as large scale, cross sectional, postal questionnaire-based research, which examine the interaction of a limited number of variables.
>
> (Chapman 1997:189)

Langfield-Smith (2007) in a review of quantitative research in control systems and strategy listed 27 studies from 1972 to 2005 dealing with the relationship between control systems and strategy. Surveys and questionnaires, sometimes developed from interviews, were used in all. The widespread use of surveys in contingency research was confirmed by Merchant and Otley (2007) and by Gerdin and Greve (2008).

Where the specific source of the data was given, it was invariably from senior managers (Langfield-Smith 2007: Table 1, 759–765). Khandwalla (1972) administered a questionnaire to company presidents, as did Miller and Friesen (1980) to managers at divisional, VP or higher levels (cited in Langfield-Smith 1997). Simons (1987), Nouri and Parker (1998) and Chenhall and Langfield-Smith (1998) surveyed senior managers exclusively in order to test whether formal organisation systems and structures matched their environments, organisational commitments and product differentiation strategies. Gordon and Narayanan (1984) investigated the relationship between an organisation's structure and information systems by interviewing decision makers; Mia and Chenhall (1994) collected data from managers about managers' performance – data to which, arguably, their subordinates might have been able to contribute (Islam and Hu 2012). This is another instance of structuring (Bourdieu 1998) or delimiting (Chia 1996), as to who was deemed to have the requisite knowledge.

The forming, framing and delimiting of Burns and Stalker's book in many mainstream research applications of their ideas has been in keeping with the scholarship outlined above: simplification and objectification. The focus has been on the ideal types mentioned in the book: mechanistic and organic organisational structures and systems, appropriate for different environmental conditions (Green 2005). A second aspect of the frame has been the implicit and sometimes overt assumption that managers alone had the knowledge necessary to answer research questions about organisational systems and structures, and the prerogative, power and capability to effect structural change (Green 2005). Employees resisting changes through group and individual action, largely absented from these representations, might be examples of

Chia's obdurate and intractable elements. The preferred methodology was usually a survey such as a questionnaire, with a statistical analysis carried out of the quantitative data collected.[4]

Critiques of contingency research

Over the decades there have been analyses of mainstream research by organisation theorists critical of functionalist, objectivist approaches. More interesting, perhaps, is the fact that mainstream scholars themselves have been critical of this research. Some, writing in the same journals, have strongly criticised the methodologies used, as Otley did in an influential paper in *AOS* in 1980. What is significant is that although this article was widely cited, it had surprisingly little effect on subsequent scholarship. This is also true of criticisms by other prominent writers.

Otley, himself a leading management accounting scholar, pointed to an over-confident handling of organisational concepts and the relationships between variables; an insufficient examination of the claims made and the inadequacy of research methodologies based on questionnaires. In sum, over-simplification was wiping out complexity and tentativeness. The first problem was that of vagueness: there were no practical guidelines as to how to order a relationship between management accounting systems and organisational efficacy; contingency variables were themselves ill-defined, as was organisational success; nor was the effectiveness of accounting systems adequately measured.

The same contingent variables were likely to affect both organisation structures and accounting information systems, so organisation structures could not be used as the sole intervening variable between accounting information systems, as this would constitute a circular argument (Otley 1980). There was insufficient rigour with respect to the claims about management accounting information systems embodying the controls in organisations. They were only one among a number of other organisational controls and had to be studied in this wider context. Other potential contributors to or detractors from organisational effectiveness were managerial flair and inter-organisational relations. Antagonistic power structures in organisations also needed to be examined (Otley 1980).

Managerial flair was an issue that had concerned Burns and Stalker, mostly in connection with the abilities of the chief executive to interpret organisational contingencies, adapt organisational structures appropriately and implement and manage these changes, including eliciting commitment from employees. Burns and Stalker found 'extraordinary importance ascribed to the personal qualities of the managing director' by respondents in all the companies they studied (Burns and Stalker 1961:211). One of the three independent variables crucial to the success of organisations adapting to new environments was:

> the relative capacity of the directors of a concern to 'lead' – i.e. to interpret the requirements of the external situation and to prescribe the

extent of the personal commitments of individuals to the purposes and activities of the working organisation.

(Burns and Stalker 1961:96)

Otley's observations, as mentioned, appear to have had surprisingly little impact on subsequent management accounting scholarship. The separation and lack of response by authors with different views and approaches to the subject was particularly striking in *AOS*. Researchers after 1980 continued to engage in the same research with the same objects of inquiry and research methodologies outlined above in the same journal where Otley's paper had been published.

Similar criticisms were made fifteen years later. Ashton et al. made the point that if human behaviour was seen as being wholly determined by organisational structures and processes, it left no room for human self-determination or creativity, and therefore for politics, resistance and the recognition that things might not turn out altogether as expected. It allowed no room for questioning the presumed natural order and its legitimacy (Ashton et al. 1995).

Loft criticised the non-reckoning with humans as active agents in organisation processes:

> In Johnson and Kaplan's world view employees of the firm are 'merely' a factor of production with a cost to be minimised, they are not sentient beings but economic ciphers controlled by the wage contract.

(Loft 1995:41)

Preston, analysing the links between budgeting and organisational structure, pointed to the inadequacy of conventional emphases on formalised, hierarchical structures with quantitative, economic budgeting systems forming part of the formal information system. In-date budgeting information was difficult to get from formal information systems in high environmental uncertainty; and formal information could not encompass complex and unfamiliar environmental conditions (Preston 1995). Based on earlier research (Preston 1986), Preston emphasised the fragility and fictional side to formal organisation communication systems and the different constructions that were placed upon them by senior management compared with lower level managers (Preston 1995).

Chapman (1997) too had criticisms of contingency studies. In a discussion on research by Bruns and Waterhouse (1975), Gordon and Miller (1976) and Waterhouse and Tiessen (1978), Chapman pointed out that these articles were contradictory. The problem with looking only at formal control systems meant that one could develop hypotheses that were plausible but opposed. Information seen as something only managers could process was not addressed in any detail and was not problematised (Chapman 1997).

Even after these criticisms of contingency theory much management accounting research continued with the same focus of inquiry, research methods and respondents. Nouri and Parker (1998) tested budget participation, perception of budget adequacy, organisational commitment and performance through a questionnaire sent to a sample of American managers and supervisors with senior management's endorsement. Chenhall and Langfield-Smith (1998) looked at company strategy in terms of management techniques and management accounting practices by sending a questionnaire to senior managers and accountants.[5] Abernethy and Brownell (1999) researched strategic change through a questionnaire to CEO's at Australian hospitals.[6]

Critiques have continued into the twenty-first century. According to Langfield-Smith (2007), although most empirical research about controls and strategy focussed on formal controls, informal controls such as those deriving from shared values and norms or the organisation's culture were important and could have an influence on the effectiveness of the organisation's formal controls. Merchant and Otley (2007:788) were of the opinion that it was 'not clear whether positivistic prescriptions that are stable across time and national and organizational culture are likely to be found, even with a much greater volume of contingency research'.

Resistance to these critiques have been remarked on by various writers. Hopper and Powell were among those who pointed out that despite criticisms by various authors in the 1970s and 1980s, researchers engaged with contingency theory did not pay enough attention to the discretion of key decision-makers, nor to the influence of values, beliefs and ideologies. Appeals for a more interpretive approach with a focus on understanding the participants themselves in order for researchers to get a better grasp of accounting practices and processes were largely ignored (Hopper and Powell 1985).

In a broader discussion March colourfully described the lack of engagement between different approaches to organisation studies in the 1990s as exhibiting '*persistent symptoms of isolation*, engaging in intermittent internecine worldview cleansing' and all in the name of 'technical purity and claims of universality'. He acknowledged that this might be a 'grim necessity' as developing interesting ideas might need commitment, narrowness and cohesiveness (March 1996:280) (emphasis in the original). Interesting ideas, however, might also arise from an engagement with more eclectic approaches.

Alternative approaches: management

There are alternative research practices in the management field. Examples include interpretive approaches, where humans, far from being ignored as part of the research data, were central to the research project. Their understandings of their situations were subjective, socially constructed realities which influenced their actions. Because the role of the researcher was to find the actors' definitions of their situation rather than seeking an objective external reality, 'soft' qualitative research methods such as participant observation, semi-structured interviews and other studies of social interactions were seen to be appropriate (Preston 1986; Sinclair 1995). Researchers were not neutral, but in a relationship with the actors in the situation. This required researchers to be critical both of the actors' definitions and of their own (Denzin and Lincoln 1998). Researchers using these approaches would question the neutrality of social science research.[7] Critical theorists saw research and the knowledge produced to be situated in a societal context influenced by dominant social, political and economic structures and ideologies (Clegg 2002). This awareness could lead to a broader, more complex epistemology, producing knowledge that was likely to be closer to organisational as well as social realities.

Alternative approaches: management accounting

Not all management accounting research was conducted along the lines described above. There are examples of research done since 1980 about similar relationships between structure and control systems that would have met some of the above criticisms. Markus and Pfeffer (1983) for example, set out to examine the effectiveness of accounting and control systems in terms of their relationship to other sources of power within organisations. Miller and O'Leary (1987) had a paper published in *AOS* titled 'Accounting and the Construction of the Governable Person' in which certain accounting techniques were conceived to be part of a wider system of power. Kalagnanam and Lindsay (1999) in order to study relationships between management control systems and organisation structures went to three sites, spent three days at each, looked at work processes and the degree of interaction and participation. They wrote up case studies of the sites and developed questionnaires which they gave to plant managers in order to investigate consultation and decision-making processes.

Alternative representations of *The Management of Innovation*

Alternative representations of *The Management of Innovation* emphasised the authors' *caveats* with regard to the implementation of organic structures and the importance they gave to intraorganisational politics (Green 2009a). In a book review in the *ASQ* two years after the publication of the first edition of *The Management of Innovation*, the reviewer praised the work for being within the sociological tradition, and emphasised the importance it assigned to politics:

> Central ... is the analysis of the relationship between work–organization, political, and status structures of the concern. The dynamics of this relationship are the crucial relations emerging between the laboratory (development) and the workshop (production) ... analyzed on several levels; as a threat to the existing code of conduct, as a disturbance of the existing status and political systems, and as an expression of contrasting occupational ideologies of scientists and managers.
>
> The last section focuses on top management and the extent to which it can interpret the changing technical and commercial situations, adapt work

organization to change, and elicit individual commitment to change. Obstacles and paths of action necessary for administration to induce innovation as a continuous process are suggested by the analysis.

(Form 1963:271–272)

This is a different interpretation of *The Management of Innovation* and emphasises the centrality given to status and political interests, rivalry and conflict. The capacities of senior executives in interpreting changing environmental contingencies, making appropriate changes and motivating staff, are identified by Form as issues addressed in the book.

In another book review in *The Economic Journal*, Burns and Stalker's work was described as producing 'rich' material in their comparisons of successful with unsuccessful innovating organisations (Freeman 1969). Some years later Miller and Friesen (1980) identified topics in Burns and Stalker's book as including internal communication processes, dynamism, technocratisation and delegation.

Kilduff and Dougherty in their overview of the 'classics', cited Burns and Stalker who

may have been the first to spot ... the importance of a common culture ... It is the very strength of this common culture, this 'way of dealing with people' at the organizational level, that allows the diversity of viewpoints, decision-making, and creativity from which innovation flows.

(Kilduff and Dougherty 2000:780)

Conclusion

These different representations pose epistemological questions to do with what counts as knowledge, the nature of academic scholarship and its usefulness for management practice. Different aspects of Burns and Stalker's theory have been presented by different writers. Despite scholars such as Form portraying a fuller and more problematised version of their theory soon after the publication of the first edition of *The Management of Innovation*, this was not acknowledged by many writing after him. There were two parallel lines of thought not engaging with one another, with the unproblematised, objectivist version more frequently presented. The continued publication of papers ignoring the critiques made by Otley and others, often in the same *AOS* journal, indicates the strength and persistence of mainstream objectivist scholarship.

Writers who subscribed to a functionalist view may have decided that what *The Management of Innovation* was really about was Burns and Stalker's recommendation for organic structures to be introduced in times of environmental instability. They would therefore have interpreted Burns and Stalker's ideas as being more about the importance of establishing appropriate structures in organisations than about the difficulties or failures to achieve these. The fact that these mainstream approaches have been dominant in organisation theory for a long time, have probably contributed to mimetic representations of the book. These interpretations may also have been influenced by the objectivist approaches in other contingency theory research. One of the most important and most objectivist studies in contingency theory, the Aston Studies by Pugh et al., extended over a period from 1976–1981, with further papers published at least until 2007 (Pugh and Hickson 2007). Objectivist versions of contingency theory were often viewed as the template for all contingency theory, and represented accordingly.

Notes

1 This chapter is based on published papers by Green (2005, 2009b) (Springer), and on book chapters (2016) (Emerald) and (2017) (Routledge). The author would like to thank Springer, Emerald and Routledge for copyright permission.
2 Bourdieu defined *habitus* as the different positions taken by people through the mediation of their particular social spaces or classes, their practices, goods and tastes, and above all their principles of classification, perceptions, values and opinions, constituting 'a veritable *language*' (Bourdieu 1998:8) (emphasis in the original).
3 Luft and Shields (2014:550) have described positivist accounting research as 'empirically validating general causal explanations... to a given phenomenon...independent of the characteristics of the individual researcher'. The research is intended to be replicable, reliable and influential within the particular research community. However, they refute the idea that accounting researchers in general agree with the classic positivist position that the social sciences are identical with the natural sciences in a quest for stable laws or that the former should aim for predictive research rather than understand causal processes.
4 In later chapters more detailed analyses are given of the management accounting paper mentioned earlier by Simons (1987), who used Burns and Stalker's work as a basis for his research.
5 Interestingly, Chenhall also did very different research using a range of ideographic approaches in a paper he wrote with Euske in 2007, examined in Chapter 8.
6 See Chapter 8 for a more detailed analysis of this paper.
7 It is also maintained that natural scientists are not neutral. See Chapter 7.

References

Abernethy, M. and Brownell, P. (1999). The Role of Budgets in Organizations Facing Strategic Change: An Exploratory Study. *Accounting, Organizations and Society*, 24 (3), pp. 189–204.
Alvesson, M. and Skoldberg, K. (2000). *Reflexive Methodology: New Vistas for Qualitative Research*. London: Sage.
Argyris, C. (2013). The Discipline of Management and Academic Defensive Routines. In: R. Mansfield, ed., *Frontiers of Management: Research and Practice*. London: Routledge Revivals, pp. 8–20.
Ashton, D., Hopper, T., and Scapens, R.W. (1995). The Changing Nature of Issues in Management Accounting. In: D. Ashton, T. Hopper and R.W. Scapens, eds., *Issues in Management Accounting*. 2nd ed. London: Prentice Hall, pp. 1–20.
Bourdieu, P. (1990). *The Logic of Practice*. Trans. R. Nice. Stanford, CA: Stanford University Press.

Bourdieu, P. (1998). *Practical Reason: On the Theory of Action*. Cambridge: Polity Press.

Bruns, W.J. and Waterhouse, J.H. Jr. (1975). Budgetary Control and Organization Structure. *Journal of Accounting Research*, 13 (2), Autumn, pp. 177–203.

Burns, T. and Stalker, G.M. (1961). *The Management of Innovation*. London: Tavistock Publications.

Chapman, C.S. (1997). Reflections on a Contingent View of Accounting. *Accounting, Organizations and Society*, 22 (2), pp. 189–205.

Chenhall, R.H. and Langfield-Smith, K. (1998). The Relationship between Strategic Priorities, Management Techniques and Management Accounting: An Empirical Investigation, Using a Systems Approach. *Accounting, Organizations and Society*, 23 (3), pp. 243–264.

Chia, R. (1996). *Organizational Analysis as Deconstructive Practice*. Berlin: Walter de Gruyter.

Clegg, S.R. (2002). "Lives in the Balance": A Comment on Hinings and Greenwood's "Disconnects and Consequences in Organization Theory?" *Administrative Science Quarterly*, 47 (3), pp. 428–441.

Denzin, N.K. and Lincoln, Y.S. (1998). Introduction: Entering the Field of Qualitative Research. In: N.K. Denzin and Y.S. Lincoln, eds., *The Landscape of Qualitative Research: Theories and Issues*. Thousand Oaks, CA: Sage, pp. 1–34.

Derrida, J. (2005). *Sur Parole: Instantanés*. La Tour d'Aigues: Éditions de l'aube.

Eco, U. (1992). Overinterpreting Texts. In: S. Collini, ed., *Interpretation and Over-interpretation: Umberto Eco with Richard Rorty, Jonathan Culler and Christine Brooke-Rose*. Cambridge: Cambridge University Press, pp. 45–66.

Form, W.H. (1963). Book Review of the Management of Innovation 1962 [Sic]. *Administrative Science Quarterly*, 8 (2), pp. 271–272.

Freeman, C. (1969). The Management of Innovation 1961, 1966. *The Economic Journal*, 79 (314), pp. 403–405.

Gerdin, J. and Greve, J. (2008). The Appropriateness of Statistical Methods for Testing Contingency Hypotheses in Management Accounting Research. *Accounting, Organizations and Society*, 33 (7/8), pp. 995–1009.

Gordon, L.A. and Miller, D.A. (1976). Contingency Framework for the Design of Accounting Information Systems. *Accounting, Organizations and Society*, 1 (1), pp. 59–69.

Gordon, L.A. and Narayanan, V.K. (1984). Management Accounting Systems, Perceived Environmental Uncertainty and Organization Structure: An Empirical Investigation. *Accounting, Organizations and Society*, 9 (1), pp. 33–47.

Green, M. (2005). Are Management Texts Produced by Authors or by Readers? Representations of a Contingency Theory. *Philosophy of Management*, 5 (1), pp. 85–96.

Green, M. (2009a). The Embedding of Knowledge in the Academy: "Tolerance", Irresponsibility or Other Imperatives? *Social Responsibility Journal*, 5 (2), pp. 165–177.

Green, M. (2009b). Analysis of a Text and Its Representations: Univocal Truth or a Situation of Undecidability? *Philosophy of Management*, 7 (3), pp. 27–42.

Green, M. (2012). Can Deconstructing Paradigms Be Used as a Method for Decon-structing Texts? *Philosophy of Management*, 11 (2), pp. 85–113.

Green, M. (2016). Organisational Governance and Accountability: Do We Have Anything to Learn from Studying African Traditional Societies? In: D. Crowther and L. Lauesen, eds., *Accountability and Social Responsibility: International Perspectives*. Developments in Corporate Governance and Responsibility. Vol. 9. Bingley: Emerald.

Green, M. (2017). Behaviour in Academe: An Investigation into the Sustainability of Mainstream Scholarship in Management Studies. In: G. Aras and C. Ingley, eds., *Corporate Behavior and Sustainability: Doing Well by Being Good*. Finance, Governance and Sustainability: Challenges to Theory and Practice Series. London: Routledge.

Hellriegel, D. and Slocum, J.W. (1973). Organizational Design: A Contingency Approach. *Business Horizons*, xvi (2), pp. 59–68.

Hopper, T. and Powell, A. (1985). Making Sense of Research into the Organizational and Social Aspects of Management Accounting: A Review of Its Underlying Assumptions. *Journal of Management Studies*, 22 (5), pp. 429–465.

Hopwood, A.G. (1976). Editorial: The Path Ahead. *Accounting, Organizations and Society*, 1 (1), pp. 1–4.

Islam, J. and Hu, H.A. (2012). Review of Literature on Contingency Theory in Managerial Accounting. *African Journal of Business and Management*, 6 (15), pp. 5159–5164.

Kalagnanam, S.S. and Lindsay, R.M. (1999). The Use of Organic Models of Control in JIT Firms: Generalising Woodward's Findings to Modern Manufacturing Practices. *Accounting, Organizations and Society*, 24 (1), pp. 1–30.

Khandwalla, P.N. (1972). Environment and Its Impact on the Organization. *International Studies of Management and Organization*, 2 (3), pp. 297–313.

Kilduff, M. and Dougherty, D. (2000). Change and Development in a Pluralistic World: The View from the Classics. *Academy of Management Review*, 25 (4), pp. 777–782.

Langfield-Smith, K. (1997). Management Control Systems and Strategy: A Critical Review. *Accounting, Organizations and Society*, 22 (2), pp. 207–232.

Langfield-Smith, K. (2007). A Review of Quantitative Research in Management Control Systems and Strategy. In: C.S. Chapman, A.G. Hopwood and M.D. Shields, eds., *Handbook of Management Accounting Research*. Vol. 2. Amsterdam: Elsevier, pp. 753–783.

Lawrence, P.R. and Lorsch, J.W. (1967a). *Organization and Environment: Managing Differentiation and Integration*. Boston, MA: Harvard Business School Press.

Lawrence, P.R. and Lorsch, J.W. (1967b). Differentiation and Integration in Complex Organizations. *Administrative Science Quarterly*, 12 (1), pp. 1–47.

Lewin, A.Y. and Volberda, H.W. (2003). The Future of Organization Studies: Beyond the Selection-Adaption Debate. In: H. Tsoukas and C. Knudsen, eds., *The Oxford Handbook of Organization Theory*. Oxford: Oxford University Press, pp. 568–595.

Loft, A. (1995). The History of Management Accounting: Relevance Found. In: D. Ashton, T. Hopper and R.W. Scapens, eds., *Issues in Management Accounting*. 2nd ed. London: Prentice Hall, pp. 21–44.

Luft, J. and Shields, M.D. (2014). Subjectivity in Developing and Validating Causal Explanations in Postivist Accounting Research. *Accounting, Organizations and Society*, 39 (7), pp. 550–558.

March, J.G. (1996). Continuity and Change in Theories of Organizational Action. *Administrative Science Quarterly*, 41 (2), pp. 278–287.

Markus, M.L. and Pfeffer, J. (1983). Power and the Design and Implementation of Accounting and Control Systems. *Accounting, Organizations and Society*, 8 (2/3), pp. 205–218.

Merchant, K.A. and Otley, D.T. (2007). A Review of the Literature on Control and Accountability. In: C.S. Chapman, A.G. Hopwood and M.D. Shields, eds., *Handbook of Management Accounting Research*. Vol. 2. Amsterdam: Elsevier, pp. 785–802.

Mia, L. and Chenhall, R.H. (1994). The Usefulness of Management Accounting Systems, Functional Differentiation and Managerial Effectiveness. *Accounting Organizations and Society*, 19 (1), pp. 1–13.

Millar, J.A. (1978). Contingency Theory, Values and Change. *Human Relations*, 31 (10), pp. 885–904.

Miller, D. and Friesen, P.H. (1980). Archetypes of Organizational Transition. *Administrative Science Quarterly*, 25 (2), pp. 268–299.

Miller, P. and O'Leary, T. (1987). Accounting and the Construction of the Governable Person. *Accounting, Organizations and Society*, 12 (3), pp. 235–265.

Nouri, H. and Parker, R. (1998). The Relationship between Budget Participation and Job Performance: The Roles of Budget Adequacy and Organizational Commitment. *Accounting, Organizations and Society*, 23 (5), pp. 467–483.

Otley, D. (1980). The Contingency Theory of Management Accounting: Achievement and Prognosis. *Accounting, Organizations and Society*, 5 (4), pp. 413–428.

Preston, A.M. (1986). Interactions and Arrangements in the Process of Informing. *Accounting, Organizations and Society*, 11 (6), pp. 521–540.

Preston, A.M. (1995). Budgeting, Creativity and Culture. In: D. Ashton, T. Hopper and R.W. Scapens, eds., *Issues in Management Accounting*. 2nd ed. London: Prentice Hall, pp. 273–297.

Pugh, D.S. and Hickson, D.J. (2007). *Writers on Organizations*. 6th ed. London: Penguin Books.

Sarbin, T.R. and Kitsuse, J.I. (1994). A Prologue to Constructing the Social. In: T.R. Sarbin and J.I. Kitsuse, eds., *Constructing the Social*. London: Sage, pp. 1–18.

Simons, R. (1987). Accounting Control Systems and Business Strategy: An Empirical Analysis. *Accounting Organizations and Society*, 12 (4), pp. 357–374.

Sinclair, A. (1995). The Chameleon of Accountability: Forms and Discourses. *Accounting, Organizations and Society*, 20 (2–3), pp. 219–237.

Vansina, J.M. (1965). *Oral Tradition: A Study in Historical Methodology*. Trans. H.M. Wright. London: Routledge & Kegan Paul.

Waterhouse, J.H. and Tiessen, P. (1978). A Contingency Framework for Management Accounting Systems Research. *Accounting Organizations and Society*, 3 (1), pp. 65–76.

Woodward, J. (1965). *Industrial Organization: Theory and Practice*. New York, NY: Oxford University Press.

4 Textual analysis

Introduction[1]

This chapter further fleshes out differences between Burns and Stalker's book and its mainstream representations. The first part of the chapter shows the deep concerns in *The Management of Innovation* with factors affecting organisational change other than the structural factors focussed on in much mainstream scholarship. A comparison is then drawn between Burns and Stalker's book with the chosen textbooks. Derrida's advice to engage in detailed textual analysis (Derrida 1981; Norris 1987) and Eco's (1992b) prescription for the focus being on *intentio operis* are followed. The textbooks are used as Burns and Stalker's theory is more clearly laid out in these than in research papers. The chapter concludes with a comparison of pages of the original text with pages in the textbooks based on Fairclough and Hardy's (1997) critical discourse analysis.

Textual analysis

Textual analysis is one of the major approaches in social science to the meanings in texts, focussing on recurring themes, and the weight given to issues in terms of emphasis, time and space (Denzin and Lincoln 1998). The analysis here is based on Burns and Stalker's (1961) book, and significantly on the prefaces by Burns to the later 1966 and 1994 editions. These prefaces include comments on the difficulties in achieving structural change because of resistance by employees for career and political interests, bureaucratic inertia, and on the problems faced by chief executives in implementing structural change policies. Most interesting perhaps is the hint by Burns in 1966 that the book had been misinterpreted in subsequent uses and references, through 'some wrongly placed emphasis' (1966:xxi).

Themes in *The Management of Innovation*

Certain themes in Burns and Stalker's work stand out, some of which have been emphasised by mainstream theorists and researchers and others identified in alternative interpretations.

Theme 1: variables

Independent variable (i) different rates of technical and market change (with the management system as a dependent variable)
In Chapter 6 of Burns and Stalker's book, the chapter in which mechanistic and organic systems are discussed in some detail, the authors, after describing management systems as a dependent variable, set out their three independent variables: the first being the familiar one in the academic literature of different rates of technical and market change; along with the two less familiar ones (Burns and Stalker 1961:96–125). This first theme is highlighted by Burns in the preface to the second edition:

> The core of all the twenty studies on which the book is based is the description and explanation of what happens when new and unfamiliar tasks are put upon industrial concerns organized for relatively stable conditions. When novelty and unfamiliarity in both market situation and technical information become the accepted order of things, a fundamentally different kind of management system becomes appropriate from that which applies to a relatively stable commercial and technical environment. This general thesis is set out in detail and argued at length in Chapters 4, 5, and 6.
>
> (Burns 1966:vii)

This theme is repeated in various chapters in the book, and examples are given of successful mechanistic organisations operating within stable programmes, and successful organic organisations in situations of rapid change (e.g. Burns and Stalker 1961:83–92). And conversely, there are analyses in the book about organisation structures and systems in which there were difficulties and failures in adaptation. The Scottish firms in particular encountered problems in adapting to change because of their inexperience in coping with market-led developments rather than with the government-supported contracts they had been used to (Burns and Stalker 1961:126–132, 138–142).

In some organisations uncertainties were created by the removal of hierarchical structures, leaving managers anxious about what they should be doing and fears that others were doing better (Burns and Stalker 1961:91). Where the pull of bureaucratic habits was too strong to change to organic systems, this resulted in the reintroduction of mechanistic structures (Burns and Stalker 1961:130–132, 152–154). Weaknesses in mechanistic structures, even in stable conditions, were also discussed (Burns and Stalker 1961:6, 11).

Not only were difficulties raised regarding organisations changing from mechanistic to organic structures, but there were also problems inherent in organic structures themselves and their consequences for efficient functioning in organisations. One difficulty with organic structures, which impinged on their personal lives, were further demands for employees to immerse themselves in their work, and for increased emotional and intellectual commitment, including closer relationships with colleagues (Burns and Stalker 1961:122–123, 233–234). This was the first independent variable specified by Burns and Stalker and it is evident that the connection between organisation structure and its technical and commercial environment was important to them.

Independent variable (ii) the relative strengths of individual commitments to political and status-gaining ends

This variable forms a large part of the content of numerous chapters in the book because of Burns and Stalker's findings that employees' career and political interests were often at variance with managerial goals in their organisations. The threats to individuals' rights, privileges, duties and obligations and what actions they might take in defence of these were discussed. Examples included employees making decisions in their own interests and using or withholding information to their own advantage, all of which could distort the workings of the organisation and lead to dysfunction.

Citing various authors including Taylor (1911), Selznick (1948), Mayo (1949) and Gouldner (1956), Burns and Stalker showed how informal structures could be used for individuals' own ends rather than in the interests of their organisations, and the potential harm these informal groupings could have on efficiency, particularly when faced with an external contingency necessitating organisational change (Green 2009a). Individual loyalties in organic structures, instead of going to the firm, could go instead to informal groups where people sought to bind others in association, resulting in commitments that might not be for the good of the organisation (Burns and Stalker 1961:98–100).

Independent variable (iii) the relative capacity of the directors of the concern to 'lead' – i.e. to interpret the requirements of the external situation and to prescribe the extent of the personal commitments of individuals to the purposes and activities of the working organisation

This variable was crucial for successful adaptation (Green 2005). It was the main subject of the last three chapters of the book, and had been mentioned in previous chapters. The main roles of the chief executive were to define goals for the whole organisation, set parameters for the tasks and activities of groups and individuals, gauge the rate of change, strategically allocate resources in the system and determine the structure of management. The chief executive had to ensure that people were more committed to organisational goals than to the pursuit of their own self-interest. There was also the constant need to adjust the internal structures of the organisation to its external environment. These were not minor tasks and reflect the first and second variables.

The problems faced by senior executives were substantial: isolation from the rest of the organisation, making it difficult for them to know how employees were thinking and feeling (Burns and Stalker 1961:212–213); having to deal with increased complexity as the firm expanded in size and functions, with the knowledge and skills required by the new technical and market demands (Burns and Stalker 1961:231); the ability to handle political manoeuvrings from people and groups (Burns and Stalker 1961:228) and the threat to senior executives' (and other managers') positions by the new teams of laboratory engineers who often acted outside the norms and rules of their organisations (Burns and Stalker 1961:177–205).

Theme 2: reversion to bureaucratic structures

This was taken up in the preface to the second edition of the book. Subsequent representations of the text had included some 'wrongly placed emphasis', and people's commitment to adapting to organic structures was hampered both for individuals and groups by a deeply ingrained ideology of bureaucracy (Burns 1966:xxi). This resulted in appealing to the chief executive's authority, overloading him[2] and at the same time bypassing senior managers and causing resentment (Green 2005). Bureaucratic structures with intermediaries were then brought in because of communication difficulties, often between the new design engineers and other managers, especially production managers. The separation of the laboratory engineers from the rest of the organisation was seen by Burns as an attempt to reinforce mechanistic structures. Solutions through the imposition of bureaucratic systems on organic structures were often unsuccessful and were described by Burns as 'dysfunctional' (1966:xxiv).

Theme 3: process

This may be part of the wrongly placed emphasis Burns had referred to in the preface to the 1966 edition. Later on in that preface, in a section titled 'Organizational Dynamics', Burns emphasised that the direction in which the social world was being studied was through process rather than 'structured immobility'. This was necessary because of the 'essential ambiguity' of human experience. If it was seen in dynamic rather than structural terms, with behaviour as a 'constant interplay and mutual redefinition of individual identities and social institutions', change, development and historical processes could be understood (1966:xxix–xxx). In the 1994 preface Burns reiterated his interest in the structure and dynamics of interpersonal relationships.

Theme 4: managerialism

In the 1994 preface Burns pointed out that social, political and economic circumstances had changed between the 1940s and the 1970s. The change was from a more inclusive view of society with improved economic welfare to a narrower, less generous outlook. In the 1950s scholarship in the social sciences had been influenced by the ideology of consensus. One of the tasks undertaken by social scientists was to identify the impediments to the proper functioning of organisations. Burns quoted authors in the organisation/management areas such as Taylor (1947), Roethlisberger and Dickson (1939) and Mayo (1949), who had engaged in that kind of analysis.

Burns declared informal organisations to be pivotal to organisational efficiency and effectiveness, with rational structures in the 1950s seen as obstacles to efficient and effective management (Burns 1994:ix–x). By the end of the 1950s scholars in organisation studies were becoming more critical. Burns quoted March and Simon's *Organizations* (1958) as the first example of scholarship where human problem-solving and choice were given prominence over organisational structure or managerial control and seen as 'fundamental to the structure and functioning of organisations' (Burns 1994:xii).

However economic pressures because of rises in oil prices, interest rates, inflation and Pacific Rim competition led to changes in organisation studies. Interest was revived in management structures and bureaucracy because of technology or powerful interests in government, business and industry (Burns 1994:xviii–xx). Burns concluded that overall thinking about management structure sought to 'block, cushion or somehow seek accommodation with adverse and competing circumstances or innovative and dissenting opinion so as to preserve the system and the context of beliefs and values which sustains it – and by which it sees itself sustained' (1994:xix). This, along with a revived interest in economics, may have been partly responsible for the 'recrudescence of the hard-line managerialism which has manifested itself in recent years' (1994:xx).

Theme 5: methodology

In more than one place, Burns and Stalker described the research they had engaged in and their selection of respondents. They had gathered information through various techniques – interviews, meetings, casual remarks in social situations and observation in the different work locations such as offices, factories and laboratories. They had interviewed a wide range of employees working in many of the areas in the organisation: industrial scientists, company directors, draughtsmen, technicians, production engineers, foremen and skilled workers (see e.g. Burns and Stalker 1961:12–14). This is very different from the more quantitative, statistical methods adopted by management accounting researchers, with respondents normally limited to senior executives, often to the most senior.

Main thesis

An argument might still be put that these broader ideas and methodologies should not be privileged over the basic premise of different organisational structures and systems being necessary for organisations facing different external contingencies. It could be claimed that this was still the nub of the book, with everything else subservient to it, and with objectivist, quantitatively-based methodologies being more suited to investigating the relationship between structure and environment. But it can also reasonably be put that even if the need for a correlation between organisation systems and external contingencies is the main point of the book, the other variables emphasised by the authors – the commitment of employees and the quality of the leadership of the senior executive – were also significant for the success of structural organisational change.

Burns and Stalker's own comments and their citations of contemporary authors support this analysis of their book. The achievement of organic systems is shown by them to be difficult, not least because of strong social, political, managerial and environmental considerations. Some thirty years later in the preface to the 1994 edition, Burns, while acknowledging that *The Management of Innovation* was partially about suggesting specific systems of management for different rates of change in technology and the market, claimed that it was also about resistance to such changes:

> In *most* of the firms studied, their reluctance to depart from the manage-ment structure and operational practices to which they had become habituated proved too strong. The solutions they in practice sought to apply were mainly to reinforce the old 'mechanistic' system and – very often – to shield it from the impact of the new ventures...
>
> (Burns 1994:xvi) (emphasis added)

According to Burns internal politics had played a dominant role in the organisations they studied:

> Careerism and internal politics were visibly present in *every one of the sixteen or so firms, English as well as Scottish,* that the study eventually covered. Nor did they seem necessarily to resolve themselves either in orderly settlement or in reconciling differences by reconstructing the firm's policy.
>
> (Burns 1994:xvii) (emphasis added)

Burns and Stalker themselves complained that the 'main preoccupation' of organisation theory was with internal structures, and that students 'have directed their attention especially to what had previously been accepted as a datum – the rationality of the formal organization' (Burns and Stalker 1966:109). And as shown, this is the direction textbook writers and academic researchers followed predominantly, rather than concerning themselves with internal organisational processes. Burns and Stalker themselves had opposed this view. In many of the social sciences there:

> has been the attempt ... to replace or supplement the static theoretical models of their textbooks with dynamic models .... with the conduct of actual people, although the existence of a large number of abstract terms in common usage and technical language allows us to ignore this ... Aware-ness of this has led to a number of assaults on accepted theories, which presume an order in equilibrium.
>
> (Burns and Stalker 1961:110)

The connections made in their book with the work of other scholars support their appreciation of the complexity and significance of organisational processes over fixed structures. They quote Carter et al. (1954) who gave sociologists the choice of being

> content with mechanical systems which ignore the complexity of men's thoughts and motives and treat past and future as essentially indistinguishable from each other; or else they must try to understand how men decide upon their courses of action when they cannot feel sure, even within wide limits, what the outcome of any course will be.
>
> (Burns and Stalker 1961:111)

Support by other writers

Burns and Stalker have certainly not been alone in emphasising these wider factors. More recently Dobbin (2009) in his review of a book on institutional studies supported the idea that sociologists overestimated the power of institutional constraint and underestimated individuals' ability to change those institutions. He emphasised how little understood was the capacity of human agency to determine the success or failure of institutions. In a book review on organisational commitment, Ross pointed to some of the authors' suggestions for the need for further research into organisational commitment, its various forms, its relationships to performance and most pertinently, into policies which would maintain high levels of commitment during periods of change (Ross 2009).

Employee commitment has been acknowledged as being important. Kanter emphasised the importance for organisational success of employees who were committed to their organisations – through the provision of the support, resources, information and opportunity enabling them to feel empowered and be creative (see e.g. Kanter 1977, 1983). Williams made the point that from the early 1970s there had been a shift of focus for some to cultural and micropolitical issues in organisations. Examples he gave included the 'garbage can' model (March and Olsen 1976) which

> presented a direct challenge to the rational, analytical perspective and gave a view of anarchic organizations pervaded with ambiguity in which their emergent properties were seen to be far more significant than their designed or intended properties.
>
> (Williams 2013:66)

The inevitability of internal politics has been recorded by many writers. Knights and Murray, researching into the development of IT in commercial organisations, saw politics as:

> the very stuff, the marrow of organisational process … managerial and staff concerns to secure careers, to avoid blame, to create success and to establish stable identities within competitive labour markets and

organisational hierarchies where the resources that donate relative success are necessarily limited.

(Knights and Murray 1994:xiv)

This was seen by them as a constraint on, or disruption to, successful strategic planning and decision-making. They cited Burns and Stalker among others as having emphasised disjunctions between individual career objectives and official organisational goals.

But according to Knights and Murray individual self-interest did not have to be at odds with organisational goals. This would depend on how successful and inclusive previous managerial exercises of power had proved, and how open subordinates had been allowed to be about their own career goals. However, much politics was kept 'under wraps' by managers, and the whole process of management was 'a vast political game of intrigue, skulduggery, backroom deals and career carve-ups' (Knights and Murray 1994:32). Ultimately they saw this not as a distortion, but as dynamic and necessary to organisational life, given the considerable inequalities in organisations.

Burns and Stalker's reservations about senior managers' abilities to devise and implement successful change strategies have been supported by other writers. Mills found that although senior managers were active in trying to create a culture change in the Nova Scotian power company she studied, employees did not find their efforts altogether plausible, and had different perceptions from their management's about the change strategies implemented (Mills 2003a).

Kanter in more practically oriented and eye-catching prose imposed an almost impossible list of requirements on leaders seeking to achieve successful innovation in their organisations. These included recommendations for senior managers to: publicise the values and vision linked to change; consider the whole chain from 'suppliers' suppliers to customers' customers; create processes which could easily be adopted and free up people for more creative work; organise cross-functional teams; cultivate empathy and respect; and make sure people 'have fun together' (Kanter 2009:259–260). One of the many difficulties with all this, according to Frenkel, was that managers had been found not to pay attention to research findings and that the gap between theory and practice was wide (Frenkel 2009).[3]

The importance of chief executives to the success of their companies has been confirmed by other researchers. Dickson et al., in their study of innovation in interfirm collaboration, attributed successes in these ventures to senior officers. The founder of a small and successful electronics firm managed to create a strong research network, due to his strong personality, entrepreneurial style and his careful and painstaking development of links with other scientists by keeping his scientific and technical knowledge up to date and impressing his collaborators. They also credited the success of a medical research company to their director and senior researcher who had the entrepreneurial skills to organise the necessary industrial collaboration needed (Dickson et al. 2013).

The selected textbooks

The testimonies above, both by Burns and Stalker and by a range of scholars over several decades, demonstrate that people, politics and process can be key to organisational change outcomes. Such ideas are considered in relation to the selected textbook representations of Burns and Stalker's book. This more detailed comparison with the selected textbooks centres mainly on the dialectic present in their content between structure and process, including formal and informal systems. This is followed by a discourse analysis, where a reading of a few pages of *The Management of Innovation* (Burns and Stalker 1961:96, 97, 99–100, 211–22, 267), is compared with pages in the textbooks by Daft (2001:144), Robbins (2003:440) and Mullins (2005:641–642). Fairclough and Hardy's (1997) constructs are used, as are some of Derrida's (Derrida 1981; Norris 1987) and Eco's (1992a, 1992b) ideas outlined earlier. The analysis will discuss the different texts in terms of 'competing' discourses (Fairclough and Hardy 1997:147).

Structure and process

How the interrelationship between structure and process is conceived (in this instance the extent to which mechanistic and organic systems are seen as independent of each other or as interleaved and influencing each other) has important consequences for the understanding and outcomes of organisational change strategies. This question is similar to asking whether formal and informal organisation structures are separate ontologically or part of the same system. Mainstream organisation theory has tended to uphold binary distinctions by conceptualising formal structures as separate, and as 'something solid, enduring, and stand[ing] in a causal relation to both human agency and its environment' (Tsoukas 2003:608). This chapter and the next are about problems of the ontological reality of formal structures as against informal ones. As the evidence has shown, the reality of formal structure is ontologically prior in much mainstream literature, with informal structures generally excluded.

In the three textbooks, informal systems are discussed only as features of organic in comparison with mechanistic structures. The mechanistic and organic models are seen as polar opposites, with formal and informal structures separate and different. Daft, as previously mentioned, describes Burns and Stalker's mechanistic system in these terms:

> When the external environment was stable, the internal organization was characterized by rules, procedures, and a clear hierarchy of authority. Organizations were formalized. They were also centralized with most decisions made at the top.
>
> In rapidly changing environments, the internal organization was much looser, free-flowing, and adaptive … Decision-making authority was decentralized.
>
> (Daft 2001:144)

There is no suggestion here of any influence or dynamic interplay between one system and the other.

Robbins too presents the characteristics of mechanistic and organic structures as two extreme models. Although they are in a continuum, there is again no suggestion that they are connected. One of the questions Robbins poses is 'What are the forces that influence the design that is chosen?' The implication is that he is thinking about two separate systems, with organisations perhaps having characteristics of some of both, but not as part of a single system (Robbins 2003:440).

Mullins describes mechanistic structures as bureaucracies, and organic structures as more fluid because of new problems requiring actions outside defined hierarchical roles. The informal organisation is mentioned only once - in relation to an organic system where 'it becomes more difficult to distinguish the formal and informal organisation' (Mullins 2005:642).

What is not pursued in the mainstream literature is the notion that formal structures are influenced by less visible processes such as informal systems (Green 2009a). In *The Management of Innovation*, alternative discourses exist in which formal and informal structures are more closely linked. Passages in the book show how mechanistic systems are compromised by informal groupings. Burns and Stalker quote Selznick to support this view:

> All formal organizations are moulded by forces tangential to their rationally ordered structures and stated goals ... However, the individuals within the system tend to resist being treated as means. They interact as wholes, bringing to bear their own special problems and purposes ... It follows that there will develop an informal structure within the organisation which will reflect the spontaneous efforts of individuals and subgroups ... the sociologist ... will look upon the formal structure ... as the special environment within and in relation to which the informal structure is built.
>
> (Selznick 1948:250–251, cited in Burns and Stalker 1961:99)

Burns and Stalker recognise that there is a merging of binary opposites in organisation structures. This muddies the picture of clear-cut alternatives between mechanistic and organic structures. It points to complexities in how a change to an organic structure would work, given that there could be something of an organic structure there already, but not one that is formally recognised or even known about. Conversely, an informal structure might have mechanistic elements re-imposed where changes to an organic structure might result in difficulties. In the preface to the 1994 edition Burns claimed that bureaucratic ideologies were so strong that more hierarchical elements were reintroduced into organic structures in the face of unfamiliar and novel conditions (Burns 1994). Mechanistic characteristics could also already be present in informal structures:

> Commitments to others involve loss of autonomy in that the right to spontaneous, divergent action outside the group is surrendered in respect of the objectives the private combination has been constituted to attain ...
>
> (Burns and Stalker 1961:100)

A robust disregard for the ontological reality of discrete hierarchies in organisations has been upheld by many writers. Derrida wanted the dismantling of binary distinctions to the point where 'opposition itself – the very ground of dialectical reason – gives way to a process where opposites merge in a constant *undecidable* exchange of attributes' (Norris 1987:35) (emphasis in the original). Put another way, some binary oppositions are 'only held in place by a failure to pursue their logic wherever it may lead' (Norris 1987:134). These ideas have resonance with Burns and Stalker's views on the relationships of formal to informal structures, with aspects of formal mechanistic organisation in informal structures merging with and impinging on the autonomy of organic structures, and vice versa.

According to Munro sociologists have long viewed the organisation chart as 'little more than an expression of wishful thinking, a persistently failing attempt to superimpose rational thought over human emotion' (Munro 1998:142–143). He reinforces the view that aspects of formal organisation could have an impact on informal groupings as well as the opposite, and his ideas support Derrida's objections to the ontological credibility of binary divides:

> Contrary to its stereotype, contemporary managerialism does not proceed, top down, through the formal, the official, the hierarchical, dragging the informal, the unofficial, the social behind it ... Both forms exist, but not separately. They exist mutually in interaction.
>
> (Munro 1998:156)

Cooper and Fox (2013) argued for the interdependence of formal organisations, which they called the 'control mode' characterised by 'rationality, coherence and identity', with the 'nomadic mode', characterised by 'flux, change and contradiction' which they saw as the 'source' of the control mode, both being interrelated and interdependent (Cooper and Fox 2013:247).

Critical discourse analysis

Knowledge, many theorists have claimed, is determined by language. Discourse is important in the deciphering of meaning. It is one of the agents determining the reality we perceive (Foucault 1972). The term 'discourse' like many others, has been used in different ways without necessarily being defined (Ferguson 2007). Here the term is used to legitimate what is seen to be out there ontologically, and therefore what counts as reality and a legitimate object of study. This is close to Foucault's view that discursive practices serve as a delimitation of a field of objects, the definitions of a legitimate perspective for the agent of knowledge, and the fixing of norms for the elaboration of concepts and theories.

(Bouchard and Simon 1977:199)

Language constructs the way organisations are understood: their structures, processes and activities and the identities in them (Westwood and Linstead 2001). Organisational discourse has been viewed by critical realists in terms of what it 'does' and 'how it does it' (Reed 2009:64). The absenting of language from an issue can lead to its being ignored and considered not to be a legitimate object of inquiry. Discourse constructs meaning by ruling 'in' ways of discussing matters that make them intelligible and legitimate; conversely by ruling 'out' other issues, the knowledge constructed about them can be limited as can our conduct in relation to them. Critical discourse analysis focusses on how linguistic forms of textual analysis can influence and illuminate or obscure power relations (Grant et al. 2009:216).

Nominalisation

Differences in the language and grammar used in texts can result in substantial differences in meaning (Fairclough and Hardy 1997).[4] A comparison is made here between the use of abstract nouns (sometimes followed by passive verbs) compared with the use of active verbs. Examples of abstract nouns include 'structure' instead of 'structuring', 'participation' instead of 'participating', and indeed 'organisation' instead of 'organising'. Abstract nouns, which Fairclough and Hardy refer to as 'nominalisation', are not uncommon in analyses of organisations. One of the consequences of this use of language is that a sense of process is absent. The term 'organisation' instead of 'organising' is liable to obscure what can be learned about who is doing the organising (and by implication who is not), how it is being done, and what is and what is not being achieved (Fairclough and Hardy 1997:154).

It is now proposed to examine Robbins', Daft's and Mullins' writings in their representations of Burns and Stalker's ideas from the viewpoint of nominalisation. Robbins, in answering the question as to why some organisations are mechanistic and others organic, explains that 'objectives are derived from the organization's overall strategy'. He then continues to make connections between an organisation's structure and strategy:

... it is only logical that strategy and structure should be closely linked ... If management makes a significant change in its organization's strategy, the structure will need to be modified ... Most current strategy frameworks focus on three strategy dimensions ... and the structural design that works best with each.

(Robbins 2003:440–441)

In this example the subjects of these sentences are the abstract nouns 'objectives', 'strategy', 'structure', 'management', strategy frameworks' and 'structural design'. This does not reveal much about process – about who is doing the strategic and structural design, and how it might be done. We only know that it is 'management' which can use structure to help achieve its (management's) objectives, and that it has the prerogative to change the organisation's strategy (Robbins 2003:440). This is an example of Fairclough and Hardy's nominalisation. It is acknowledged that because the amount of space given to Burns and Stalker's ideas is small – about a page – it may help account for the use of abstract nouns as a way of condensing ideas.

Daft, also discussing Burns and Stalker's ideas in hardly more than one page, uses similar terminology. His first sentence reads: 'Another response to environmental uncertainty is the amount of formal structure and control imposed on employees'. Here 'response', 'formal structure' and 'control' are the driving ideas of the sentence, and again they are abstract concepts giving little sense of who is deciding on the structure and imposing controls on employees, what the controls are and any difficulties that might arise, not least on the part of employees.

Daft, in transmitting Burns and Stalker's ideas, describes organisations in rapid environmental change as 'looser, free-flowing, and adaptive'. These are adjectives, which do not give a picture of what such an organisation might look like, nor its attendant problems. A later sentence does give more of an idea of process. When describing organic structures Daft writes: 'People had to find their own way through the system to figure out what to do'. But after that we are told that 'Decision-making authority was decentralized'. We do not have information as to who decentralised the decision-making, how it was done, who were the beneficiaries of such decentralisation and what problems might have arisen. Similarly, in the sentence 'As environmental uncertainty increases, organizations tend to become more organic, which means decentralizing authority and responsibility to lower levels...' Daft does not specify who would do this and how it might be done (Daft 2001:144).

Mullins' description of organic systems is less abstract and although also not much more than a page in length, is more informative about how a decentralised system might work: 'The location of authority ... is by consensus and the lead is taken by the "best authority", that is the person who is seen to be most informed and capable'. After that there are abstractions similar to those employed by Robbins and Daft. For example, 'Commitment to the goals of the organisation is greater in the organic system ...' And the 'development of shared beliefs in the values and goals of the organisation in the organic system runs counter to the co-operation and monitoring of performance achieved through the chain of hierarchical command in the mechanistic system' (Mullins 2005:642).

Mullins gives a clearer idea of some of the differences between mechanistic and organic systems and their advantages in particular situations. Mechanistic structures because they require stability are appropriate in an up-market hotel and in major fast-food chains; an organic structure is suitable in a different kind of hotel, where there is unpredictable demand, many functions and many different types of customers. But there are still abstractions which obscure the processes and the problems in each structure – how shared beliefs are achieved in the organic system, for instance. What nominalisation has obscured in these representations is the presence of participants or actors, their power relationships and the effects of these on structure and vice versa.

Language of process

Although there is nominalisation in *The Management of Innovation,* for example 'management system' and 'the organization's goals', there is also analysis showing process (Burns and Stalker 1961:106, 108). Nominalisation is avoided more easily than in the textbooks when the consequences of employee action are analysed in terms of the second variable mentioned by Burns and Stalker – individual commitment to political and status interests. In the chapter on mechanistic and organic systems of management, after outlining some employee rights and obligations and how they are conferred, Burns and Stalker recognise employees' own interests which may be at variance with management's:

> But the men and women it [a firm] employs bring in with them other, private purposes of their own ... these purposes may be achieved partly by the return they get from the contract ... to allow themselves, their physical and mental capacities, to be used as resources. But men and women do not ordinarily yield themselves wholly to use as resources by others ...
>
> (Burns and Stalker 1961:97)

Here the language shows employees as active agents and highlights possible employee action. The grammar contains human subjects, active verbs showing process which includes the potential for individuals to show an independence which might work against their managers' interests.

Burns and Stalker consider organisational processes and the actions of participants when they discuss how employees' informal groupings can compromise managerial change initiatives:

> ... informal structures may exert a decisive influence over the efficiency of the working organization .... In pursuing these private purposes which are irrelevant to the working organization, individuals affiliate themselves to groups, and seek to bind others in association. They acquire commitments. These commitments may persist in the face of an express need for the working organization to adapt itself to new circumstances.
>
> (Burns and Stalker 1961:99)

While the first part of the quote contains the abstract noun 'informal structures', the next sentence makes it clearer who populates these structures and what happens in them. Overall this is a different picture showing employees as actors in these situations through the use of active verbs which largely are not abstract. The passage emphasises the role and potential obstruction of management's plans by employees informally organising. It avoids the effects of nominalisation, particularly its ideological significance indicated by Fairclough and Hardy (1997): the hiding of aspects of power. In this case it shows the influence that employees can have on the implementation of organisational change.

Burns and Stalker make it clear through their language what they see as particular to the senior manager's role. As already demonstrated, it is an awesome set of responsibilities, which Burns and Stalker judge to be crucial for effective organisational change:

> he [the head of the concern] sets the goals the whole concern is to achieve, and so sets the parameters of the tasks and the activities of groups and persons ... he specifies ... the measure of privilege and rights attached to lower positions. The system and structure of management are both determined largely by him. Above all, he is the ultimate authority for appointment and promotion.
>
> (Burns and Stalker 1961:211)

They then describe some of the difficulties with this role:

> He enters what is ... an unreal world, one in which all responses to his actions and to himself are filtered through the knowledge that he is in supreme command, and in a position to control the careers and occupational lives of all the members of the organization. People below him have to be ... circumspect in their dealings with him...
>
> (Burns and Stalker 1961:212)

Here again the actual duties, as envisaged by Burns and Stalker, are spelled out more specifically, with the chief executive shown to be an active but fallible agent.

Construction of identity: actors

Differences between *The Management of Innovation* and the selected textbooks are shown up when applying Fairclough and Hardy's (1997) notion of texts as constructing identities (Green 2009a). In the textbooks cited, the identities of the actors are not discussed explicitly – neither the chief executive, the managers, nor the employees lower down the hierarchy. The most we can see from Mullins' book is the comment that Burns and Stalker suggested that both mechanistic and organic systems represented a 'rational' form of organisation 'which could be created and maintained explicitly and deliberately to make full use of the human resources in the most efficient manner' (Mullins 2005:642).

No subject is attributed to such creation and maintenance – one can assume that it is from among the managers. The location of authority in the organic system, according to Mullins, was 'by consensus and the lead is taken by the "best authority", that is the person who is seen to be most informed and capable' (Mullins 2005:642). Robbins' text gives one more rope in assuming that the authority envisaged in organisational action is management's, but not which managers or at what level. After arguing that strategy and structure should be closely linked, Robbins, as already seen, writes:

> More specifically, structure should follow strategy. If management makes a significant change in its organization's strategy, the structure will need to be modified to accommodate and support this change.
>
> (Robbins 2003:440)

The lack of problematisation present in these and other textbooks in respect of the implementing of organic structures, as the above quotations show, might be seen as part of a general socio-cultural practice which gives managers the prerogative and power to effect organisational change. The last quote by Robbins makes this more explicit. One might deduce that the sub-text in this literature is that managers are given a message of confidence and certainty around their judgments, decisions and implementation capabilities.

Chenhall, in a review of contingency-based management accounting research confirms that conventional scholarship has assumed that management control systems are designed to assist in managers' decision-making and in achieving their organisational goals (Chenhall 2007). There are similarities in whether the identity of managers is overtly accorded authority through their being selected as the main and often only respondent, as in the research papers cited earlier, or where less overtly, there are a set of formulae which assume certain truths and ignore other potential influences in organisations, as in the textbooks cited. Some writers have criticised conventional conceptions of the idea that organisational practices are controlled by management, calling this a management myth (e.g. Puxty and Chua 1989). According to Tourish,

> The general assumption is that managers are the experts' on the multiple issues that confront most workplaces, and thus are the ultimate arbiters of what matters ... managerial decisions can be placed beyond dispute ... It is equally plausible to suggest that expertise may be more widely distributed than such hierarchical models suggest.
>
> (Tourish 2012:179)

Fairclough and Hardy's (1997) argument that nominalisation 'can be seen as reinforcing shared taken-for-granteds and adding to the authority of the writer through its aura of technicality' is relevant here (Fairclough and Hardy 1997:154). Through the nominalisation techniques referred to above, this unproblematised picture about the implementation of structural change in organisations indicates a decontextualised, idealised picture of organisations, with power naturally assumed to be with management.

Construction of identity: readers

Texts can also shape the identities of readers. Burns and Stalker's text is open in the sense that it draws the reader into their discoveries; it theorises problems and shows their application in situations in the companies they studied without necessarily offering clear solutions. It presents certain dilemmas and to a large extent leaves them undecided. This allows the reader to reflect on the issues and come up with her own ideas. One can say that the reader is invited to participate in the discussion and retains a measure of independence in analysing and evaluating these situations.

One example of this in *The Management of Innovation* can be seen from the description of a meeting between the chairman of a company and a foreman. Burns and Stalker, after analysing the different intentions and use and style of language in the conversation, pose problems rather than suggest solutions:

> His [the chairman's] employment of the word 'we' at a critical point in the discussion was of the first importance. We need not decide whether he was right to do so or not ... such simplicity [formalism with narrow limits set by management] is usually deceptive; or rather, it exacerbates organizational and personal problems by refusing to acknowledge their reality. No firm has found a style of conduct ideally adapted to the requirements of its situation.
>
> (Burns and Stalker 1961:257)

Textbook writers, on the other hand, have adopted a different discourse – telling us how it is, without leaving the reader room for questioning or reflection. Daft, after giving the outline of Burns and Stalker's definitions of mechanistic and organic structures writes:

> As environmental uncertainty increases, organizations tend to become more organic, which means decentralizing authority and responsibility to lower levels, encouraging employees to take care of problems by working directly with one another, encouraging teamwork, and taking an informal approach to assigning tasks and responsibility. Thus, the organization is more fluid and is able to adapt continually to changes in the external environment.
>
> (Daft 2001:144–145)

Mullins, having distinguished between mechanistic and organic systems as defined by Burns and Stalker, asserts that:

> The development of shared beliefs in the values and goals of the organisa-tion in the organic system runs counter to the co-operation and

monitoring of performance achieved through the chain of hierarchical command in the mechanistic system.

(Mullins 2005:642)

In both these instances the authors have highlighted decentralisation, participation, informality, flexibility and shared values, which were for Burns and Stalker fundamental characteristics of organic organisation. The emphasis is on structure, and a structure that is successful, but, as mentioned above, with no hint of who is to do the structuring and what difficulties there may be in the process. An alternative reading might provide a different focus – on the problems and pitfalls in achieving successful organic structures. Such an interpretation might make it easier for the reader to think more independently about the problems and be in a stronger position to question the authors' own analyses and judgements. It would provide a firmer base for understanding the issues and problems with regard to organisational change raised by Burns and Stalker.

More than telling us how it is, textbook writers have also told us how they see Burns and Stalker telling it. This retelling is supported by Foucault's idea that any discourse is not simply a coherent set of statements but 'a complex set of practices' which support some statements and exclude others (Mills 2003b:54). One of these practices is, according to Foucault, commentary on another's statements. As with other practices, commentary is concerned with classifying and ordering discourse and distinguishing between what is authorised and what is not, an activity supported by many practices and institutions such as universities (Foucault 1981).

What have not been authorised in these mainstream interpretations are the problems arising from the actions of chief executives and employees (Green 2009a). Discourses different from but complementary to the structural emphases in mainstream representations and deducible from Burns and Stalker's text, would enable richer scholarship and more informed practice. Like the journal articles discussed in the previous chapter, there is a simplification here of organisational change processes with the assumption that it is managers' prerogative and within their capability to implement change strategies successfully.

Conclusion

Textual analyses have shown that Burns and Stalker's book has produced different and competing discourses from its textbook representations, highlighting the dialectical oppositions between them. Mainstream textbook representations have focussed on structure as the means for achieving successful organisational change. Complementary discourses based on Burns and Stalker's book could just as well have added employee commitment and action and how these might affect the implementation of workable change strategies. Special attention might also have been given to the chief executive's role and its importance in achieving successful organisational outcomes.

One way of looking at texts is as a 'mode of practice', 'socially shaped but also socially shaping' (Fairclough and Hardy 1997:145). In this case the excerpts can be said to be shaping our understanding of structural adaptation of organisation systems in conditions of external uncertainty. From *The Management of Innovation* itself, the overlap between mechanistic and organic characteristics contests simple conceptualisations of polarised structures and opens up ways to question analyses of structural change. Readers are made aware of possible difficulties because of employee attitudes, the pull of bureaucratic structures, political interests, informal organisation processes and the capacities of chief executives.

The complexity of organisation structures highlighted by Burns and Stalker and by other contemporary scholars confirms Derrida's suspicions of the ontological validity of binary opposites. This throws into further relief differences with the mainstream representations cited, the epistemological difficulties and questions raised in connection with this 'monovalent' scholarship with its emphasis on one focus, one object of inquiry and one ontological position (Bhaskar 1993:11).

Notes

1 This chapter is based on published papers by Green (2005, 2009a, 2012a) (Springer); and Green (2009b, 2012b) (Emerald). The author would like to thank Springer and Emerald for copyright permission.
2 At that time chief executives were likely to be exclusively male.
3 Difficulties of matching theory with practice are discussed in the last chapter of the book.
4 Fairclough and Hardy's concept of discourse as an analysis of written text is used here. Critiques such as Widdowson's, of a lack of distinction between text and discourse in some of Fairclough's work should not apply here (Ferguson 2007).

References

Bhaskar, R. (1993). *Dialectic: The Pulse of Freedom*. London: Verso.
Bouchard, D.F. and Simon, S. (1977). *Michel Foucault: Language, Counter-Memory, Practice: Selected Essays and Interviews* (D.F. Bouchard and S. Simon, eds., Trans. D.F. Bouchard and S. Simon). Oxford: Basil Blackwell.
Burns, T. (1966). Preface to the Second Edition. In: T. Burns and G.M. Stalker, eds., *The Management of Innovation*. 2nd ed. London: Tavistock Publications, pp. vii–xxii.
Burns, T. (1994). Preface to the Third Edition. In: T. Burns and G.M. Stalker, eds., *The Management of Innovation*. 3rd ed. Oxford: Oxford University Press, pp. vii–xx.
Burns, T. and Stalker, G.M. (1961). *The Management of Innovation*. London: Tavistock Publications.
Carter, C.F., Meredith, G.P., and Shackle, G.L.S. eds. (1954). *Symposium on Uncertainty and Business Decisions*. Liverpool: Liverpool University Press.
Chenhall, R.H. (2007). Theorizing Contingencies in Management Control Systems Research. In: C.S. Chapman, A.G. Hopwood and M.D. Shields, eds., *Handbook of Management Accounting Research*. Vol. 1. Oxford: Elsevier, pp. 163–206.
Cooper, R. and Fox, S. (2013). Two Modes of Organization? In: R. Mansfield, ed., *Frontiers of Management: Research and Practice*. London: Routledge Revivals, pp. 247–261.

Daft, R.L. (2001). *Organization Theory and Design*. 7th ed. Cincinnati, OH: South-Western College Publishing.

Denzin, N.K. and Lincoln, Y.S. (1998). Methods of Collecting and Analyzing Empirical Materials. In: N.K. Denzin and Y.S. Lincoln, eds., *Collecting and Interpreting Qualitative Materials*. Thousand Oaks, CA: Sage, pp. 35–45.

Derrida, J. (1981). *Dissemination*. Trans. B. Johnson. London: Athlone Press.

Dickson, K., Lawton Smith, H. and Smith, S. (2013). Interfirm Collaboration and Innovation: Strategic Alliances or Reluctant Partnerships? In: R. Mansfield, ed., *Frontiers of Management: Research and Practice*. London: Routledge Revivals, pp. 140–160.

Dobbin, F. (2009). Book Review of T.B. Lawrence, R. Suddaby and B. Leca, Eds., Institutional Work: Actors and Agency in Institutional Studies of Organizations. *Administrative Science Quarterly*, 55 (4), pp. 673–675.

Eco, U. (1992a). Interpretation and History. In: S. Collini, ed., *Interpretation and Over-interpretation: Umberto Eco with Richard Rorty, Jonathan Culler and Christine Brooke-Rose*. Cambridge: Cambridge University Press, pp. 23–44.

Eco, U. (1992b). Overinterpreting Texts. In: S. Collini, ed., *Interpretation and Over-interpretation: Umberto Eco with Richard Rorty, Jonathan Culler and Christine Brooke-Rose*. Cambridge: Cambridge University Press, pp. 45–66.

Eco, U. (1992c). Between Author and Text. In: S. Collini, ed., *Interpretation and Over-interpretation: Umberto Eco with Richard Rorty, Jonathan Culler and Christine Brooke-Rose*. Cambridge: Cambridge University Press, pp. 67–88.

Fairclough, N. and Hardy, G. (1997). Management Learning as Discourse. In: J. Burgoyne and M. Reynolds, eds., *Management Learning: Integrating Perspectives in Theory and Practice*. London: Sage, pp. 144–160.

Ferguson, J. (2007). Analysing Accounting Discourse: Avoiding the "Fallacy of Internalism". *Accounting, Auditing and Accountability Journal*, 20 (6), pp. 912–934.

Foucault, M. (1972). *The Archaeology of Knowledge*. Trans. A.M. Sheridan Smith. London: Routledge.

Foucault, M. (1981). The Order of Discourse. In: R. Young, ed., *Untying the Text: A Post-Structuralist Reader*. London: Routledge & Kegan Paul, pp. 48–79.

Frenkel, S. (2009). Critical Reflections on Labor Process Theory, Work, and Management. In: M. Alvesson, T. Bridgman and H. Willmott, eds., *The Oxford Handbook of Critical Management Studies*. Oxford: Oxford University Press, pp. 525–535.

Gouldner, A.W. (1956). *Patterns of Industrial Bureaucracy*. London: Routledge.

Grant, D., Iedema, R., and Oswick, C. (2009). Discourse and Critical Management Studies. In: M. Alvesson, T. Bridgman and H. Willmott, eds., *The Oxford Handbook of Critical Management Studies*. Oxford: Oxford University Press, pp. 213–231.

Green, M. (2005). Are Management Texts Produced by Authors or by Readers? Representations of a Contingency Theory. *Philosophy of Management*, 5 (1), pp. 85–96.

Green, M. (2009a). Analysis of a Text and Its Representations: Univocal Truth or a Situation of Undecidability? *Philosophy of Management*, 7 (3), pp. 27–42.

Green, M. (2009b). The Embedding of Knowledge in the Academy: "Tolerance", Irresponsibility or Other Imperatives? *Social Responsibility Journal*, 5 (2), pp. 165–177.

Green, M. (2012a). Can Deconstructing Paradigms Be Used as a Method for Deconstructing Texts? *Philosophy of Management*, 11 (2), pp. 85–113.

Green, M. (2012b). Objectivism in Organization/Management Knowledge: An Example of Bourdieu's "Mutilation"? *Social Responsibility Journal*, 8 (4), pp. 495–510.

Kanter, R.M. (1977). *Rosabeth Moss Kanter on the Frontiers of Management*. Boston, MA: Harvard Business Review Press.

Kanter R.M. (1983). *The Change Masters: Corporate Entrepreneurs at Work.* London: Unwin Paperbacks.

Kanter, R.M. (2009). *Supercorp: How Vanguard Companies Create Innovation, Profits, Growth and Social Good.* London: Profile Books.

Knights, D. and Murray, F. (1994). *Managers Divided: Organisation Politics and Information Technology Management.* Chichester: John Wiley and Sons.

March, J.G. and Olsen, J.P. (1976). *Ambiguity and Choice in Organisations.* Bergen: Universitetsforlaget.

March, J.G. and Simon, H.A. (1958). *Organizations.* Oxford: Wiley.

Mayo, E. (1949). *The Social Problems of an Industrial Civilization.* London: Routledge.

Mills, J.H. (2003a). *Making Sense of Organizational Change.* London: Routledge.

Mills, S. (2003b). *Michel Foucault.* London: Routledge.

Mullins, L.J. (2005). *Management and Organisational Behaviour.* 7th ed. Harlow: Prentice Hall.

Munro, R. (1998). On the Rim of Reason. In: R.C.H. Chia, ed., *In the Realm of Organization: Essays for Robert Cooper.* London: Routledge, pp. 142–162.

Norris, C. (1987). *Derrida.* London: Fontana Press.

Puxty, A.G. and Chua, W.F. (1989). Ideology, Rationality and the Management Control Process. In: W.F. Chua, T. Lowe and T. Puxty, eds., *Critical Perspectives in Management Control.* Houndmills: The Macmillan Press, pp. 115–140.

Reed, M.I. (2009). Critical Realism in Critical Management Studies. In: M. Alvesson, T. Bridgman and H. Willmott, eds., *The Oxford Handbook of Critical Management Studies.* Oxford: Oxford University Press, pp. 52–75.

Robbins, S.P. (2003). *Organizational Behavior.* 10th ed. Upper Saddle River, NJ: Pearson Education.

Roethlisberger, F.V. and Dickson, W.J. (1939). *Management and the Worker.* Cambridge, MA: Harvard University Press.

Ross, W. (2009). Book Review of H.J. Klein, T.E. Becker and J.P. Meyer, Eds., Commitment in Oganizations: Accumulated Wisdom and New Directions. *Administrative Science Quarterly,* 54 (4), pp. 680–683.

Selznick, P. (1948). *T.V.A. And the Grass Roots: A Study of Politics and Organization.* Berkeley, CA and Los Angeles, CA: University of California Press.

Smith, J.K.A. (2005). *Jacques Derrida: Live Theory.* New York: Continuum Books.

Taylor, F.W. (1947). *The Principles of Scientific Management 1911.* Reprinted in: *Scientific Management.* New York: Harper.

Tourish, D. (2012). 'Evidence Based Management', or 'Evidence Oriented Organizing'? A Critical Realist Perspective. *Organization,* 20 (2), pp. 173–192.

Tsoukas, H. (2003). New Times, Fresh Challenges: Reflections on the Past and the Future of Organization Theory. In: H. Tsoukas and C. Knudsen, eds., *The Oxford Handbook of Organization Theory.* Oxford: Oxford University Press, pp. 607–622.

Westwood, R. and Linstead, S. (2001). Language/Organization: Introduction. In: R. Westwood and S. Linstead, eds., *The Language of Organization.* London: Sage, pp. 1–19.

Williams, G. (2013). Experimentation in Reflective Practice: A Conceptional Framework for Managers in Highly Professionalized Organizations. In: R. Mansfield, ed., *Frontiers of Management: Research and Practice.* London: Routledge Revivals, pp. 65–75.

5   Paradigm commensurabilities

Introduction[1]

The previous chapter included a close reading of Burns and Stalker's work, and a comparison with the three textbooks. Critical discourse analysis was one of the approaches used. The knowledge produced in the textbooks fell within an objectivist frame, focussing on structural adaptation. Yet as the evidence from the detailed analysis of Burns and Stalker's own text showed, a not inconsiderable part of the book was devoted to the difficulties in effecting change from a hierarchical to a flexible, decentralised model and to showing how change strategies without the commitment of employees or an able chief executive could result in dysfunction and failure.

Paradigms

Different discourses, resulting in different types of knowledge, have been derived from the original text. A comparison between the different discourses is now made from the perspective of their location across the spectrum of the different ontological[2] and epistemological[3] approaches in this field. The model of sociological paradigms constructed by Burrell and Morgan (1979) is used as the framework for this analysis. One definition of a paradigm is

> a set of assumptions, concepts, values and practices that constitute a way of viewing reality for the community that shares them, especially in an intellectual discipline.
>
> (The Free Dictionary)

Burns and Stalker's (1961) original text is compared with its mainstream representations through their paradigmatic similarities and differences. The extent to which Burns and Stalker's approach is located within the same paradigm as their textbook representations and research applications is examined. The same textbooks are used and a further comparison is made between *The Management of Innovation* and Simons' (1987) research paper as an example of orthodox contingency research methodology. This enables further investigation into the kind of knowledge produced in each case and into the implications for scholarship and practice.

The problem of accessing the various texts remains – how can one interpretation be justified over another, given earlier *caveats*, and the problems of gaining access to a text outside an interpretation of it. This cannot be done, and it is acknowledged that there could well be more than one valid interpretation. However, following Derrida (2002) and Eco (1992a, 1992b), one can mount an argument for a particular interpretation, provided the analytical footwork is done through detailed investigations of the texts in question. It is proposed in this chapter to examine the paradigmatic underpinnings of the original text and its mainstream representations, perforce through yet another interpretation.

The most pertinent set of criteria concerns epistemology. Whether there are any common standards for what counts as knowledge is examined, and, if there are different types of knowledge, whether there are any universal criteria for determining such differences. If it can be shown that the knowledge in the original text and its representations, as interpreted here, are within the same paradigm boundaries, there could be closure to the problematisation of these representations. If, however, it can reasonably be shown that the knowledge in each text is substantially different, this would give new impetus to the original question as to whether these different discourses are, or are not, commensurable, and ultimately what this means for the question of what counts as knowledge in the academy.

One way in which this question has been evaluated is through considering the ontological realities and epistemological criteria assumed in different approaches to knowledge. This issue has been addressed in the natural and social sciences through the concept of paradigms: the knowledge produced in different paradigms; criteria for determining the boundaries of knowledge between paradigms and their commensurabilities. Kuhn, one of the earliest writers on paradigms, stated that for a time, scientific knowledge consisted of universally recognised achievements providing model problems and solutions, with the same range of phenomena described and interpreted in the same way, and with the same rules, standards and methods for scientific practice (Kuhn 1970). This has been claimed to be true also for early organisation studies, commonly based on beliefs in science, rationality and progress (Green 2012).

For this to be the case there had to be fundamental agreement about the entities in the universe (its ontology), how they interacted with each other, and also about entities the universe did not contain. A situation when certain problems could not be solved by an existing paradigm through 'repeated failure to make an anomaly conform' was the most prevalent cause for the emergence of a new paradigm (Kuhn 1970:9). The survival of new paradigms would depend on their success over competing paradigms in their explanations of phenomena and solutions of problems. This would involve a shift in the nature of the problems and a change in the standards for what counted as admissible problems, legitimate solutions and rules or methodologies governing practice (Kuhn 1970).

Different paradigms would paint different pictures about the population of the universe and its behaviour. New paradigms, or what Kuhn called 'the incommensurability of the pre- and post-revolutionary normal-scientific tradition' would often give tangible form to a disagreement about which problems needed to be resolved, and might generate different definitions as to what science was (Kuhn 1970:148). Scientists would now be working in and responding to a different world. Old terms, concepts and experiments might still be used, but they would now fall into different relationships with each other. Different meanings attributed to these terms could lead to partial communication and to the inability to evaluate different theories on comparable terms (Kuhn 1970:103). One of his definitions of paradigms included

> problems available for scientific scrutiny and in the standards by which the profession determined what should count as an admissible problem or as a legitimate problem solution.
>
> (Kuhn 1970:6)

Natural scientific paradigms were dependent for their survival on their ability to provide solutions to problems (Kuhn 1970). No such proviso appears to exist currently for paradigms in the social sciences. It is true that the development of alternative epistemologies and methodologies in the social sciences might occur because of perceived inadequacies in the particular constructions of organisational structures, processes and individual agency. So for example Neimark and Tinker emphasised the epistemological failings of positivist approaches in which mainstream management accounting theory was grounded:

> [positivist epistemology] offers criteria for theory assessment that are readily and regularly undermined in practice because they fail to recognise both the social mutability of the reality they seek to discover and the part the social scientist plays in the social construction of that reality.
>
> (Neimark and Tinker 1986:376)

Chua (1986), while acknowledging strengths in objectivist approaches in relation particularly to accounting research, remarked on the many limitations in their beliefs about physical and social reality, and about knowledge. More damning is Frenkel's evaluation of positivist research which

> proceeds by simplifying and hence inappropriately posing problems and then seeks to resolve these by measuring and quantitatively analysing variables that are devoid of their likely contested meanings generated in complex social settings.
>
> (Frenkel 2009:531)

Such criticisms have not displaced the original and still dominant paradigm. Widely different paradigms in the social sciences exist simultaneously, often with very little communication between the scholars espousing them. The absence of communication even among scholars in the same discipline and writing in the same journal has been mentioned. MacIntyre recognised the existence of generalisations with counter examples coexisting in the social sciences, which he described as a 'tolerant' attitude (MacIntyre 2007:90). Starbuck pointed to there being differences among social science researchers about the nature of knowledge, the value of different kinds of knowledge and of particular contributions to knowledge (Starbuck 2016). Differences in representation may be partly explained by the coexistence of these diverse approaches.

Paradigm similarities and differences

The first question that arises regarding *The Management of Innovation* and its mainstream representations is whether there are any objective or commonly accepted standards and criteria for these different texts. One of Kuhn's[4] criteria for comparable standards to evaluate whether various approaches were in the same or different paradigms, was to do with the definitions of problems and solutions. If one accepts these criteria for the social sciences, one can examine the extent to which problems and solutions as defined by Burns and Stalker and their mainstream interpreters are similar or different. These texts can then be explored in terms of the paradigms they encompass, and ultimately whether they lie within the same paradigmatic boundaries. The findings would have implications for an evaluation of the knowledge transmitted in representations of *The Management of Innovation* compared with that presented in Burns and Stalker's original book.

Ontological issues

The original problem posed by Burns and Stalker is the same as that presented in mainstream textbooks: organisations facing a situation of rapid technological and market change were compromised if they had hierarchical, mechanistic structures. In order to succeed in this environment their structures needed to be changed to more flexible, organic systems. In this scholarship the ontology presented focussed on structure, as that is what was understood to be 'real' and the stuff of organisations. This has been challenged by postmodern theorists, among others (Green 2005). The exclusion of other factors in this ontology has implications for the question of paradigm location.

An alternative analysis including the other problems raised by Burns and Stalker with their focus on organisational processes, could arrive at an ontology where structures might be a given, but they would also be influenced by and interdependent with human interests and agency. These and other factors inimical to the development of different organisation structures had been seen by Burns and Stalker to constitute threats to structural change.

Different interpretations are likely to give rise to different ontologies, as is evident if one compares Daft's (2001), Robbins' (2003) and Mullins' (2005) positions with Burns and Stalker's. Kuhn's (1970:41) 'fundamental entities' would in the one case be formal organisation structures; in the other, organisational processes and human factors alongside structural issues. The difference in these ontologies constitutes a dialectical opposition, largely to do with absences – the exclusions in mainstream textbooks and in research publications of human, political and career interests, the susceptibilities of formal structures to informal groups and the responsibilities and capacities of chief executives – Burns and Stalker's second and third independent variables.

Norris has pointed out that while defending values of truth, reason and critique, Derrida

> defends those values while also calling attention to blind spots of prejudice – the symptomatic moments of exclusionary violence that have often emerged within the discourse of enlightened modernity.
>
> (Norris 2002:xxiv)

Exclusionary interpretations of the original text are central to the issues raised in this book. Derrida's concepts of supplementarity and binary oppositions, which he used to contest and overturn overt meanings in texts (Green 2005), highlight the differences in the discourses prevalent in management texts about *The Management of Innovation*.[5]

Derrida's description of binary oppositions as a violent hierarchy and his encouragement for them to be replaced with a new concept without dual oppositions (Derrida 2002), or in critical realist terms, a more holistic approach without absences (Bhaskar 2008), support Burns and Stalker's questioning the power and workings of formal structures. Burns and Stalker advocated a dialectical synthesis in their contesting the notion that formal organisation alone can achieve organisational goals without mobilising human resources. Their reference to Selznick (1948), as mentioned earlier, reinforces their view that the agency of individuals is significant and closely linked with other organisational processes and structures:

> They interact as wholes, bringing to bear their own special problems and purposes ... It follows that there will develop an informal structure within the organization.
>
> (Selznick 1948:250–251, cited in Burns and Stalker 1961:99)

In Derridean terms the concept of formal organisation is overturned in Burns and Stalker's book, and the boundaries between formal and informal organisation breached. But as has been seen, this has not been the case in many mainstream representations, which focus on an ontological reality based exclusively on formal structures.

Epistemological issues

If the claim is contested that formal organisation structure is the only or overriding ontological reality, then so must its corresponding epistemology, in which such structures are studied to the exclusion of other entities. An argument, easily applicable to Burns and Stalker's ideas, can be made for an alternative epistemology including a focus on human agency, informal organisation and process as essential for an understanding of factors affecting the successful delivery of organisational change.

If we return to one of Kuhn's (1970:viii) definitions of a paradigm – 'model problems and solutions to a community of practitioners' it can be demonstrated that problems in the two sets of texts have been differently conceived, with different solutions, differently arrived at. In mainstream research applications of Burns and Stalker's work, the task has been to assess the environmental contingencies facing organisations together with an evaluation of the appropriateness of their structures and systems. The relevant data is acquired from senior managers, who presumably are seen as being in a position to have comprehensive knowledge both of their organisations' systems and of the environments in which they are situated.[6]

In an alternative epistemology, organisations could be conceived as operating on the basis of human decisions, actions and reactions rather than according to what have been described as objective laws (Scherer 2009). People's constructions of their social worlds and consequent actions would be ontologically significant. Researchers' intentions then might be to study the vulnerabilities of organisation structures to human agency. This would require a study of people and processes in organisations in order to understand the outcomes of the implementation of managerial policies. What would then be epistemologically necessary would be an understanding of the organisation systems in place, such as the communication and decision-making processes and both managers' and other employees' impacts upon them. Legitimate and relevant knowledge in this epistemology would then include an examination of people's constructions of and reactions to what was happening in their organisations, particularly to their own situations (Burrell and Morgan 1979).

Solutions follow the same principles. It has been shown throughout this book that mainstream solutions have been about structural change. Previous theories (even when the subject was ostensibly about employees, as were social psychological/motivation theories) were usually based on the premise that employees were essentially passive, that their behaviour could be determined by external stimuli and that the initiative to set up appropriate systems and procedures or to use suitable motivation techniques to achieve goals lay largely with managers (Hopper and Powell 1985). But Burns and Stalker, in addition to advocating organic structures in unstable technological and market environments, looked for solutions outside structure to the problems senior executives and managers faced in trying to achieve these changes. Burns and Stalker's ideas in the early 1960s have been seen as providing a new way of looking at the world. These authors have been described as being possibly the first scholars to understand the importance of the beliefs and interests of a working community (Kilduff and Dougherty 2000).

Burns and Stalker's attention to the influence of employees on the successes or failures of managers' strategies constitutes a different way of understanding organisational events and processes, with different relationships between managers and employees, managers and organisational structures and employees and organisational structures. As set out previously, in *The Management of Innovation* the matching of appropriate structures to environmental and technological conditions is there, and, some would claim, central to the purpose of the book. But the other issues raised put into question the workings of the formal system and the ways in which management intended it to work. Much of Burns and Stalker's book through their choice of independent variables, the space given to these and the line of argument throughout, is about the effects of human agency on change processes. These, as will be seen, constitute different ontological and epistemological positions according to Burrell and Morgan's (1979) construction of sociological paradigms and their boundaries, and provide a deeper understanding of the knowledge and discourses present in these different texts.

Methodological issues

Comparisons can be made between Burns and Stalker's research techniques and mainstream research applications of their theory. Many management accountant researchers, having adopted similar ideas to the textbook representations outlined earlier as to what was the essential Burns and Stalker, used methodologies[7] focussed on structural features of organisations. As in the journal articles cited earlier, adaptations to the influence of environment and technology were directed to the design of information and control systems, budgeting and strategic planning (Covaleski et al. 1996). These were often researched through questionnaires and then subjected to complex statistical analyses, justified at some length by the author. The aim was to establish enduring relationships between such variables. Hopper and Powell thought that an underlying assumption behind this type of management accounting research was that optimal accounting systems could be created for any situation (Hopper and Powell 1985).

Simon's (1987) article is one example of this approach. His paper is used here for purposes of comparison with Burns and Stalker's research and methodology.[8] Simons set out to test Burns and Stalker's model of a synergy between control systems and strategy in successful firms. The control systems, Simons is careful to point out, were

> formalized procedures and systems that use information to maintain or alter patterns in organizational activity.
>
> (Simons 1987:359)

Simons hypothesised that there would be correlations between control system and strategy. Organisation 'defender' strategies would pursue formal accounting procedures, while firms adopting 'prospector'[9] strategies would have more flexible systems allowing for individual creativity (Simons 1987:360). This hypothesis was in line with a contingency approach and was designed to test Burns and Stalker's (1961) theory that 'unstructured, organic organizations were best suited to a strategy of innovation' (Simons 1987:357).

Thus far, Simons' approach is similar to that of the textbook writers and the many researchers mentioned earlier: what was considered to be ontologically real and epistemologically valid were formalised structures and systems – in this case accounting control systems and their relationships with organisation strategies in different contingent situations. Organisational processes including the influence of human agency were not included.

Simons, as has been pointed out, was meticulous in choosing his sample selection of external experts and company executives. The design of his questionnaire was carefully tested with senior managers in randomly selected firms. He used overlapping data from respondents within the industry and from senior managers in the randomly selected firms, to arrive at a double confirmation of the categorisation of the companies' strategies into prospector and defender firms. The questionnaire, which consisted of 33 Likert-type scale questions for control system factors, was sent out to senior managers and its results subjected to a detailed statistical analysis.

Simons' intention was to find out about control systems through interviewing and surveying senior managers in order to come to an evaluation of whether Burns and Stalker's ideas held in the companies he researched. One can, as has been stated, focus on the systems and structures in Burns and Stalker's analysis as Simons did. But if one accepts the complexities of organisation structures because of human interference, one might speculate as to whether Simons, with different research methods and a broader research base, might not have come up with different findings. Simons had acknowledged in a footnote that one could not impute causality from his findings, as his research was not aimed at investigating differences between reported and actual control systems. Rather, it was aimed at looking at control system features on the assumption that 'when certain organizational attributes are beneficial to the ... success of a set of firms, the use of these attributes by firms in the set will be more prevalent' (Simons 1987:358 fn.2). Arguably this result from Simons' research has value in itself both to the academy and as guidance to professional managers and consultants in their roles as change agents.

A broader interpretation of *The Management of Innovation* is supported by Burns' comments in the preface of the 1966 edition, where he claimed that the book was about actions and happenings according to people's personalities and commitments on the one hand, and about organisations as political systems or status hierarchies on the other, with relationships between people and events explicable in terms of organisational, political and career significance (Burns 1966). It is here that Burns made his strong plea that in order to understand changes, developments and historical processes, the social (and organisational) world should be seen as a dynamic process, rather than as 'an anatomy frozen into structured immobility'

(Burns 1966:xxx). Burns and Stalker's research, in that it had adopted idiographic methods,[10] facilitated this approach. It constitutes a very different methodology from Simons', which was essentially nomothetic.[11]

Others, albeit a minority, have acknowledged these differences. According to Hall, early contingency-based research used a variety of research methods including field-based investigations. These resulted in important insights, for example with respect to the psychological processes surrounding management accounting practices, whereas subsequent research was limited primarily to surveys and experiments (Hall 2016). Granlund and Lukka, in a recent paper on contingency-based management accounting research, also differentiated early contingency research from later approaches. Burns and Stalker's research methods were seen by them as 'a qualitative approach, allowing for penetration to the emic[12] domain of the organisations examined' (Granlund and Lukka 2017:fn.3).

These authors recommended 'a return to the original ideas of the early contingency theorists' which would involve 'shaking up the current box of institutionalised research practices in the field' where the use of routine instruments such as survey-based research could show only a limited understanding of the complexity of organisations. These functionalist etic methods should be combined with emic approaches, allowing more varied, open approaches in which organisational actors would have a 'less predetermined' voice. This would result in more contextually relevant scholarship, more thorough analyses of management control practices and a greater understanding of organisational complexities and change, something difficult to do using only cross-sectional methods (Granlund and Lukka 2017:76–78).

Otley, whose work on contingency theory research was cited earlier, recommended in a recent paper that contingency theory change from using solely traditional, functionalist methods to combining these with more interpretive and critical approaches. Traditional contingency research methods had 'run their course', and new approaches were needed in addition to deal satisfactorily with such a complex topic (Otley 2016:46). While his survey of contingency theory research in major accounting and management journals between 1980 and 2014 showed an increase in scholarship in this area, he found that quantitative studies based on survey questionnaires, usually unsupported by fieldwork, continued to be the dominant research method with little combination of this method with qualitative interpretive or critical approaches. It was important to distinguish between the existence of formal controls and how these were used in practice by managers (Otley 2016).

Burrell and Morgan's sociological paradigms

Burrell and Morgan's (1979) work on paradigms was addressed to the social sciences generally, and to organisation scholarship more specifically. Their criteria for determining where theories lay in their paradigmatic schema were the familiar ones of ontology, epistemology and methodology with another criterion, 'human nature' – assumptions about individuals being either products of their environment, or having free will and creating their environment (Burrell and Morgan 1979:2). Their work provides a way of comparing *The Management of Innovation* with textbook writers' and management researchers' interpretations. This analysis seeks to establish paradigm boundaries for the original text compared with those for its representations in order to arrive at a further understanding of their similarities and differences. As mentioned, this has implications for the kind of knowledge produced, and for what is imparted to scholars, students and practitioners.

Like Kuhn (1970), Burrell and Morgan defined paradigms as 'founded upon mutually exclusive views of the social world' (Burrell and Morgan 1979:viii). They constructed four paradigms, which they defined in their introduction as follows:

> Each stands in its own right and generates its own distinctive analyses of life. With regard to the study of organisations, for example, each paradigm generates theories and perspectives which are in fundamental opposition to those generated in other paradigms.
>
> (Burrell and Morgan 1979:viii)[13]

But unlike Kuhn's description of how natural scientific theories are arrived at, different sociological paradigms have been adopted by scholars as new knowledge and approaches have developed without the earlier ones being invalidated (Burrell and Morgan 1979). This makes Burrell and Morgan's initial objective in constructing their paradigm boundaries more difficult as these theories often do not have clear and discrete ontological, epistemological and methodological boundaries, as will be shown in relation to *The Management of Innovation*. A theorist could also be unclear about their own stance and 'oscillate precariously from one position to another according to his purpose' as in the case of Silverman, an 'action frame of reference' theorist (Burrell and Morgan 1979:199, 195).

Burrell and Morgan's paradigm constructs referred to for the purposes of this analysis are the functionalist and the interpretive. Functional organisation theory in their schema covered a wide range of approaches, which on the surface did not all subscribe to a particular perspective on social life, nor were they always in opposition to ideas in other paradigms. This complicates the question as to where the paradigm boundaries of *The Management of Innovation* might be seen to lie.

The functionalist paradigm

Burrell and Morgan categorised functionalism as being about the study of formal organisations, focussing on empirical studies all highly oriented to managerial concerns (Burrell and Morgan 1979). There were within functionalism four theoretical perspectives, which they claimed were only superficially different, as there was a strong common base to the theories grouped under the functionalist umbrella. Most prevalent, on the most extreme boundary, and relevant to this discussion, was social system theory which had the most objectivist and determinist approach, treating the organisation as if it were in:

> the world of natural phenomena, characterised by a hard concrete reality which can be systematically investigated in a way which reveals its under-lying regularities ... it is a world of cause and effect; the task of the management theorist is the identification of the fundamental laws which characterise its day to day operation ... the individual is assigned an essentially passive ... role ... [and where] objective factors in the work situation have a major influence upon behaviour.
>
> (Burrell and Morgan 1979:127–129).

Burrell and Morgan described it as 'abstract empiricism', an approach where the social structure became increasingly concretised from being an idea and manifested itself in 'a host of empirical snapshots of reified social structures' (Burrell and Morgan 1979:53–54).

Burns and Stalker's book

Burrell and Morgan claimed that many of the interpretations of contingency theories lay within this theoretical perspective. They criticised such interpreta-tions from a viewpoint that would sit comfortably with the alternative representations of Burns and Stalker's work. They found it 'questionable' that the ontological and epistemological foundations of contingency theories which were essentially processual should be ignored at the expense of structure (Burrell and Morgan 1979:180). Research based on such interpretations fitted into their extreme version of functionalism:

> Much of the research which has been conducted under the guiding notion of the contingency approach has been of this nature [the equation of organisations with their structural characteristics] and as such stands as an abstracted form of empiricism.
>
> (Burrell and Morgan 1979:180)

This seems an apposite description of the focus by mainstream writers on Burns and Stalker's mechanistic and organic models. Burrell and Morgan themselves were critical of this approach. They recognised the importance of a 'human subsystem'. Although management subsystems superseded human subsystems in most representations of contingency theory, contingency theorists themselves saw intended changes to organisational systems as far from being assured in uncertain and turbulent environments (Burrell and Morgan 1979:174).

It is significant that notwithstanding these arguments, Burrell and Morgan's own interpretation of *The Management of Innovation* seems not far removed from what they criticised mainstream writers for doing. They themselves placed Burns and Stalker's and other contingency theorists' work firmly within the functionalist paradigm. Various contingency theories including Burns and Stalker's occupy a prominent 18 pages in the chapter titled 'Functionalist Organisation Theory'. According to Burrell and Morgan:

> Burns and Stalker (1961) had demonstrated that successful firms adopted an approach . . . which was consistent with demands placed upon them by their environment, particularly with regard to the degree of market and technological change.
>
> (Burrell and Morgan 1979:166)

and

> The distinction offered by Burns and Stalker (1961) between mechanistic (bureaucratic) and organic organisations has become well established. . .
>
> (Burrell and Morgan 1979:175)

Their emphasis on the objective and deterministic factors of technology and the market, and on Burns and Stalker's ideal-type model of mechanistic and organic structures, went against their own judgement that contingency theories were essentially processual and cognisant of the latent influence of human agency.

Reasons for this categorisation

The question then arises as to how Burrell and Morgan could classify Burns and Stalker's work as they did and fit contingency theories into their functionalist paradigm, given their own criticisms of objectivist interpretations of these theories. Of course, *The Management of Innovation* does have functionalist elements: managerial concerns were a major area of interest in Burns and Stalker's book, and Burns and Stalker's text can further be related to that part of functionalism claimed by Burrell and Morgan to encompass sociological approaches based on Weber's work, where subjective meanings and actions by human actors are important. The categorisation of this as functionalist, however, is questionable, as discussed below.

One explanation for their apparent *volte-face* is that Burrell and Morgan may ultimately have been among those influenced by more objectivist contingency approaches such as the Aston Studies, 1976–1981 (Pugh and Hickson 2007), which they then may have generalised to all contingency research (Hopper and Bui 2016; Granlund and Lukka 2017). But it seems unlikely that this is the full explanation for the placing of Burns and Stalker's and other contingency theories squarely within the functionalist paradigm. Burrell and Morgan themselves were among those who had acknowledged that there was more to Burns and Stalker's and other contingency theorists' ideas than an abstract empiricism: human and processual factors were important as were difficulties in implementing organisational change in conditions of uncertainty. The problem is broader or deeper than that, and involves Burrell and Morgan's own construction of their paradigm boundaries, as pointed out, a daunting task in itself with such boundaries always likely to be contested.

Willmott has pointed to a difference between Kuhn and Burrell and Morgan, which is relevant to the latter's interpretation of contingency theories and their location in their framework. Kuhn was interested in theory development and therefore emphasised theory continuity and overlap between old and the new paradigms replacing them, whereas Burrell and Morgan engaged in 'rival ways of seeing' (Willmott 1993:686). But if one examines further the different categories within Burrell and Morgan's construction of functionalist theory, they include strange bedfellows. Burrell and Morgan themselves asserted that this paradigm 'reflects the dominant influence of sociological positivism' yet was 'fused' with elements of German idealism, the 'most subjectivist' part of the paradigm (Burrell and Morgan 1979:48).

Sociological positivist ideas at one end of this spectrum were best represented in social system theory, in turn divided into structural functionalism and system theory. Both to different degrees adopted mechanical and biological analogies for the study of society and for organisations. At the other end was subjectivism, described by Burrell and Morgan as reality constructed by individuals rather than being separate from it. Instead of being passive recipients, people independently and actively created their own realities. Knowledge would derive from how individuals interpreted their world and acted in it, rather than from external factors such as structure (Burrell and Morgan 1979, Chapter 1 *passim*).

Order-conflict axis

The logic outlined by Burrell and Morgan behind the construction of their paradigm framework is crucial in explaining why their boundaries were placed in the ways they were. Rather than relying solely on ontological and epistemological differences in social theories, they found themselves 'on firmer ground' by developing a 'two by two' model. One axis was divided between 'objective' and 'subjective' theories; the other between 'regulatory' and radical approaches focussing on the 'order-conflict' debate of the 1960s, when theories were classified according to whether they focussed on order or on conflict and change (Burrell and Morgan 1979:x).

Burrell and Morgan saw the 'order-conflict' debate as underpinning the differences between leading social theorists in the nineteenth and early twentieth centuries (Burrell and Morgan 1979:11). They developed these into a dichotomy between 'regulation' and 'radical change' theories, which they saw as one of the 'powerful means for identifying and analysing the assumptions which underlie social theories in general'. The sociology of regulation was about the need for regulation in society, with an assumption of its underlying unity and cohesiveness. Theories containing critiques of capitalist society were part of a 'sociology of radical change' – a sociology essentially focussed on deep-rooted societal domination and conflict and excluded from the function-alist paradigm (Burrell and Morgan 1979:17).

Problems with order-conflict axis

Yet there are similarities between some of the theories in Burrell and Morgan's functionalist and radical structuralist paradigms, the latter being one of the paradigms addressing conflict and change. In both, the world is ontologically prior to individual cognition and both emphasise objective relationships independent of individual agency (Hopper and Powell 1985). Conversely, theories that might on ontological and epistemological grounds be seen to be largely incompatible, were placed by Burrell and Morgan in the same paradigm because of their political priorities.[14]

Burns and Stalker's book: a rebuttal

Although Burns and Stalker's work can at first glance reasonably be placed on the order or regulation side of this debate, their stance is more complex. In their quest for understanding and achieving regulation, Burns and Stalker were at the same time very much concerned with politics and perceived conflicting interests among employees (and also among managers[15]), their constructions of reality and consequent actions. This connection between conflict and regula-tion had been recognised by Burrell and Morgan, but was ultimately rejected by them, despite their acknowledging Dahrendorf's criticism that order and conflict were not disconnected and that order could result from coercive social control. Morgan and Smircich made the same point a year after the publication of Burrell and Morgan's book. According to them Burrell and Morgan were

> wedded to ideological perspectives that overplay the tendency to sponta-neous order and regulation in social affairs, while ignoring modes of domination, conflict, and radical change.
>
> (Morgan and Smircich 1980:492)

Burrell and Morgan's argument had been that their revised terminology of 'regulation' and 'radical change' showed up the 'stark contrast' between the two (Burrell and Morgan 1979:17). While there could be a 'middle ground' between regulation and conflict, the two were fundamentally different as they were 'based upon opposing assumptions' (Burrell and Morgan 1979:19).

This may have been the main reason why Burrell and Morgan's boundaries for the functionalist paradigm included such diverse and different schools of thought, ranging from those under the rubric of objectivism and social system theory to interactionism and social action theory (Burrell and Morgan Chap-ter 4, *passim*). And this may also be why Burns and Stalker's work had been positioned in the functionalist paradigm. In their introduction to contingency theory, in which Burns and Stalker's ideas were given prominence, Burrell and

Morgan placed contingency theory firmly within the framework of a regulated, potentially unified system:

> The results of empirical research have been interpreted within the context of a managerially oriented set of propositions, which assert that the effective operation of an enterprise is dependent upon there being an appropriate match between its internal organisation and ... its tasks, its environment and the needs of its members.
>
> (Burrell and Morgan 1979:164)

Burrell and Morgan's categorisation of other contingency theories such as the Aston Studies (1976–1981) as objectivist scholarship in the functionalist paradigms are appropriate given the latter's objectivist approaches. But it is questionable whether Burns and Stalker's research wholly belongs there, unlike its textbook representations, which, as the evidence has shown, can clearly be located in the functionalist paradigm. Put another way, an essentially political stance with respect to contingency theories about regulation was given priority over ontological and epistemological differences among these contingency theories. Alternative readings of Burns and Stalker might pick up that their analyses of self-interested action, conflict, tension, rivalry, resistance to structural change and uncertainty from respondents in different parts and at various levels of the organisations they studied, fitted more comfortably into the interpretive paradigm. Willmott pointed to the playing down of such factors in Burrell and Morgan's construction of their paradigm boundaries:

> By paradigmatic fiat, ambiguity and tension within all forms of analysis is backgrounded
>
> (Willmott 1993:685)

The question that must then be asked is whether opposing political assumptions are sufficient to position such schools of thought in different paradigms, and more pertinently whether schools of thought with similar assumptions naturally fit into the same paradigm. As mentioned earlier, Burrell and Morgan themselves discuss the determinism of abstract empiricism as being very different from Burns and Stalker's concerns and research methods, and which in Kuhnian terms conjured up very different problems and solutions (Kuhn 1970:6).

Although Burns and Stalker recommended particular structures to suit different technological and market environments, it can be demonstrated that their study was essentially a study in dysfunction because of the politics and power considerations driving human actions and resistance. Burrell and Morgan's decision to place *The Management of Innovation* wholly in the functionalist paradigm could lead to the conclusion that they had taken an essentially political (regulatory) stance regarding the meaning of Burns and Stalker's book. And that this stance had been allowed to override Burns and Stalker's ontological, epistemological and methodological conceptualisaton of organisations – as malleable systems governed by political interest and human agency rather than by formal concrete structures.

Objective-subjective axis

The objective-subjective axis is the second of Burrell and Morgan's two principles. Ontologically, is reality external or internal to the individual – objectively imposing itself on human consciousness or its product? Is knowledge concrete, objective and easily transmissible, or unique, subjective and personal? At the extreme, can it be acquired or does it have to be personally experienced? The differences in this axis include differences concerning human nature – between people responding deterministically to their environment and people creating their environment through free and independent action. Methodologically those researchers inclining to the objectivist view would focus on relationships and regularities between the various external, concrete elements of this reality. The subjectivist view would entail the inquiry being centred on individuals' interpretations of and actions in and on the world as they understood it (Burrell and Morgan 1979 Chapter 1 *passim*).

Objectivist scholarship using Burns and Stalker's concept of mechanistic and organic organisations might fit in with Burrell and Morgan's (1979) human nature dimension of determinism rather than voluntarism.[16] Organisation systems would be ontologically real and epistemologically important in testing Burns and Stalker's theory, while the latter's other concerns – human perceptions and actions – would not need to be investigated. The former research is closer to Burrell and Morgan's (1979) description of the extreme objectivist position in the functionalist paradigm as

> a swing towards a highly objectified and static view of social reality – towards a positivism of an extreme, narrowly empirical and, indeed, atheoretical form .... [which] carried with it a relatively determinist view with regard to human nature.
>
> (Burrell and Morgan 1979:54–57)

Problems with the objective-subjective axis

As with the order-conflict debate, the distinctions between subjectivism and objectivism are not clear cut in all instances in Burrell and Morgan's schema. They grouped together in the functionalist paradigm both strongly objectivist schools of thought such as behaviourism and abstracted empiricism with strongly subjectivist ones such as symbolic interactionism, one version of which (Blumer's 1966) was 'essentially concerned with the meanings which underlie the process of interaction', and social action theory – a version of neo-idealist philosophy where subjective meanings were all important (Burrell and Morgan 1979:81). Subjectivist positions within this paradigm such as Mead's, saw man as living in a realist world of symbolic and physical objects, and Weber's social action approach, which, while placing importance on the subjective meanings held by individuals, still aimed at developing an objective social science offering causal explanations of social phenomena (Burrell and Morgan 1979:83). The situation thus is complicated and again one must appreciate Burrell and Morgan's groundbreaking work with respect to this complexity.

There have been criticisms of definitions of this axis and its relationship to Burrell and Morgan's paradigmatic boundaries. Willmott has questioned whether radical theories, in this case radical structuralism, did not contain enough characteristics of the (subjectivist) interpretive paradigm so that these exclusive boundaries of radical/regulatory and subjective/objective could be questioned (Willmott 1993). He favoured an incorporation of the subjective dimension into orthodox labour process theory without abandoning the dimension of radical change.

Hopper and Powell raised doubts as to the extent to which 'social sciences literature' could be 'pigeonholed' into Burrell and Morgan's objective-subjective dimension, which they saw as a continuum rather than as being mutually exclusive (Hopper and Powell 1985:430, 451). Williams too from his own research experience thought there should be freer movement between the functionalist and interpretive paradigms than seemed to be the case in Burrell and Morgan's construction. He recommended that Burrell and Morgan's schema be regarded as a 'heuristic device rather than a set of rigid definitions' (Williams 2013:68).

The interpretive paradigm

The question remains as to why Burns and Stalker's theory should not also have been placed in Burrell and Morgan's subjectivist paradigm *par excellence* – the interpretive paradigm. An argument can be made that according to Burrell and Morgan's own definitions, Burns and Stalker's approach fits there as well, if not better, than in the functionalist paradigm,

Burrell and Morgan had described the interpretive paradigm as seeking explanation of the social world

> within the realm of individual consciousness and subjectivity, within the frame of reference of the participant as opposed to the observer of the action.
>
> (Burrell and Morgan 1979:28)

The world through the interpretive paradigm is seen as 'an emergent social process ... created by the individuals concerned' (Burrell and Morgan 1979:29). Dilthey (1976), among its proponents, pointed to the notion of *verstehen* (understanding) as appropriate to internal mental processes. There had, therefore, to be a different approach from one searching for general laws and causal explanations. More appropriate would be a method whereby human experience was re-lived or re-enacted (Burrell and Morgan 1979:230).

The Management of Innovation in many respects fits comfortably within the interpretive paradigm. It certainly cannot on any grounds be located at the extreme end of the subjectivist approach. It cannot be described as solipsistic or in any way denying the possibility of an external reality. Burns and Stalker's research methodology and outcomes seem reasonably close to Weber's (1947) position of wanting to have human actors' subjective meanings and enactments understood, probably in order to arrive at causal explanations for social action, as well as acknowledging objective realities in organisations and their environments. Weber was interested in the subjective meanings attached to action as a way of understanding the world. However, he took a position closer to positivism in that he wanted to arrive at a causal explanation of the causes and events of social action (Burrell and Morgan 1979:230). Burrell and Morgan maintained that Weber was ultimately an objectivist as he believed in the objective reality of the social world, albeit interpreted by human agents, and that this is why they located his work partly in the functionalist paradigm.[17]

Another point of similarity between Burns and Stalker and Weber is the use of ideal types. According to Burrell and Morgan, Weber used ideal types to

> incorporate the 'spirit' which characterises individual phenomena into a wider, generalised whole ... the method of *verstehen* is assimilated into a typological scheme of analysis which provides a means of ordering and explaining human action.
>
> (Burrell and Morgan 1979:231)

Burns and Stalker's mechanistic and organic depictions of structure can be said to do the same. If the claim holds that Weber's work, with particular reference to his ideal types is essentially functionalist and that Burns and Stalker's is similar enough to Weber's, the justification for their work being positioned in the functionalist paradigm would be sustained. But there is still more to be explored in terms of where their work should be positioned. This is obviously a difficult question to answer conclusively because theories are complex and have different facets which may be contradictory. There is also the artificial problem of trying to fit such theories into Burrell and Morgan's construction of paradigm boundaries, which has been shown to be contestable in some respects.

There are characteristics which Burrell and Morgan described as constituting the 'underlying unity' of the interpretive paradigm, which are applicable to Burns and Stalker's approaches. Burrell and Morgan claimed that interpretive scholarship was 'based upon fundamentally different assumptions about the ontological status of the social world'. In the interpretive paradigm knowledge was constructed from individual actors' experiences and standpoints and not from those of observers. Theories were antipositivist in that they were based on human subjectivities and did not seek objective relationships and regularities common to research in the natural sciences.[18] Methods of study were idiographic rather than nomothetic, and social reality was constructed according to the views of the actors in the situation (Burrell and Morgan 1979:254). Many of these features apply to Burns and Stalker's research (except perhaps Burns and Stalker's mechanistic/organic characterisation of organisation systems). If one includes their findings regarding human agency, these are clearly different from major characteristics of the functionalist paradigm as defined by Burrell and Morgan.

If the argument is upheld that largely objectivist and subjectivist theories cannot be placed in the same paradigm because of substantive differences in their ontologies, epistemologies and methodologies, one must then conclude that they are located in different paradigms. In many of these objectivist-subjectivist distinctions it is quite feasible to rank *The Management of Innovation* on the subjectivist side if one includes the human and political factors analysed in that book. On the other hand, the evidence from analyses of mainstream textbook representations and research applications points to these falling squarely within the objectivist camp. They are objectivist because of their presentations of organisation structures as real and concrete; and knowledge as objective and scientific. People in organisations (apart from managers) are nowhere deemed to be active agents capable of affecting the success or otherwise of managerial change strategies.

This chapter is limited to an exploration of whether all the types of knowledge produced in Burns and Stalker's original text are within the same paradigm as constructed by Burrell and Morgan or whether they differ substantially. If one interprets *The Management of Innovation* more narrowly, one can reach the conclusion that the book falls within the functionalist paradigm. But because of the many subjectivist elements shown to be present in the book, a case can be made for Burns and Stalker's work lying also in the interpretive paradigm. This raises questions to be discussed in a later chapter about the relationship between paradigms. Are they incommensurable with each other as Burrell and Morgan and others have claimed, or can an argument be made for their commensurability?

Chua (1986) criticised what she has called the 'dichotomic features' of Burrell and Morgan's paradigm construct, described by her as 'illogical, relativistic and superficial' (Chua 1986:627). More recently, debates about paradigm boundaries, particularly in management accounting, have centred on the notion that paradigms straddle objectivism and subjectivism (Ahrens 2008; Kakkuri-Knuuttila et al. 2008; Lukka 2010, 2014). Ultimately the argument needs to be about the desirability and possibility of rising above the dialectic constructed between these two approaches and incorporating then into more inclusive knowledge (Green 2005).

Conclusion

Burns and Stalker may have been objectivist in that their conclusions from their research constituted objective and transmissible knowledge. There was no reflection on their part, as indeed there was unlikely to be in the early 1960s in their academic *milieu*, about problematising what knowledge they were producing as researchers and their 'situatedness' (Sarbin and Kitsuse 1994), although Burns in the 1994 edition's preface was aware of the changing political, social and economic pressures put on the academy. They also did not raise the question of possible bias[19] in their respondents' information. Their use of the ideal types of mechanistic and organic may be a further reason for seeing them as functionalists.

Thus a claim can be made, as Burrell and Morgan ultimately did, that Burns and Stalker's work falls into the objectivist, structuralist, functionalist paradigm, given their focus on the relationship between organisational structure and its technological and market environment. If, however, one gives equal weight to the other two independent variables in the book – employee commitment and the role and capacity of the senior executive – one can as well make the point that their conceptual framework, methodologies, analyses of the problems and conclusions are subjectivist and should be located in the interpretive paradigm.

It has been suggested throughout this book that there is a strong subjectivist bent in Burns and Stalker's work. Their ontology strongly encompasses human consciousness and actions influencing organisational systems. Their epistemology follows from this. Their analysis includes liberal attention paid to the perceptions and actions of employees. Their research shows the importance they placed on finding out how the actors in the organisations they studied interpreted the changes that were being introduced, their intentions, and the effects of their responses on their organisations. Their methodology reflects this in the number and range of employees they interviewed, observed and spent time with.

We have a situation where mainstream representations of *The Management of Innovation* in textbooks and research are based on objectivist ideas and can be said with confidence to be located in the functionalist paradigm. Because subjectivist factors also have a strong presence in their book as do the dysfunctional and failed attempts at structural change, it can be shown, using Kuhnian concepts, that what Burns and Stalker considered to be legitimate problems with implied solutions were more akin to ideas in the interpretive paradigm as they were more dependent on human understanding, intention and agency. The claim here is that *The Management of Innovation* and its mainstream representations are located to a significant extent in different paradigms. The underlying question then becomes what counts as knowledge if a text lying substantially in one paradigm is interpreted and represented by texts in another.

This ends the first part of the book which has sought to establish, from different perspectives, that there are significant differences between *The Management of Innovation* and its mainstream representations. The comparison made between Burns and Stalker's book and these representations was analysed from the perspectives of meanings in texts, problems of representation, and textual analyses. The discourse and knowledge produced in Burns and Stalker's (1961) original text was compared with those in mainstream representations. These differences constituted one set of discourses focussing on structural change for organisations in environmental and market instability, while the original and alternative set of discourses, without excluding issues of structures and systems, was based largely on an analysis of human agency, power, politics and resistance and their effects on the success or otherwise of change strategies in organisations. It was demonstrated in this chapter that these discourses lie largely in different paradigms. Significant implications for what counts as knowledge in the academy and for what is most meaningful for managers, other practitioners and employees in the planning and implementation of change strategies follow from this.

Notes

1 This chapter is based on published papers by Green (2009) (Emerald); (2012) (Springer); and a book chapter (2017) (Routledge). The author would like to thank Emerald, Springer and Routledge for copyright permission.
2 The 'form and nature of reality, and, therefore, what can be known about it' (Guba and Lincoln 1998:201).
3 The 'nature of the relationship between the knower . . . and what can be known', or what counts as knowledge (Guba and Lincoln 1998:201).
4 One criticism of Kuhn is that he used several definitions of paradigm (see e.g. Burrell 1996). Kuhn responded to this in the 1970 edition of his book, defining his use of the concept in two different ways: the beliefs and values shared by a scientific community and secondly the more specific shared problems and solutions (Kuhn 1970). Here both these meanings are referred to; the second is used to define paradigms and relate them to the different texts under discussion.
5 Supplementarity and binary oppositions in Derrida's schema both deal with the problem of boundaries. He uses the concept of supplement to show something added on to something to enrich it further, but at the same time it is something that makes up for some lack. This is a contradiction as it implies the original 'something' is in the one instance whole and in the other, lacking. This leads Derrida to the idea that the supplement is neither 'inside' nor 'outside' and perhaps both inside and outside at the same time. Derrida's 'law of the supplement' means that no one idea or object is definitively separable from another. The context would determine this. Derrida's concept of binary oppositions similarly rejects an 'ideal purity' where there are clear distinctions or 'oppositional logic' such as serious/non-serious; and intentional/non-intentional. Derrida suggests instead 'a supplementary complication that calls for other concepts, for other thoughts beyond the concept' (Derrida 1988:117).
6 Researchers using objectivist, structural approaches normally did not justify their research strategies – nor their research instruments, the questions asked or the respondents chosen. This is discussed in Chapter 8.
7 How researchers find what they believe can be known (Guba and Lincoln 1998:201).
8 Simons' research paper is analysed again in more detail in Chapter 8 in discussions on scientifically based research in the management accounting field.
9 These are Miles and Snow's (1978) categories for organisations facing relatively stable product/market development as against those constantly seeking new market opportunities (Simons 1987). This is similar to Burns and Stalker's framework. Miles and Snow's ideas have also been used extensively in management accounting research.
10 Knowledge is obtained of the subjects at first hand (Burrell and Morgan 1979).
11 This involves scientific testing and quantitative analyses of data (Burrell and Morgan 1979).

12 'Emic' is defined as ideographic: from within the social group (from the perspective of the subject), as opposed to 'etic', which is positivist, from outside (from the perspective of the observer) (Guba and Lincoln 1998).

13 There are many interpretations of Burrell and Morgan's book, and it has been claimed that they did not mean to support incommensurability among the paradigms. Morgan (1990:28) in fact invited scholars to engage in 'dialectical modes of research which attempt to counterpose the insights generated from competing perspectives'. Likewise Burrell (1996) stated that the aim of the book was to show that a plurality of legitimate and competing perspectives would be normal especially for the social sciences.

14 Burrell and Morgan had also placed regulation in the interpretive paradigm, which, it will be shown, is more in keeping with broader interpretations of Burns and Stalker's ideas. But what was more important for Burrell and Morgan with regard to that paradigm was its subjectivist approach, with regulation being 'often implicit rather than explicit', whereas the functionalist paradigm on the other hand was clearly and firmly 'rooted in the sociology of regulation' (Burrell and Morgan 1979:28, 25).

15 For example, many managers saw as a threat to themselves the newly appointed engineers and laboratory technicians, who saw themselves and acted as a privileged group.

16 According to them 'determinist' was used to describe humans as products of their environments and conditioned by the circumstances in which they were placed. 'Voluntarist' described people exercising free will and creating rather than being created by their environments (Burrell and Morgan 1979:2).

17 It may be that critical realism solves this problem, allowing for both objective entities in the world, mediated by and interdependent with subjective human agency (Fleetwood 2005).

18 Burns and Stalker's ideal types may be an exception, as indeed may Weber's, and this is where one might argue that *The Management of Innovation* has some functionalist characteristics.

19 The word 'bias' carries with it an epistemological stance – that one can understand the world free of biased or value-filled perspectives.

References

Ahrens, T. (2008). Overcoming the Subjective-Objective Divide in Interpretive Management Accounting Research. *Accounting, Organizations and Society*, 33 (2–3), pp. 292–297.

Bhaskar, R. (2008). *Dialectic: The Pulse of Freedom*. London: Routledge.

Blumer, H. (1966). Sociological Implications of the Thought of George Herbert Mead. *American Journal of Sociology*, 71 (5), pp. 535–544.

Burns, T. (1966). Preface to the Second Edition. In: T. Burns, and G.M. Stalker, eds., *The Management of Innovation*. 2nd ed. London: Tavistock Publications, pp. vii–xxii.

Burns, T. and Stalker, G.M. (1961). *The Management of Innovation*. London: Tavistock Publications.

Burrell, G. (1996). Normal Science, Paradigms, Metaphors, Discourses and Genealogies of Analysis. In: S.R. Clegg, C. Hardy and W.R. Nord, eds., *Handbook of Organization Studies*. London: Sage, pp. 642–658.

Burrell, G. and Morgan, G. (1979). *Sociological Paradigms and Organisational Analysis: Elements of the Sociology of Corporate Life*. Aldershot: Ashgate.

Chua, W.F. (1986). Radical Developments in Accounting Thought. *The Accounting Review*, lxi (4), pp. 601–632.

Covaleski, M.A., Dirsmith, M.W., and Samuel, S. (1996). Managerial Accounting Research: The Contributions of Organizational and Sociological Theories. *Journal of Management Accounting Research*, 8, pp. 1–35.

Daft, R.L. (2001). *Organization Theory and Design*. 7th ed. Cincinnati, OH: South-Western College Publishing.

Derrida, J. (1988). *Limited Inc*. Trans. S. Weber. Evanston, IL: Northwestern University Press.

Derrida, J. (2002). Implications: Interview with Henri Ronse. In: J. Derrida, ed., *Positions*. Trans. A. Bass. 2nd ed. London: Continuum, pp. 1–14.

Dilthey, W. (1976). *Selected Writings*. In: H.P. Rickman, ed. London: Cambridge University Press.

Eco, U. (1992a). Interpretation and History. In: S. Collini, ed., *Interpretation and Over-interpretation: Umberto Eco with Richard Rorty, Jonathan Culler and Christine Brooke-Rose*. Cambridge: Cambridge University Press, pp. 23–44.

Eco, U. (1992b). Overinterpreting Texts. In: S. Collini, ed., *Interpretation and Over-interpretation: Umberto Eco with Richard Rorty, Jonathan Culler and Christine Brooke-Rose*. Cambridge: Cambridge University Press, pp. 45–66.

Fleetwood, S. (2005). Ontology in Organization and Management Studies. *Organization*, 12 (2), pp. 197–222.

Frenkel, S. (2009). Critical Reflections on Labor Process Theory, Work, and Management. In: M. Alvesson, T. Bridgman and H. Willmott, eds., *The Oxford Handbook of Critical Management Studies*. Oxford: Oxford University Press, pp. 525–535.

Granlund, M. and Lukka, K. (2017). Investigating Highly Established Research Paradigms: Reviving Contextuality in Contingency Theory Based Management Accounting Research. *Critical Perspectives on Accounting*, 45, pp. 63–80.

Green, M. (2005). Are Management Texts Produced by Authors or by Readers? Representations of a Contingency Theory. *Philosophy of Management*, 5 (1), pp. 85–96.

Green, M. (2009). The Embedding of Knowledge in the Academy: "Tolerance", Irresponsibility or Other Imperatives? *Social Responsibility Journal*, 5 (2), pp. 165–177.

Green, M. (2012). Can Deconstructing Paradigms Be Used as a Method for Deconstructing Texts? *Philosophy of Management*, 11 (2), pp. 85–113.

Green, M. (2017). Behaviour in Academe: An Investigation into the Sustainability of Mainstream Scholarship in Management Studies. In: G. Aras and C. Ingley, eds., *Corporate Behavior and Sustainability: Doing Well by Being Good. Finance, Governance and Sustainability: Challenges to Theory and Practice Series*. London: Routledge.

Guba, E.G. and Lincoln, Y.S. (1998). Competing Paradigms in Qualitative Research. In: N.K. Denzin and Y.S. Lincoln, eds., *The Landscape of Qualitative Research: Theories and Issues*. Thousand Oaks, CA: Sage, pp. 195–220.

Hall, M. (2016). Realising the Richness of Psychology Theory in Contingency-Based Management Accounting Research. *Management Accounting Research*, 31, pp. 63–74.

Hopper, T. and Bui, B. (2016). Has Management Accounting Research Been Critical? *Management Accounting Research*, 31, pp. 10–30.

Hopper, T. and Powell, A. (1985). Making Sense of Research into the Organizational and Social Aspects of Management Accounting: A Review of Its Underlying Assumptions. *Journal of Management Studies*, 22 (5), pp. 429–465.

Kakkuri-Knuuttila, M.-L., Lukka, K., and Kuorikoski, J. (2008). Straddling between Paradigms: A Naturalistic Philosophical Case Study on Interpretive Research in Management Accounting. *Accounting, Organizations and Society*, 33 (2–3), pp. 267–291.

Kilduff, M. and Dougherty, D. (2000). Change and Development in a Pluralistic World: The View from the Classics. *Academy of Management Review*, 25 (4), pp. 777–782.

Kuhn, T.S. (1970). *The Structure of Scientific Revolutions*. 2nd ed. Chicago, IL: Chicago University Press.

Lukka, K. (2010). The Roles and Effects of Paradigms in Accounting Research. *Management Accounting Research*, 21 (2), pp. 110–115.

Lukka, K. (2014). Exploring the Possibilities for Causal Explanation in Interpretive Research. *Accounting, Organizations and Society*, 39 (7), pp. 559–566.

MacIntyre, A. (2007). *After Virtue*. 3rd ed. London: Duckworth.

Miles, R.E. and Snow, C.C. (1978). *Organizational Strategy, Structure and Process*. New York: McGraw Hill.

Morgan, G. (1990). Paradigm Diversity in Organizational Research. In: J. Hassard and D. Pym, eds., *The Theory and Philosophy of Organizations: Critical Issues and New Perspectives*. London: Routledge, pp. 13–29.

Morgan, G. and Smircich, L. (1980). The Case for Qualitative Research. *Academy of Management Review*, 5 (4), pp. 491–500.

Mullins, L.J. (2005). *Management and Organisational Behaviour*. 7th ed. Harlow: Prentice Hall.

Neimark, M. and Tinker, T. (1986). The Social Construction of Management Control Systems. *Accounting, Organizations and Society*, 11 (4–5), pp. 369–395.

Norris, C. (2002). Derrida's *Positions*, Thirty Years on: Introduction to the Second English Language Edition. In: J. Derrida, ed., *Positions*. Trans. A. Bass. 2nd ed. London: Continuum, pp. ix–liv.

Otley, D. (2016). The Contingency Theory of Management Accounting and Control: 1980–2014. *Management Accounting Research*, 31, pp. 45–62.

Pugh, D.S. and Hickson, D.J. (2007). *Writers on Organizations*. 6th ed. London: Penguin Books.

Robbins, S.P. (2003). *Organizational Behavior*. 10th ed. Upper Saddle River, NJ: Pearson Education.

Sarbin, T.R. and Kitsuse, J.I. (1994). A Prologue to Constructing the Social. In: T.R. Sarbin and J.I. Kitsuse, eds., *Constructing the Social*. London: Sage, pp. 1–18.

Scherer, A.G. (2009). Critical Theory and Its Contribution to Critical Management Studies. In: M. Alvesson, T. Bridgman and H. Willmott, eds., *The Oxford Handbook of Critical Management Studies*. Oxford: Oxford University Press, pp. 29–51.

Selznick, P. (1948). *T.V.A. and the Grass Roots: A Study of Politics and Organization*. Berkeley, CA and Los Angeles, CA: University of California Press.

Simons, R. (1987). Accounting Control Systems and Business Strategy: An Empirical Analysis. *Accounting Organizations and Society*, 12 (4), pp. 357–374.

Starbuck, W.H. (2016). 60th Anniversary Essay: How Journals Could Improve Research Practices in Social Science. *Administrative Science Quarterly*, 61 (2), pp. 165–183.

TheFreeDictionary.com

Weber, M. (1947). *The Theory of Social and Economic Organisation*. Trans. A. Henderson and T. Parsons. Glencoe, IL: Free Press.

Williams, G. (2013). Experimentation in Reflective Practice: A Conceptional Framework for Managers in Highly Professionalized Organizations. In: R. Mansfield, ed., *Frontiers of Management: Research and Practice*. London: Routledge Revivals, pp. 65–75.

Willmott, H. (1993). Breaking the Paradigm Mentality. *Organization Studies*, 14 (5), pp. 681–719.

6 The academy

Introduction[1]

Questions need to be answered as to why these particular constructions of the text are dominant in the literature. Why did they emerge with widespread agreement among mainstream scholars? Was there, as Kuhn (1970) had suggested for scientific paradigms, a narrowing in order to be able to carry out research? Was it to suit prevailing orthodoxies in the academy? Did the disciplines such as Management Accounting influence interpretations and research applications in management more generally? Or should one turn to more substantive social and political factors, as would critical theorists, to answer these questions? Explanations range across different levels of constituency and different levels of analysis. One can divide the factors into micro, meso and macro levels involving individual actors, academic artefacts, university departments and dominant political ideologies.

Explanations for mainstream representations of *The Management of Innovation*

Unlike in the natural sciences, scholars working in different paradigms in the social sciences seem to be able to coexist in the same world of academia often with very little communication between them, and with separate careers and publishing outlets. This echoes MacIntyre's description of tolerance to alternative views:

> social scientists themselves characteristically and for the most part do adopt just such a tolerant attitude to counter-examples, an attitude very different from that of either natural scientists themselves or of Popperian philosophers of science ...
>
> (MacIntyre 2007:90)

This diversity, exemplified by Burrell and Morgan (1979), may be one of the reasons enabling the multiplicity of paradigms regarding original texts and their representations. Reasons are suggested in this chapter for the choices made in dominant scholarship for objectivist, quantitative approaches. The academy is examined. It is the context in which most scholars work and where this scholarship is grounded. Journal articles, journal editors' prerogatives and other issues to do with the academy are considered. Journal rankings have been shown to be a significant factor. Other pressures on the academy are discussed: corporate influences on business schools particularly in the US, the strength of sister disciplines, technological developments and wider political and social pressures.

The academy

In investigating the academy, examples are drawn from both US and UK scholarship. The sources used here are mainly from the US academy, mostly the *Administrative Science Quarterly (ASQ)*. This journal is one of the most influential US journals in the organisation/management field. It has a high reputation in the US and internationally because of its high ranking and citation indices (Meriläinen et al. 2008; Willmott 2011). It has been used because of the strong influence of North American on British (and European) scholarship (Alvesson 2013). The top ten management journals have all been from the US (Legge 2001).

North American (and Australian) scholarship has been intertwined with the British academy. The many examples from the UK and Australia published in the *ASQ* include articles by prominent scholars – Child (1973), Willmott (1981), Hickson (1996) and Clegg (2002). Among the UK and Australian books reviewed in the *ASQ* were those by Clegg and Dunkerley (1980), Burrell and Morgan (1979), Hassard and Pym (1990), and Clegg (2002). One explanation for main-stream representations of Burns and Stalker's and other contingency theorists' work in the UK is because of the demands of the US academy, particularly the requirements of editors of prominent US journals for particular types of scholarship.

Similarities and differences between US and UK scholarship are complex. Hickson (1996) claimed that it was difficult to come to one conclusion. Writers have highlighted important transatlantic similarities and differences over the decades. A working group soon after the establishment of EGOS (the European Group for Organization Studies) reported in the *ASQ* that superficially there were similarities within Anglo-American scholarship, which they described as having an

> empirical and positivist trend in favour of quantitative methods ... [in comparison with] a Latino-European trend, closer to socio-historical analysis and inclined to use ethnographical type surveys.
>
> (Vignolle 1976:511)

However, the diversity of 'local' approaches was thought by some to be more important than 'any hypothetical unity of national schools'. There was a marked divergence between British scholars who favoured quantification and modelling, an approach which had become a dominant tradition in the US and in the *ASQ*, and those who used a Marxist frame of reference (Vignolle 1976:512). Hickson (1996) certainly confirmed that the Aston objectivist studies he had been involved in with Pugh, Hinings and Pheysey between 1963 and 1969 were more warmly received in North American journals than in British ones.

Quantification and modelling was considered to constitute an important difference between North American and British scholarship. Hickson pointed to the contrast between North American interest in developing and testing causal theory, and European preferences for qualitative studies (Hickson 1996). Hopper and Bui (2016) confirmed this twenty years on for management accounting research, claiming that the distance between US and European scholarship was growing, with American scholars engaging less with their European counterparts. US scholarship was less multi-paradigmatic than European research. This is supported by many scholars who have described the highest-ranking US journals as pursuing managerialist and positivist agenda (Meriläinen et al. 2008).

Hickson also emphasised the ethnocentrism of North Americans, who cited few other than North Americans. The influence of research was uneven – mainly from west to east and not the other way round (Hickson 1996). A comparison in the early 1990s with *Organization Studies*, a European journal, showed a far greater diversity in the origins of its authors than in the *ASQ* (Grey 2010). Hickson (1996) and Clegg (2002) described European scholarship as having a sociological approach with an interest in power including discursive power, through the legitimation of certain rationalities, dominant coalitions of interest and the actors, their interests and their connections.

In North American scholarship politics became minimised by 'rationalized rationality' with a 'singular focus on efficiency and effectiveness' (Clegg 2002:437). Dunne et al. (2008) examining high-ranking US business and management US journals 2003–2004 similarly found 'a remarkable lack of attention being paid to the pressing social and political issues of our day' (Dunne et al. 2008:272). Critical research, according to one doctoral student at a US university, was generally not encouraged in highly rated American journals, nor in the business school at which he was studying (Prasad 2013).

This is relevant to interpretations of *The Management of Innovation* in both the UK and the US. These may be an important exception to the differences claimed to straddle both continents, and are a further justification for the inclusion of North American scholarship to discuss influences on mainstream representations of Burns and Stalker's book. There is the added complication in that what were called contingency theories were conceived in the mainstream literature as uniformly objectivist, as has been seen in the case of interpretations of Burns and Stalker's work.

Journals

Publications, particularly journal publications, are central to the academy. The types of writing and uses of language published in academic journals are crucial for the legitimation of what counts as knowledge, of what count as valid methodologies to establish such knowledge, and ultimately of what constitutes reality in the field. A reviewer in the *ASQ* identified with Cummings et al. (1985) about the 'apparent influence that the publishing mandate and practices had on both the content and process of organizational inquiry' (Donnellon 1986:313).

Parker and Thomas went further. It had an effect on the 'politics of the places we inhabit'. Parker and Thomas were discussing the social sciences and humanities generally, claiming that the type of research undertaken and problems explored could contribute either to an underpinning of the status quo or, if the inquiry adopted a critical approach, to a change in current social arrangements (Parker and Thomas 2011:420).

Being published plays a large part for academicians in advancing or quashing their academic careers. The individual actors here are scholars in the academy, scholars aspiring to be successful, first as undergraduate then postgraduate students, and then as lecturers, professors and respected scholars. One of the crucial markers of accepted scholarship is work accepted for publication in a high-ranking academic journal. The link between journal editors and academicians is close as the latter are often not only journal editors but also reviewers for articles submitted for publication to journals (Putnam 2009).

The *Administrative Science Quarterly*

The *ASQ* was selected for detailed examination as it was a journal specifically cited by scholars writing both within the journal (e.g. Palmer 2006) and outside it (e.g. Burrell and Morgan 1979) as requiring objectivist scholarship for acceptance for publication (Green 2009, 2012). Burrell and Morgan described the *ASQ* as packed with research in the objectivist tradition. According to them it 'helped to raise objectivism as applied to the study of organisations to the status of an orthodoxy' (Burrell and Morgan 1979:162).

Burrell and Morgan had specifically justified objectivist approaches in connection with contingency theory because of these *ASQ* requirements. Contingency authors while recognising that contingency models of organisation were 'essentially processual' had nevertheless deemed it politic to conceptualise their work in terms of structure. This was for the purposes of empirical research which could generate the hard quantitative measures from surveys about structure required by journals such as the *ASQ*. The methodology in such studies was, however, nowhere as sophisticated as the concepts on which it was based (Burrell and Morgan 1979:223–224, fns.37,38).

This claim about *ASQ* requirements for objectivist scholarship was investigated through an examination of publications in the *ASQ* from the 1960s to the 2010s. It was found that this was not entirely the case (Green 2009). There were examples of alternative approaches published in the journal, including Marxist, interpretive and social constructionist-based scholarship. Although the lion's share of articles published in the *ASQ* and in other primary US journals devoted to organisations was indeed in the objectivist camp (Scott 1996:164), the fact that there was a substantial minority of articles based on subjectivist scholarship tempers the claim that scholars basing their research on contingency theories had no option but to follow an objectivist epistemology and methodology.

The type of scholarship seen as valid and desirable, in comparison with what has actually been published in academic journals, is a subject that has interested scholars particularly in the US, and very much those writing in the *ASQ*. Interestingly, there were conflicting views about the type of scholarship actually published in the *ASQ* (and in other high-ranking journals). This opens up a disagreement about the nature and trends of scholarship in that journal and in organisation/management studies more widely. Some have felt that the scholarship was narrow and objectivist; others that it was multi-paradigmatic and eclectic. These differences leave open the possibility for there being room, albeit probably limited, for eclectic approaches.

Objectivist research

Many have affirmed that the *ASQ* and other major journal editors supported the notion of a restrictive, scientific set of criteria in research acceptable for publication. This has resulted in a narrowness in content, style and paradigm (Palmer 2006). Many writing in the journal were of the firm opinion that journals, particularly the *ASQ*, had contributed to the kinds of limiting knowledge and methodologies referred to above in connection with representations of Burns and Stalker's work. Those believing that this type of scholarship was dominant but who were against it as were Stern and Barley, exhorted journal editors to begin to take risks and include papers with broad perspectives and non-traditional methodologies (Stern and Barley 1996). A well-articulated paper with a sound methodology could be rejected 'simply because it clashes with their [the editors' or reviewers'] particular conceptual tastes' (Sutton and Staw 1995:372). The criteria included a preference for similar approaches and for empirical over theoretical work:

> it is much easier for a set of reviewers ... to agree on a carefully crafted empirical piece that has little or no theory than it is for them to go along with a weak test of a new theoretical idea ... papers chosen ... tend to be those with acceptable methods and undeveloped theory.
>
> (Sutton and Staw 1995:381–382)

One reason for this suggested by Astley was that journal editors were inclined to select papers for publication that were similar to their own epistemological and methodological preferences. Unlike in the sciences, there were no objective scientific criteria by which to judge the value of an article, so reviewers used their own socially grounded frames of reference rather than ones based purely on scholarship. Such social factors included institutional affiliations and personal ties. Uncertainty and paradigm dissensus were further reasons for employing social cues such as similar social networks for the selection of papers for publication (Astley 1985).

This view of US journals and their influence over UK journals was supported more recently in an article in *Organization*. Willmott criticised British journals for fostering a 'monoculture', in which a

> preoccupation with shoehorning research into a form prized by elite, US-oriented journals overrides a concern to maintain and enrich the diversity of topics, the range of methods and the plurality of perspectives ... in business and management research.
>
> (Willmott 2011:429)

It is possible that this culture has had a strong influence on the representation of texts like Burns and Stalker's, and may have played a part in channelling positivist research to journals in both the US and the UK, including articles based on Burns and Stalker's work.

Research in the ASQ

The kind of scholarship actually produced in the *ASQ* has however included more eclectic approaches. Much of the scholarship was indeed objectivist and statistically based (Scott 1996), but there were articles in that journal advocating broader approaches and criticising narrower ones. For example Selznick (1948) (whom Burns and Stalker had cited in relation to informal groups' abilities to subvert formal organisation structures and strategies) claimed in a later paper published in the *ASQ*, that rational-actor models and a focus on formal structures were mythical and served as legitimations of particular organisational forms and practices, providing displays of confidence and satisfaction rather than being reflective of whether they were efficient and whether they coped with uncertainties. Such models in fact denied the inspection and evaluation of concrete organisational processes with their tensions and problems. What was ignored was the organisation's culture and social structure with its social entanglements or commitments, which Selznick described as the 'underlying reality – the basic source of stability and integration' (Selznick 1992:232 cited in Selznick 1996:271). When discussing organisational change Selznick, again quoting from his earlier work, affirmed that

> [N]o social process can be understood save as it is located in the behavior of individuals, and especially in their perceptions of themselves and each other.
> (Selznick 1957:4 cited in, Selznick 1996:274)

Criticisms by those who regarded organisation/management studies or the *ASQ* specifically as too functionalist or traditionalist continued to be published in that journal. Clegg wrote about the narrowness and political and moral bias in North American organisation studies as a whole:

the discipline has focused on the efficiency and effectiveness dimension ...
In effect the dominant institutionalizations of North American organization
theory discourse have resulted in the rationalization of rationality without a
moral dimension ... through seeing truth as something that is outside of
social practices, being instead located in an autonomous sphere of science.

(Clegg 2002:430–431)[2]

Over the years many book reviews were written from pluralist perspectives.
Praise was given to Edwards' book, *Contested Terrain*, which had been written
from a Marxist standpoint. The reviewer in the *ASQ* described this as a
'welcome counterpoint to the customary models employed by most students of
organization' (Mitchell 1981:293). Bolman and Deal wrote a book about the
need for 'conceptual pluralism' – the analysis of organisational actors and
processes from different schools of thought: structural, interpretive, political
and symbolic. This was reviewed positively in the *ASQ* (Van Meter 1985:135).
Meyer and Scott's book on ritual and rationality, according to the *ASQ*
reviewer, focussed on the idea that 'modern organizations have been described
incompletely by prevailing theories of formal structure' (Clark 1985:295).

Morgan's chapter in Cummings et al. (1985) which criticised control and
domination by positivist gatekeepers was sympathetically received in a review in
the *ASQ*. The reviewer favourably described chapters in the book concerned with
non-traditional subjects such as diversity, emotion and culture (Hunt 1986). A
decade later, Hickson, who had worked closely with Pugh and had engaged in
positivist research was of the view, based on Usdiken's and Pasadeos' assertions
about the prominence in the *ASQ* of institutional theory, that American researchers were not all hard any more than all Europeans were soft in their methodological stance (Hickson 1996). Because of this not inconsiderable eclecticism in the
ASQ, further explanations than editors' requirements are needed to explain the
preponderance and tenacity of objectivist research in the academy.

Trends: narrowings

Just as there are differences as to the type of scholarship published in the *ASQ*,
so too there are different analyses of trends in organisation scholarship, in
particular in the *ASQ*. Some have claimed that the type of knowledge in that
journal has steadily become narrower, more scientific and less sociological.
Palmer, himself an editor of the *ASQ*, went into some detail about the
founding editors' vision and what had happened in practice across the decades
from the first issue of the journal. Litchfield and Thompson, the first editors,
had wanted scholars to develop a theory of administration through a scientific
methodology, with models which evaluated empirical relationships (Litchfield
1956). Significantly, they were agnostic about the merits of qualitative or
quantitative analysis (Palmer 2006:538). Whisler had predicted in 1974 that
scientific-type research was there to stay and grow in strength. He was writing
more generally about knowledge in the academy, which he saw as continuing

to develop analytic and measurement techniques relevant to business problems and performance measurement systems growing out of econometrics and statistical decision-making (Whisler 1974).

In a series of papers published in 1996 to mark the 40th anniversary of the *ASQ* and reflect on its history, there were differences of opinion as to whether the journal had broadened in content and approach or become narrower (*ASQ*, 41 (1) 1996). In that year Stern and Barley also claimed that the trend was towards narrower scholarship. They highlighted the administrative emphasis in the *ASQ*. Parson's (1956) paper, published in the first issue of the journal had been taken up in terms of his second agenda – the 'mechanisms of implementation' – a study of structures, processes and decision-making internal to organisations (Stern and Barley 1996:151). Parsons' third requirement, an examination of the role of organisations in relation to the broader sociocultural system, had in the main not been pursued. This had led to a narrowing of the content of the field and of its ideological direction (Stern and Barley 1996). Scott agreed with Stern and Barley that the 'primary' journals dealing with organisations including the *ASQ* had 'abandoned [sociological] traditions', though Weber's and Parson's traditions were still being upheld in journals in the broader social science area and outside what he called the 'core organizational journals' (Scott 1996:164).

Hinings and Greenwood (2002) too felt that the *ASQ* in its beginnings had been sociological in its approach, with an interest in questions of power and privilege in organisations. They claimed that this quest had been abandoned from the 1970s and replaced by questions to do with efficiency and problem-solving from a managerial point of view. Parker and Thomas confirmed this about sociology more broadly. Writing in *Organization*, they pointed to the criticality of sociology in the 1960s, which by the 1990s had gone the way of other disciplines 'towards positions where they could speak directly to those providing funding for policy advice and evaluation' (Parker and Thomas 2011:423).

Burns, writing more widely about the field in the preface to the third edition of *The Management of Innovation*, was of the view that until the end of the 1950s, post-war reconstruction, political change and economic prosperity had led to scholarship about the social concerns of people, societal processes, consensus and a desire to identify obstacles in the way of the efficient functioning of organisations. One example of such research was the Human Relations school which promoted the idea of informal organisations, focussing on the behaviour, relationships, values and commitment of employees (Burns 1994).

Possibly influenced by representations of *The Management of Innovation*, Burns wrote that notions of organisational efficiency had begun to change. It was now considered to be best achieved through rational organisational structures for decision-making and control. From the 1970s economic difficulties, precipitated by increases in oil prices, had led to a revived interest in bureaucracy and a search for general principles determining organisations structures, such as technology, or wider governmental, business and industrial systems. Above all, there had to be accommodation with adverse and competing circumstances. Innovative opinion and dissension were blocked as a way of preserving the system and the beliefs and values sustaining it (Burns 1994).

Trends: broadenings

Interestingly, opposing views on the direction of the discipline were also put forward in the *ASQ*. Dunbar, analysing trends in the journal from its early volumes until the 1980s, concluded that the *ASQ* had attempted to represent all approaches to administrative science, and that although many administrative researchers continued to use 'natural science' methods, a 'significant minority' such as Weick (1979) had placed more value on the subjective aspects of organisational relations and processes. And while some theorists were interested in underlying order, others were interested in the forces bringing about change (Dunbar 1983:129).

Scott gave a brief history of organisation studies, which he saw as emerging in the 1950s and 1960s. Because the discipline was new, it could not establish a discrete field, but 'infiltrated all of the social sciences – psychology, political science, economics and (but not just) sociology' (Scott 1996:166). Scientistic models had been more prevalent in the development of organisation studies at an earlier period – in the mid-1960s. Now, some thirty years later, the danger of organisational sociology being 'submerged under administrative science' was 'quite remote'. The *caveat* was scholarship in the professional schools such as business, which had to be applied with a focus on practice in work environments, as opposed to departments dealing with liberal arts programmes (Scott 1996:167).[3] This is perhaps another reason for the way Burns and Stalker's work has been represented in mainstream scholarship.

Scott's arguments were echoed by Porter, who, in his own overview of organisation studies over several decades, pointed to the 'absence of any clear and compelling paradigms' and praised the discipline for being 'truly multidisciplinary' (Porter 1996:266, 262). Porter felt that the field of organisation studies was broadening from its psychological base, with the *ASQ* a 'major force' for providing an outlet for scholars wishing to adopt multi-disciplinary approaches (Porter 1996:263).

March agreed with this. He attested to a variety of approaches and research methodologies becoming 'common' (March 1996:279). Zald wrote in the *ASQ* in the same year about the 'fragmentation and lack of shared paradigms that have come to characterize the field'. He attributed this to new topics, new theories and methodologies from wider influences within and outside the social sciences, such as linguistics, literary and feminist theories and historical approaches (Zald 1996:252). Later on, a set of editors from the *ASQ* also took a broad view. They claimed to be receptive to articles on diverse topics, theories, practices and research methods, provided the papers included some theoretical grounding.

One editor's summation

An overview of organisation studies over those forty years by Palmer, then editor of the *ASQ*, gives a confused picture. He singled out the *ASQ* for being relatively multi-disciplinary in its orientation from its beginnings, as opposed to the field of organisation studies in general, which, in the 1950s had been dominated by psychologists. The problem with this conclusion was that articles which had been rejected, self-censored and not submitted were excluded from his analysis. This could weigh the evidence more in favour of traditional topics and methodologies (Palmer 2006).

While many scholars followed the original editors' wishes, some took different paths. Palmer investigated whether the founding editors' wishes had in fact been upheld in the manuscripts selected for publication in the *ASQ*. He made a study of the authors who had been given the *ASQ* Award for Scholarly Contributions between 1995 and 2006 to see what types of articles had been accepted for publication. The weakness in this research, as he had stated, was that he saw only the papers chosen by the awards committees, not those that had been passed over. Palmer's assessment nevertheless allowed for some eclecticism, with the inclusion of broader, more organisational approaches (Palmer 2006).

Seven of the twelve papers did not include the administrative process, but focussed on broader aspects of organisational behaviour. Another criterion set by Litchfield and Thompson and germane to this study was that of paradigm homogeneity. Palmer found very little paradigm-building in the papers he studied, and came to the conclusion that 'the *ASQ* has not done much to promote *increased* paradigmatic homogeneity in recent years – which, of course, was not to say that it had fostered paradigmatic heterogeneity'. Four of the twelve papers had used qualitative methods, confirming his view that while the *ASQ* allowed qualitative work, it nevertheless privileged quantitative-based research. Palmer and other researchers claimed that there was ultimately an increasing use of scientific or quantitative/statistical methods in the *ASQ* particularly by the late 1960s and into the 1970s, with increasingly simple models and corresponding lower language variety (Palmer 2006:544) (emphasis in the original). Other authors sharing this view included Boulding (1958), Daft (1980) and Zald (1993).

Daft (1980) pointed out that this was by no means all encompassing. In 1979 there had been a special issue of the *ASQ* devoted to papers using a variety of qualitative methods. There were papers too in the *ASQ* in favour of case study research which also used qualitative methods. Clegg put forward a stronger counterargument: alternative views were published mainly through special issues such as the one on Foucault in 1998 (Clegg 2002). The factors identified and analysed below tend to support arguments for an increasingly scientific, objectivist, quantitative-based scholarship in the second half of the twentieth century.[4]

Differences in interpretation

There are difficulties in arriving at a fully satisfactory evaluation as to why there were these markedly different analyses of the type of knowledge produced in the *ASQ*, and elsewhere. This is resonant with the problems concerning representations of Burns and Stalker's text. Just as there were differences in interpretations of that text, so too there were differences in interpretations as to what was permissible, what was actually published in the ASQ and what the trends were.

An evaluation of scholarship over a number of decades by different scholars was likely to yield complex results, even with respect to one journal. For Weick, in a 'low-paradigm' field scholars would differ (Weick 1996:309). Palmer suggested ambiguities in editorial policy. There was indeterminacy or conflicts of opinion as to what the editorial policy was and what was published in the *ASQ*. In a 'stock-taking' of the criteria used in the *ASQ* for scholarly work, he asserted that editors were rigorously selected to evaluate scholars' papers according to criteria approved by the founding editors. But those were often 'imprecise' and guidelines to contributors and reviewers correspondingly vague, aside from editors and reviewers exercising independent judgment in their evaluations of manuscripts (Palmer 2006:536).

The criteria, whatever they were, remained 'incompletely articulated and relatively unexamined'. They were either used as a guideline by subsequent editors or were opposed by them, generating worries that the *ASQ*'s community of scholars either 'clung too closely to the vision of the journal's founders or strayed too far from it' (Palmer 2006:536). The fact that the first editors wanted scholars to develop a theory of administration and a scientific methodology with models which evaluated empirical relationships, but were indifferent as to whether the analysis was quantitative or qualitative, may have constituted additional grounds for confusion (Palmer 2006:538). This potential ambiguity as to what has counted as scientific has led to an investigation into definitions of science in the next chapter.[5]

Role of contingency theory

As discussed earlier, another source of confusion may have been to do with how contingency theory was defined, and whether it was seen as mainstream and current, or as increasingly outdated and restricted to a limited group of scholars. An identification of contingency theory with objectivist approaches may have influenced the different interpretations of the type and prevalence of scholarship published in the *ASQ*. This had been an important factor defining British scholarship, particularly in the management accounting field.

For many, contingency theory was viewed as having a static approach to organisations with an emphasis on structure, models and statistical techniques (Daft 1980). Its significance was in its prominence in organisation studies (Drazin and Van de Ven 1985). Stern and Barley (1996), in their overview of

ASQ scholarship over the previous 40 years, felt that contingency theory and the search for scientific respectability were reasons for a diminution of a broad social systems perspective. March, too, described contingency theory as involving static rules and institutions, which had become problematic for organisation theory (March 1996). These views have continued into the twenty-first century with Scherer (2009) for instance giving contingency theory as an example of 'dominant positivist approaches' (Scherer 2009:37).

The way contingency theory has been conceptualised in management accounting scholarship has influenced analyses of trends in British management accounting research. The 1970s proved to be a watershed, with the introduction of behavioural and organisational approaches. Dissatisfied with the 'static and highly statistical survey methods prevailing in contingency theory' researchers for this and other reasons such as the entry into accounting departments by social scientists, turned to case study research, organisation controls, politics and processes in organisations (Hopper et al. 2001:273–274).[6]

Relevant to this discussion is the assertion that contingency theory was among ideas that 'tended to be abandoned', and that this in part made for an increasing divergence from North American scholarship. Contingency theory was seen as marginalised, and was therefore excluded in the assessment of trends in management accounting scholarship in the UK. It was claimed that from the 1970s more eclectic approaches were beginning to be included in UK than in North American scholarship (Hopper et al. 2001:275). Others, as seen above, had placed more importance on the continuing influence of objectivist contingency scholarship. This again raises questions of differences in evaluations of contingency theories and of what counts as knowledge in the academy.

Scholarship in the ASQ: conclusions

The scholarship produced in the *ASQ* was predominantly objectivist, quantitative and narrower than more pluralist approaches. This claim is strengthened by the fact that the alternative scholarship published in the *ASQ* was often written by eminent academics such as Simon and Mintzberg rather than by those lesser known (Green 2009). Also, more eclectic views were more often located in book reviews than in full articles. Nevertheless, the point is that instead of there being a rigid and universal conformism, there were substantial differences in the type of work published in the *ASQ*, with opportunities for scholars to submit alternative types of research.

The multiplicity of views about what was published in the *ASQ*, and the fact that different types of scholarship were published in that journal have not provided full answers to the original question as to why so many of the representations and research applications of Burns and Stalker's ideas were based on survey results from data exclusively from senior managers. And why more sociological, complementary approaches with data from a larger cross-section of employees in organisations along with the inclusion of other issues such as power, control and resistance were largely absent.

Journal rankings

Academic journals are one of the pivotal influences in the academy, particularly through their rankings. Politically, the hierarchisation of journals as markers of research prowess has led to pressures on academics to publish in the highest ranked journals. This has led to work that has been subject to conformist criteria at the expense of originality and creativity in content, format and method (Butler and Spoelstra 2012). It has encouraged homogeneity and hindered innovative ideas (Putnam 2009; Alvesson 2013). Adler and Harzing (2009) have claimed that the use of ranked journal lists

> dramatically skews scholarship as it implicitly encourages conservative research that asks familiar questions using accepted methodologies rather than research addressing new, often controversial questions that are investigated using innovative methodologies.
>
> (Adler and Harzing 2009:80)

Harzing is in a good position to make a judgment on this as she has compiled and edited several versions of the Journal Quality List, an evaluation of journals in the fields of social science, economics, finance and other business subjects (Harzing 2013).

Scholars, under the constraints associated with 'publish or perish' who have managed to publish in the higher ranked journals, have for long enabled their institutions to enjoy more prestige and resources, and to attract better students (Bhagat 1979). Clegg has connected publishing outcomes in the right places with the granting of tenure (Clegg 2002). Academicians publishing in these journals have been rewarded by being recruited and promoted (Willmott 2011; Thomas and Parker 2012; Lachmann et al. 2017). In another journal quality guide, the ABS, journals were rated from 1 to 4, with 4 marking the top journals. That guide has been used to determine tenure, promotion and research allocations in various business schools in the UK (Hussain 2015).

The screw was further tightened when new authors approached an editor or professor who knew their work personally and who served as gatekeeper to the publisher. Salancik (1987) has estimated that in such circumstances the chances of the work being accepted rose to 1 in 3. The advice given to new academics was to 'play the game' by seeking to publish in the higher ranked journals according to the above criteria (Moizer 2009:289). Starbuck recently highlighted problems with orthodox, statistical methods such as null-hypothesis significance tests. He had pleaded with journal editors to experiment with innovation, particularly as this could influence researchers' practices for the better, but acknowledged the difficulties with senior scholars adopting new methodologies at the risk of implicating their previous work. There were exceptions however, such as the banning of objectivist, null-hypothesis statistical tests by the editor of a medical journal, which had resulted in others doing the same (Starbuck 2016).

Journals have become 'commodified' in that publications are exchanged for the money and resources enjoyed by the institutions whose scholars write for the most highly ranked publications. Alvesson has described it 'as a matter of *going from research to roisearch*', with the likely result that the intellectual status quo is reinforced and new, innovative ideas marginalised (Alvesson 2013:82) (emphasis in the original). These activities have been called 'list fetishism' – a situation where the publication outlet (the high-ranked journal) is valued more for its place in the rankings than for the content of its articles and for the contributions of the scholars writing in it (Willmott 2011:430).

Moizer, himself having had the experience of being the editor of a top 10-ranked accounting journal, concluded that publication in the social sciences had become a 'game' in which the original purpose of the advancement of knowledge seemed to have 'got lost' (Moizer 2009:285). The problem was that such journals had the power to attribute quality and legitimation to scholarship. According to many one cannot evaluate the worth of an article according to the ranking of the journal in which it is published. Inferior papers have ridden on the backs of high-ranked journals and been evaluated unjustifiably highly (Baum 2011; Willmott 2011; Starbuck 2016).

> Where you publish seems to have become vastly more important than what you publish
>
> (Thomas and Parker 2012)

This can translate into Bourdieu's concept of capital – the 'structure of the distribution of the forms of power' (Bourdieu 1998:32). Cultural and social capital – the power and position gained through belonging to certain networks, in this case professional networks, enables people to acquire powerful symbolic capital (the power which consolidates other types of capital) and to seize 'potential opportunities' (Bourdieu 1990:64). Because these ranking systems influence the distribution of resources in a university, it influences what counts as valued academic work and what serves as legitimate knowledge. Hogler and Gross argue that the commodification process is taken further in that high-ranking journals mark what is the 'dominant narrative', and appropriate 'learning' is produced for student consumers who 'purchase' a 'defined quantum of knowledge' which become 'services' to enhance their own careers (Hogler and Gross 2009:4).

Yet this has not precluded the publication in these journals of strongly academic scholarship, open to people outside the discipline (Alvesson 2013). The editors of some journals, for example *Management Accounting Research*, in a review of 25 years of the journal, encouraged 'whatever theoretical perspectives and methodologies ... appropriate for research in the field of management accounting (broadly defined)... provided ... [they] satisfied authoritative reviewers' (Bromwich and Scapens 2016:2–3). The breadth and diversity of topics and research methods in that journal has been confirmed by others, e.g. Hopper and Bui (2016).

Academic networks

Social networks are all important. Pfeffer, in his review of a book on organisational design, pointed to the close networking processes and influence shared by the editors and contributors to that book. He described how in the 1970s a unique niche was founded at Carnegie Mellon University by a group of scholars wanting to differentiate their work from the established Academy of Management and from the *ASQ*. They developed a focus on design and design management, and organised among other things a conference, a book based on the conference and the editorship of a journal. Pfeffer showed that eight of the twelve contributors to the volume had studied or taught at only three institutions (Pfeffer 1977).

Various authors have pointed to editors working for their own and their social networks' advantage and not for more intrinsic reasons. According to Salancik, decisions were politicised and made by a small number of people allied to key members of the academic community. Probably at its worst was the situation where

> social science books are ... often accepted for publication because a publisher's editor knows someone in the field who said it was a good book.
>
> (Salancik 1987:307)

Clegg has supported this view in his criticism of what are considered to be robust research programmes – not those that are truly the most robust, but those which are 'best located, resourced and publicized'. Being funded by the most powerful patrons, they have wider symbolic capital (Clegg 2002:435). This process is further reinforced by academics citing articles based on papers written by members of the elite groups they are familiar with, potentially strengthening the status and ranking of certain journals at the expense of others – a development predicted in the early 1970s and still ongoing (Macdonald and Kam 2011).

Control and political manoeuvring over journal publications has been analysed by Bourdieu through his definition of a 'field' – a struggle in a social network among people possessing a sufficient amount of one of the kinds of capital to dominate the field (Bourdieu 1998:34). Bourdieu describes fields in academe as exercising 'the most brutal constraints of the ordinary social world' (Bourdieu 1998:138). To have this control, academics must acquire cultural, social and symbolic capital (Green 2009). Economic power is excluded as academics are weaker in the acquisition of that type of power (Bourdieu 1998).

What is important in academic debate and politics is not about monetary resources overtly, but about what legitimately constitutes a field of study: 'discussion, refutation, and regulated dialogue', and particularly positive and negative sanctions on individual 'products' (Bourdieu 1998:139). It is not only within the field that symbolic capital is acquired by scholars. For academic work is rated by outside bodies as well – the ranking of universities for example through the assessment of doctoral programmes; the ranking of journals by outside arbiters such as the Thomson ISI Web of Knowledge in the US and the influence of external funding bodies (Putnam 2009).

Universities

Much has been written about what an ideal university should be. MacIntyre presented an idealised view of universities as communities of shared interests where practice constituted

> socially established cooperative human activity ... with the result that human powers to achieve excellence, and human conceptions of the ends and goods involved, are systematically extended.
>
> (MacIntyre 2007:187)

But universities are also subject to strong economic pressures to acquire resources, and to political pressures to produce a certain kind of knowledge. Here too there are differences of opinion among scholars about the kind of knowledge produced. Ladd and Lipset (1975) on the basis of extensive research of US academics in the late 1960s and early 1970s, postulated a wide diversity of American academics; the type of university; the social context (their research being done in the wake of the campus crises in the 1960s); the different functions of the moment such as services to public or private sectors dependent partly on whether republican or democratic administrations were in office; political persuasions and the possible influence by politics on different academic disciplines (Kadushin 1976).

Ladd and Lipset (1975) found that social scientists were more liberal than natural scientists, who in turn were more liberal than those in engineering, business and law. This again may be one of the explanations for mainstream representations of *The Management of Innovation*. Creative professors were often disloyal to majority values and norms and tended to be progressive, liberal and leftist. Some thought that the more leftist and therefore the more intellectual and theoretical, the more likely was the academician to be successful with publications, grants, top positions and government consultantships, whereas the more conservative professors were likely to be the more deprived (Kadushin 1976).

Manns and March's research found a correlation between a scarcity of resources and conservative curricula, as an institution in such circumstances would be vulnerable to the student market and would devise a curriculum attractive to students. But universities with strong reputations such as Stanford, where these authors had done their research, were less likely to be pressured in terms of their curricula (Manns and March 1978). Like Manns and March, Barley et al. (1988) claimed that declining economic productivity and competitiveness encouraged academics to adopt more managerialist agenda. Scarcity of resources induced paradigm conformity as conflict would be reduced and politics could be used more freely in decision-making (Pfeffer and Moore 1980).

Another factor encouraging conventional scholarship was length of tenure. Heads of department tended to be more conservative, as they were likely to enjoy longer tenure when there was high paradigm agreement, more conformity and fewer divergent views. This again suggests that while there were examples of a plurality of approaches, there were strong pressures for conforming to more orthodox agenda, as Burrell also found in his university in the UK. One department thought to be being involved with 'the critical project' was under constant surveillance in case of financial difficulties because its ideology was seen as a potential threat to MBA recruitment. There were pressures on that department to work with companies which were regarded as having 'highly questionable' ethics (Burrell 2009:557).

Business schools: US

Conflicting views as to the nature of the scholarship in organisation studies can be explained to some extent according to where the scholarship originated. Several writers have attributed an objectivist, managerialist turn to the establishment and power of business schools in the US. Ladd and Lipset's (1975) linking of business faculties with engineering, and their assessment of engineering as being less liberal, can lead one to expect business schools to be conservative, require high paradigm consensus and exert objectivist influences on the research and methodologies selected (Kadushin 1976).

By the 1980s corporate sponsors of business schools strongly promoted managerialist, functionalist scholarship focussed on practical problem-solving and not on sociological understanding (Stern and Barley 1996). The hospitality which business schools accorded organisation theorists seeking resources and power for their new discipline in hard-pressed sociology departments, had both 'intended and unintended' consequences (Stern and Barley 1996:154). It had a negative impact on sociologists regarding the content of what was taught and the methodologies used. This resulted in a legitimation of different ontological and epistemological positions as to what constituted the 'reality' out there and therefore what counted as knowledge. From previous interest in public service and government agencies the focus or object of inquiry shifted to commercial companies, reinforced by corresponding career incentives for academics (Stern and Barley 1996).

This new interest was intentional in that some organisation scholars were looking for access to corporations. What was not foreseen were the pressures placed on them to deal with issues of immediate interest to those corporations rather than the 'externalities' of larger, systemic questions (Stern and Barley 1996:154). Funding imperatives affected scholarship, and managers could shape research agenda through their power to choose to whom to award grants (Barley et al. 1988). Hinings and Greenwood (2002) writing about business schools in the US questioned whether professors identifying primarily with their business school, could raise issues of relationships between organisations and society, including the critical questions of power, privilege and disadvantage. This could become even more problematic if professors also benefitted from organisations by working for them as consultants (Bartunek 2002).

Some scholars have been of the opinion that managerial approaches were strengthened by the importance given them in MBA courses. In business schools in the US, students were taught the need for tight control and the monitoring of people and competition in companies, including their suppliers, customers, employees and regulators, as well as their competitors (Ghoshal 2005). Clegg attested to MBA students hardly being required to consider questions of power and performativity. In many curricula the focus was on profit and efficiency (Clegg 2002).

This was extended to PhD programmes, where professors could build their own reputations or intellectual capital through encouraging their students to buy into their own theories and research methods (Clegg 2002). A further factor increasing managerial orientations in organisation studies was that many organisation theorists themselves had studied to PhD level in business schools rather than in departments offering complementary disciplines such as political science, industrial relations or sociology (Stern and Barley 1996).

It has been claimed that business school academics over the last half-century have rejected romantic approaches which focussed on individual choice, action and achievement in favour of scientific methods (Ghoshal 2005). Because scholarship had become more concerned with practical managerial issues than with sociological questions involving the understanding of social processes, management education had become politicised in a certain direction, and its values enmeshed with corporate and free market principles (Hogler and Gross 2009). MBAs, primarily based on conservative curricula and research, earned praise from corporations like Enron and Lehman Brothers for having an entrepreneurial perspective (Alvesson et al. 2009). Merchant has supported these views by asserting that the two dominant criteria for success in US business schools were publication in the highest-ranking journals and citations in the Social Science Citation Index (SSCI), criteria which were

> closing the door on many potential important research undertakings ... [and] squeezing out topic, discipline and research method diversity, at great cost to the schools themselves, the academy and, indeed, society.
>
> (Merchant 2010:116)

Business schools: UK

A contrary development occurred in the UK. In the late 1960s there was an expansion of newly established business schools. They had a critical tradition to draw on, which had been much less the case in the US. Alternative approaches were encouraged because, unlike in the US, many scholars and courses were located in social science faculties (Hopper et al. 2001). In the 1970s, the growth of undergraduate accounting and business degrees led to expansion in the then polytechnics and civic universities, but these did not lead to closer ties with business nor to a corporatist focus on scholarship as in US MBA and PhD degrees (Fournier and Grey 2000).

In the 1980s the influence of the New Right in the UK led to cutbacks in social science departments, particularly in sociology. The antisociological sentiments and actions against sociology departments under Mrs. Thatcher's conservative government had the effect of closing many down altogether, and driving sociologists as well as organisation theorists into business schools. An unintended consequence of this was that the entry of would-be social science scholars into business schools encouraged a cross-fertilisation between management studies and critical social science scholarship (Fournier and Grey 2000).

Similarly, critical non-accounting scholars were co-opted into accounting departments, spurred on by a rapid expansion of business degrees and the simultaneous deterioration in academic salaries relative to those in the private sector. This often led to approaches more diverse than the managerialist scholarship outlined above, including the development of a strong critical and interdisciplinary tradition (Hopper et al. 2001; Alvesson et al. 2009). However, such critiques were limited, given that the vast majority of students planned to enter companies which often financed business schools and recruited from them (Hopwood 2009).

The influence of management accountants has been shown to be particularly relevant to representations of Burns and Stalker's work. Yet many management accountants developed different approaches from those cited earlier whose research was based on Burns and Stalker's ideas. Because accounting data were central to economic and political debates and developments under Thatcherism around privatisation, industrial restructuring and changes to public sector management, management accountants, whatever their political orientation, realised that their research had to be located in a broader social, political, and institutional context. Those who were more radical were stimulated to engage more directly with government policies in European social democratic traditions (Hopper et al. 2001). This again raises questions as to why management accounting research based on Burns and Stalker's book normally did not follow this direction, despite critiques of that research and more pluralist approaches published in the same journals.

Disciplinary influences

Organisation vs management studies

The separation of disciplines between organisation studies and managerial perspectives is another possible explanation for the development of differences among scholars. Barley, Meyer and Gash saw these differences stemming from two approaches to the subject. Organisation studies was seen as a sub-branch of sociology and therefore concerned with societal issues, and with a more abstract and in many cases critical quest for knowledge. A managerialist agenda was more focussed on organisational, often corporatist problems needing solutions. These differences would naturally lead to different conceptions of the subject, how it should be approached and what its imperatives were (Barley et al. 1988).

As with many other issues the distinction, according to some writers, was murky. Salancik claimed that these two approaches were confused in management textbooks. Reviewing a popular textbook by Hellriegel and Slocum (1974), Salancik defined management as interested in practical, problem-solving activities, while organisational behaviour was about theoretical understandings of the social and psychological issues for individuals and organisations in economic and political contexts. They were related to each other, with problem-solving likely to be more effective if based on an understanding of organisational and psychological processes. But theoretical perspectives were confused with management practice, and ideas about management were upgraded to the status of theory (Salancik 1975). Clegg and Dunkerley (1980) also pointed to confusion between these two approaches. They put new schools of organisation theorists in the managerialist camp, attributing witting or unwitting motives to them in providing a means to help managers in large corporations achieve their agenda – usually increased productivity and control.

Whatever separation there was of organisation from management studies, this has been played out in the different interpretations of Burns and Stalker's book. For the mainstream, the focus was on structure – something managers could relate to and handle. A change in structure was represented as unproblematic, with the implicit message that it was easily achievable by managers and was their prerogative to take on this task. The *caveats* of Burns and Stalker about employee commitment, conflicting individual and group interests and the difficulties faced by chief executives, all constituting a challenge to managerial power, were omitted. In a minority of cases Burns and Stalker's ideas were subject to more sociological interpretations.

Economics

Ferraro et al. (2005) among others have viewed economics as the most dominant discipline in the social sciences, influencing other disciplines, including organisation studies. In a survey of the subject from the 1970s onward

Clegg found that organisation theory had become increasingly influenced by economic, biological and engineering models at the expense of a sociological model in which people in organisations would be constructed as discursive beings, influenced by and influencing power relations through their several rationalities (Clegg 2002). It was the economists who

> have done most to uncouple and abandon sociological questions, especially those centered on power.
>
> (Clegg 2002:432)

The transaction cost approach was the basis of the influence of economics and what was so influential for organisational scholarship was

> its sociological disinterest, shown by its derivation of theory from market auspices and its resolute blindness to empirical matters of power and politics in organizational structuring.
>
> (Clegg 2002:432)

Palmer pointed to the growing influence of research methods with measurable variables and increased mathematical formalism, derived *inter alia* from economics (Palmer 2006). Marsden characterised the ontology of economics as 'empiricist', which limited objects of knowledge to the observable, and which conceived

> the social as a series of empirical regularities among a mass of atomistic individuals, events and things. Blind to their non-empirical connections, economics abstracts individuals from their social context to form '*homo economicus*'.
>
> (Marsden 2005:142)

Mainstream accounting research has been heavily influenced by economics-based empirical research, particularly from the US (Green 2009). This has again led to the homogenisation of paradigm and research methods, at the cost of the inclusion of other paradigms, disciplines, topics and research methods, resulting in a loss of creativity and innovation to the discipline, to the academy and to society in general (Lukka 2010; Merchant 2010; Bromwich and Scapens 2016). Although positivism was completely *passé* in the philosophy of science, it was still largely dominant in accounting research where 'law-like regularities... testable with empirical data sets' were still sought. This had the effect of limiting more varied research and intellectual activity in accounting, particularly in the US (Lukka 2010:112).

The other influence economics is thought to have had on organisation studies is in its prescriptiveness. One of the core economics assumptions – that people will behave in self-interested ways – also serves as a norm about how people should behave (Ferraro et al. 2005). An interesting anomaly in relation to representations of Burns and Stalker is that this core concept of self-interest, which Burns and Stalker saw as a potential obstruction to managers trying to introduce organic structures, is not considered in mainstream representations and applications of their ideas (Green 2012). The opposite is implied – a passive, conformist workforce which would not challenge management strategies.

Tropes

Some have claimed that ideas in the social sciences engage the attention of their academic or practitioner audiences more because they are interesting than because they are true (Ferraro et al. 2005). Particular uses of language such as metaphors and other tropes can engage attention and shape how reality is constructed for readers (and scholars). Metaphors can be reified and treated as the real thing, offering normative and ideological markers (Berger and Luckmann 1966). Theories can be turned to slogans or into 'canonical masterpieces' by talented expositions (DiMaggio 1995:396). 'Compelling visual imagery' may be abstracted from empirical reality, and may move beyond any empirical data. This may result in fictional constructs which nevertheless demand of its audience to 'join an author in a kind of make-believe' that has no basis in experience (Astley 1985:502).

What might be seen as more to do with spin than substance, are phrases that concentrate minds, and become the crucial element of a text. Atkinson (1984:47–48) examined various rhetorical devices used by politicians, which he described as 'designed to catch applause' (Green 2012). One was what he called 'claptrap', by which he meant techniques which struck a chord with the public. One of the most effective forms of claptrap was contrastive pairs. Atkinson wrote specifically about political debate, but his ideas are equally applicable to scholarly writing, which of course can also be considered to be political. Atkinson claimed that a contrast between two items was 'an extraordinarily adaptable and widely used technique for packaging and delivering applaudable messages' (Atkinson 1984:73). Although the terms 'mechanistic' and 'organic' were by no means tricks and not intended for live audiences, of all the ideas put forward by Burns and Stalker those two terms were the ones that stuck. The mechanistic/organic distinction is the element that has been seized on through the decades and remained representative as the kernel of their book.

One of the major metaphors in organisation theory is that of the organism – a system of connected and interdependent parts attempting to survive in a wider environment. Morgan saw the term 'organism' as having a 'strong and clear' link with much organisation theory. He gave Burns and Stalker's theory as one example of the development of this metaphor, which emphasised the idea that the organisation was in an open environment, in a constant situation of flux in its interactions with the wider world (Morgan 1980:614).

Burns and Stalker's ideas have been party to another type of fictionalisation – their use of mechanistic and organic systems as ideal types. Astley regarded such descriptions as 'intentional fictionalizations of the reality under examination', intended to accentuate the attributes so constructed (Astley 1985:502). He quoted Weber on the partiality and imaginary character of ideal types:

> An ideal type is formed by the one-sided accumulation of one or more points of view and by the synthesis of a great many diffuse, discrete ... concrete individual phenomena ... into a unified analytical construct ... [which] cannot be found anywhere in reality.
>
> (Weber 1963:398 cited in Astley 1985:502–503)

It would be interesting to know whether such fictionalisation was intended by Burns and Stalker, or whether it was used as an analytical tool to highlight different organisation structures. The more interesting question perhaps is whether mainstream scholars attracted by the mechanistic/organic ideal types, were themselves engaging in fictionalisation, intentional or otherwise.

Preexisting expectations, assumptions and representations without paying careful attention to the text can also lead to a kind of fictionalisation. DiMaggio and Powell's (1983) disseminated idea that organisations have a tendency to resemble each other was claimed by DiMaggio to be false. The central idea in their own work, that it was the role of interorganisational networks in institutional theory that drove organisations to become more like one another, was a concept that was wiped out. Within a few years their paper had become 'a kind of ritual citation'. The view propounded was 'that, well, organizations are kind of wacky, and (despite the presence of "collective rationality" in the paper's subtitle) people are never rational' – not what had been written in the original paper (DiMaggio 1995:395). This too is reminiscent of representations of Burns and Stalker's book.

Technological and curricular developments

Technical and curricular developments from the 1950s strengthened objectivist, scientifically based scholarship and curricula designed to support managerial concerns. Advances in the mainframe computer led to the language of cybernetics being adopted in management discourse. Competition with the USSR because of its economic gains, political influence in developing countries and the launching of the Sputnik in 1957 led to more attention and resources being put into science, engineering and their methods (Maher 2001). Willmott explains this as a

> scholarly tradition fashioned in North America during the Cold War at a time when academic rigor was conflated with respectability gained from prostration before a Method ascribed to the natural sciences, irrespective of the ontology of the phenomena under discussion.
>
> (Willmott 2011:436)

The Ford Foundation criticised business schools for their lack of coherence and rigour in the 1950s, recommended MBA degrees as a prerequisite for managers, and more importantly, that curricula in business schools be 'stiffened' with statistics and quantitative methods. From these developments arose new, more rational disciplines such as operations research and management science. Operations research used to solve military logistical problems spread to industry, and the application of quantitative techniques to management planning and control (Barley and Kunda 1992:376, Maher 2001).

In the atmosphere of the Cold War and McCarthyism, some major institutions were instrumental in making management scholarship more empirical, quantitative and scientific. The Ford Foundation further entrenched functionalist and positivist approaches in organisation studies. One way of doing this was for the foundation to stipulate that the term 'behavioural science' should be an umbrella definition for many of the social sciences, moving the approaches to these disciplines in the direction of the natural sciences. The Ford Foundation's research funding swung to the right, to projects upholding pro-business free market ideologies (Tadajewski 2009).

Conclusion

This chapter focussed on possible explanations for the fact that in much mainstream scholarship a certain view has been taken of *The Management of Innovation*. The answer as to why representations of Burns and Stalker's ideas largely adopted a narrower, more functionalist, objectivist or managerialist approach has been shown to be complex. The idea that explanations can be found wholly in the ideologies and practices of journal editors is inadequate. It might constitute a partial explanation for the continuing dominance of objectivist approaches, but what was published in the *ASQ* and other journals has been shown to contain eclectic approaches and methodologies. Related suggestions have been journal rankings, pressures in the academy, the role of business schools, the influence of economics, and wider social and political pressures, all of which served to legitimate an objectivist and managerialist ideology. They have underwritten managerial authority as all-powerful in delivering its strategies; accorded formal structures a reality which alone could bring those strategies to fruition; and ignored informal behaviours – behaviours which might be inconsistent with these policies, and have the power to render them dysfunctional.

These factors can be related back to the problems about representation raised in Chapter 3. One of the factors lay with the researchers themselves. Here ambition, the desire for status and rewards and pressures on scholars, bear out Bourdieu's view of the field being the site of constant struggles by scholars for cultural, social, political and symbolic capital (Bourdieu 1998). The rewards in the academy, awarded largely to scholars following conventional, objectivist approaches may have been a strong influence on mainstream representations of contingency theories, including of Burns and Stalker's book. If these conclusions are generalisable to the representation and research applications of other texts in the organisation, management and management accounting areas, the epistemological implications are far reaching, as may be questions about their practical value for managers and other professionals.

Leaving external governmental and other institutional pressures aside, questions still remain as to why the academy, including its journal editors, scholars, departmental heads and other players chose to continue to legitimate the functionalist paradigm specifically, with its exclusively objectivist focus and empirical, quantitative-based methodologies. Why were alternative approaches and methodologies more commonly not considered? These could have produced complementary knowledge which together with more orthodox approaches might have resulted in richer and more sustainable scholarship and more practically useful knowledge. Further answers are suggested in the next chapter, where more fundamental bases for objectivist, quantitative-based scholarship are investigated and deeper theoretical explanations offered for the direction of mainstream scholarship in the last half-century.

Notes

1 This chapter is based on published papers by Green (2009, 2012) (Emerald) and a book chapter (2017) (Routledge). The author would like to thank Emerald and Routledge for copyright permission.
2 This does not mean that the knowledge produced had results that did promote efficiency and effectiveness, particularly as crucial influences in contributing to successes and failures in organisations were generally omitted from such knowledge.
3 The difference made by business schools may be one explanation for differences among scholars about trends, in the UK as well as the US.
4 Similar discrepancies have appeared in relation to *Management Accounting Research*. Lukka wrote a paper in that journal where he expressed a concern for 'the increasing narrowness of accounting research in terms of its philosophical assumptions, methodological approaches, and theoretical underpinnings' (Lukka 2010:110). However a few years later it was judged by some of its contributors to be open, multi-disciplinary and multi-paradigmatic (e.g. Hopper and Bui 2016).
5 See Chapter 7.
6 Not all management accounting scholars saw contingency theory as being objectivist. See e.g. Hall's comments in previous chapter.

References

Adler, N.J. and Harzing, A-W. (2009). When Knowledge Wins: Transcending the Sense and Nonsense of Academic Rankings. *Academy of Management Learning and Education*, 8 (1), pp. 72–95.

Alvesson, M. (2013). Do We Have Something to Say? From Re-Search to Roi-Search and Back Again. *Organization*, 20 (1), pp. 79–90.

Alvesson, M., Bridgman, T., and Willmott, H. (2009). Introduction. In: M. Alvesson, T. Bridgman and H. Willmott, eds., *The Oxford Handbook of Critical Management Studies*. Oxford: Oxford University Press, pp. 1–28.

Astley, W.G. (1985). Administrative Science as Socially Constructed Truth. *Administrative Science Quarterly*, 30 (4), pp. 497–513.

Atkinson, M. (1984). *Our Masters' Voices: The Language and Body Language of Politics*. London: Methuen.

The Author(s). (2012). Invitation to Contributors. *Administrative Science Quarterly*, 57 (4), pp. 718–721.

Barley, S.R. and Kunda, G. (1992). Design and Devolution: Surges of Rational and Normative Ideologies of Control in Managerial Discourse. *Administrative Science Quarterly*, 37 (3), pp. 363–399.

Barley, S.R., Meyer, G.W., and Gash, D.C. (1988). Cultures of Culture: Academics, Practitioners and the Pragmatics of Normative Control. *Administrative Science Quarterly*, 33 (1), pp. 24–60.

Bartunek, J.M. (2002). The Proper Place of Organizational Scholarship: A Comment on Hinings and Greenwood. *Administrative Science Quarterly*, 47 (3), pp. 422–427.

Baum, J.A.C. (2011). Free-Riding on Power Laws: Questioning the Validity of the Impact Factor as a Measure of Research Quality in Organization Studies. *Organization*, 18 (4), pp. 449–466.

Berger, P.L. and Luckmann, T. (1966). *The Social Construction of Reality: A Treatise in the Sociology of Knowledge*. Harmondsworth: Penguin Books Ltd.

Bhagat, R.S. (1979). Book Review of Developing an Interdisciplinary Science of Organizations by K.H. Roberts, C.L. Hulin and D.M. Rousseau. *Administrative Science Quarterly*, 24 (2), pp. 333–337.

Boulding, K.E. (1958). Evidences for an Administrative Science: A Review of the Administrative Science Quarterly, Volumes 1 and 2. *Administrative Science Quarterly*, 3 (1), pp. 1–22.

Bourdieu, P. (1990). *The Logic of Practice*. Trans. R. Nice. Stanford, CA: Stanford University Press.

Bourdieu, P. (1998). *Practical Reason: On the Theory of Action*. Cambridge: Polity Press.

Bromwich, M. and Scapens, R. (2016). Management Accounting Research: 25 Years On. *Management Accounting Resesarch*, 31, pp. 1–9.

Burns, T. (1994). Preface to the Third Edition. In: T. Burns and G.M. Stalker, eds., *The Management of Innovation*. 3rd ed. Oxford: Oxford University Press, pp. vii–xx.

Burrell, G. (2009). Handbooks, Swarms and Living Dangerously. In: M. Alvesson, T. Bridgman and H. Willmott, eds., *The Oxford Handbook of Critical Management Studies*. Oxford: Oxford University Press, pp. 551–562.

Burrell, G. and Morgan, G. (1979). *Sociological Paradigms and Organisational Analysis: Elements of the Sociology of Corporate Life*. Aldershot: Ashgate.

Butler, N. and Spoelstra, S. (2012). Your Excellency. *Organization*, 19 (6), pp. 891–903.

Child, J. (1973). Predicting and Understanding Organization Structure. *Administrative Science Quarterly*, 18 (2), pp. 168–185.

Clark, D.L. (1985). Book Review of Organizational Environments: Ritual and Rationality by J.W. Meyer and W.R. Scott. *Administrative Science Quarterly*, 30 (2), pp. 295–296.

Clegg, S. (2002). "Lives in the Balance": A Comment on Hinings and Greenwood's "Disconnects and Consequences in Organization Theory?" *Administrative Science Quarterly*, 47 (3), pp. 428–441.

Clegg, S.R. and Dunkerley, D. (1980). *Organization, Class and Control*. London: Routledge and Kegan Paul.

Cummings, L.L., Frost, P.J., and Vakil, T.F. (1985). The Manuscript Review Process: A View from inside on Coaches, Critics, and Special Cases. In: L.L. Cummings and

P.J. Frost eds., *Publishing in the Organizational Sciences*. Homewood, IL: Richard D. Irwin Inc, pp. 469–508.

Daft, R.L. (1980). The Evolution of Organization Analysis in *ASQ* 1959–1979. *Administrative Science Quarterly*, 25 (4), pp. 623–636.

DiMaggio, P. and Powell, W.W. (1983). The Iron Cage Revisited: Institutional Isomorphism and Collective Rationality in Organizational Fields. *American Sociological Review*, 48 (2), pp. 147–160.

DiMaggio, P.J. (1995). Comments on "What Theory Is Not". *Administrative Science Quarterly*, 40 (3), pp. 391–397.

Donnellon, A. (1986). Book Review of Publishing in the Organizational Sciences by L. L. Cummings and P.J. Frost, Eds. *Administrative Science Quarterly*, 31 (2), pp. 313–315.

Drazin, R. and Van de Ven, A.H. (1985). Alternative Forms of Fit in Contingency Theory. *Administrative Science Quarterly*, 30 (4), pp. 514–539.

Dunbar, R.L.M. (1983). Toward an Applied Administrative Science. *Administrative Science Quarterly*, 28 (1), pp. 129–144.

Dunne, S., Harney, S., and Parker, M. (2008). Speaking Out: The Responsibilities of Management Intellectuals: A Survey. *Organization*, 15 (2), pp. 271–282.

Ferraro, F., Pfeffer, J., and Sutton, R.I. (2005). Economics Language and Assumptions: How Theories Can Become Self-Fulfilling. *Academy of Management Review*, 30 (1), pp. 8–24.

Fournier, V. and Grey, C. (2000). At the Critical Moment: Conditions and Prospects for Critical Management Studies. *Human Relations*, 53 (1), pp. 7–32.

Ghoshal, S. (2005). Bad Management Theories Are Destroying Good Management Practices. *Academy of Management Learning and Education*, 4 (1), pp. 75–91.

Green, M. (2009). The Embedding of Knowledge in the Academy: "Tolerance", Irresponsibility or Other Imperatives? *Social Responsibility Journal*, 5 (2), pp. 165–177.

Green, M. (2012). Objectivism in Organization/Management Knowledge: An Example of Bourdieu's "Mutilation?" *Social Responsibility Journal*, 8 (4), pp. 495–510.

Green, M. (2017). Behaviour in Academe: An Investigation into the Sustainability of Mainstream Scholarship in Management Studies. In: G. Aras and C. Ingley, eds., *Corporate Behavior and Sustainability: Doing Well by Being Good*. Finance, Governance and Sustainability: Challenges to Theory and Practice Series. London: Routledge.

Grey, C. (2010). Organizing Studies: Publications, Politics and Polemic. *Organization Studies*, 31 (6), pp. 677–694.

Harzing, A.W. (ed.) (2013). *Journal Quality List* 48th ed. Melbourne, Australia: www.harzing.com.

Hassard, J. and Pym, D. (eds.) (1990). *The Theory and Philosophy of Organizations: Critical Issues and New Perspectives*. London: Routledge.

Hellriegel, D. and Slocum, J.W. (1974). *Management: A Contingency Approach*. Reading, MA: Addison Wesley.

Hickson, D.J. (1996). The *ASQ* Years Then and Now through the Eyes of a Euro-Brit. *Administrative Science Quarterly*, 41 (2), pp. 217–228.

Hinings, C.R. and Greenwood, R. (2002). Disconnects and Consequences in Organization Theory. *Administrative Science Quarterly*, 47 (3), pp. 411–421.

Hogler, R. and Gross, M.A. (2009). Journal Rankings and Academic Research: Two Discourses about the Quality of Faculty Work. *Management Communication Quarterly*, 23 (1), pp. 107–126.

Hopper, T. and Bui, B. (2016). Has Management Accounting Research Been Critical? *Management Accounting Research*, 31, pp. 10–30.

Hopper, T., Otley, D., and Scapens, B. (2001). British Management Accounting Research: Whence and Whither: Opinions and Recollections. *British Accounting Review*, 33 (3), pp. 263–291.

Hopwood, A.G. (2009). On Striving to Give a Critical Edge to Critical Management Studies. In: M. Alvesson, T. Bridgman and H. Willmott, eds., *The Oxford Handbook of Critical Management Studies*. Oxford: Oxford University Press, pp. 515–524.

Hunt, J.G. (1986). Book Review of Publishing in the Organizational Sciences by L.L. Cummings and P.J. Frost, Eds. *Administrative Science Quarterly*, 31 (2), pp. 310–312.

Hussain, S. (2015). Journal List Fetishism and the 'Sign of 4' in the ABS Guide: A Question of Trust? *Organization*, 22 (1), pp. 119–138.

Kadushin, C. (1976). Book Review of the Divided Academy: Professors and Politics by E.C. Ladd Jr. And S.M. Lipset. *Administrative Science Quarterly*, 21 (3), pp. 525–530.

Kuhn, T.S. (1970). *The Structure of Scientific Revolutions*. 2nd ed. Chicago, IL: Chicago University Press.

Lachmann, M, Trapp, I., and Trapp, R. (2017). Diversity and Validity in Positivist Management Accounting Research – A Longitudinal Perspective over Four Decades. *Management Accounting Research*, 34, pp. 42–58.

Ladd, E.C. and Lipset, S.M. (1975). *The Divided Academy: Professors and Politics*. New York: McGraw-Hill.

Legge, K. (2001). Silver Bullet or Spent Round? Assessing the Meaning of the 'High Commitment Management'/Performance Relationship. In: J. Storey, ed., *Human Resource Management: A Critical Text*. London: Thomson Learning.

Litchfield, E.H. (1956). Notes on a General Theory of Administration. *Administrative Science Quarterly*, 1 (1), pp. 3–29.

Lukka, K. (2010). The Roles and Effects of Paradigms in Accounting Research. *Management Accounting Research*, 21 (2), pp. 110–115.

Macdonald, S. and Kam, J. (2011). The Skewed Few: People and Papers of Quality in Management Studies. *Organization*, 18 (4), pp. 467–475.

MacIntyre, A. (2007). *After Virtue*. 3rd ed. London: Duckworth.

Maher, M.W. (2001). The Evolution of Management Accounting Research in the United States. *British Accounting Review*, 33 (3), pp. 293–305.

Manns, C.L. and March, J.G. (1978). Financial Adversity, Internal Competition and Curriculum Change in a University. *Administrative Science Quarterly*, 23 (4), pp. 541–552.

March, J.G. (1996). Continuity and Change in Theories of Organizational Action. *Administrative Science Quarterly*, 41 (2), pp. 278–287.

Marsden, R. (2005). The Politics of Organizational Analysis. In: C. Grey and H. Willmott, eds., *Critical Management Studies: A Reader*. Oxford: Oxford University Press.

Merchant, K.A. (2010). Paradigms in Accounting Research: A View from North America. *Management Accounting Research*, 21 (2), pp. 116–120.

Meriläinen, S., Tienari, J., Thomas, R. and Davies, A. (2008). Hegemonic Academic Practices: Experiences of Publishing from the Periphery. *Organization*, 15 (4), pp. 584–597.

Mitchell, S.M. (1981). Book Review of Contested Terrain: The Transformation of the Workplace in the Twentieth Century by R. Edwards. *Administrative Science Quarterly*, 26 (2), pp. 293–296.

Moizer, P. (2009). Publishing in Accounting Journals: A Fair Game? *Accounting, Organization and Society*, 34 (2), pp. 285–304.

Morgan, G. (1980). Paradigms, Metaphors, and Puzzle Solving in Organization Theory. *Administrative Science Quarterly*, 25 (4), pp. 605–622.

Palmer, D. (2006). Taking Stock of the Criteria We Use to Evaluate One Another's Work: *ASQ* 50 Years Out. *Administrative Science Quarterly*, 51 (4), pp. 535–559.

Parker, M. and Thomas, R. (2011). What Is a Critical Journal? *Organization*, 18 (4), pp. 419–427.

Parsons, T. (1956). Suggestions for a Sociological Approach to the Theory of Organizations-1. *Administrative Science Quarterly*, 1 (1), pp. 63–85.

Pfeffer, J. (1977). Book Review of the Management of Organization Design: Strategies and Implementation Volume 1 by R.H. Kilman, L.R. Pondy and D.P. Slevin, Eds. *Administrative Science Quarterly*, 22 (4), pp. 677–682.

Pfeffer, J. and Moore, W.L. (1980). Average Tenure of Academic Department Heads: The Effects of Paradigm, Size and Departmental Demography. *Administrative Science Quarterly*, 25 (3), pp. 387–406.

Porter, L.W. (1996). Forty Years of Organization Studies: Reflections from a Micro Perspective. *Administrative Science Quarterly*, 41 (2), pp. 262–269.

Prasad, A. (2013). Playing the Game and Trying Not to Lose Oneself: A Doctoral Student's Perspective on the Institutional Pressures for Research Output. *Organization*, 20 (6), pp. 936–948.

Putnam, L.L. (2009). Symbolic Capital and Academic Fields: An Alternative Discourse on Journal Rankings. *Management Communication Quarterly*, 23 (1), pp. 127–134.

Salancik, G.R. (1975). Book Review of Management: A Contingency Approach by D. Hellriegel and J.W. Slocum. *Administrative Science Quarterly*, 20 (2), pp. 311–313.

Salancik, G.R. (1987). Power and politics in academic departments. In: M.P. Zanna and J.M. Darley, eds., *The complete academic: A practical guide for the beginning social scientist.* New York, NY: McGraw-Hill, pp. 61–84.

Scherer, A.G. (2009). Critical Theory and Its Contribution to Critical Management Studies. In: M. Alvesson, T. Bridgman and H. Willmott, eds., *The Oxford Handbook of Critical Management Studies.* Oxford: Oxford University Press, pp. 29–51.

Scott, W.R. (1996). The Mandate Is Still Being Honored: In Defense of Weber's Disciples. *Administrative Science Quarterly*, 41 (1), pp. 163–171.

Selznick, P. (1948). *T.V.A. And the Grass Roots: A Study of Politics and Organization.* Berkeley, CA and Los Angeles, CA: University of California Press.

Selznick, P. (1957). *Leadership in Administration: A Sociological Interpretation.* Berkeley, CA and Evanston, IL: Row, Peterson.

Selznick, P. (1992). *The Moral Commonwealth: Social Theory and the Promise of Community.* Berkeley, CA: University of California Press.

Selznick, P. (1996). Institutionalism "Old" and "New". *Administrative Science Quarterly*, 41 (2), pp. 270–277.

Starbuck, W.H. (2016). 60th Anniversary Essay: How Journals Could Improve Research Practices in Social Science. *Administrative Science Quarterly*, 61 (2), pp. 165–183.

Stern, R.N. and Barley, S.R. (1996). Organizations and Social Systems: Organization Theory's Neglected Mandate. *Administrative Science Quarterly*, 41 (1), pp. 146–162.

Sutton, R.I. and Staw, B.M. (1995). What Theory Is Not. *Administrative Science Quarterly*, 40 (3), pp. 371–384.

Tadajewski, M. (2009). The Politics of the Behavioural Revolution in Organization Studies. *Organization*, 16 (5), pp. 733–754.

Thomas, R. and Parker, M. (2012). Organization. *Organization@20*, 20 (1), pp. 3–5.

Van Meter, E.J. (1985). Book Review of Modern Approaches to Understanding and Managing Organizations by L.G. Bolman and T.E. Deal. *Administrative Science Quarterly*, 30 (1), pp. 135–138.

Vignolle, J-P. (1976). Working Group on Theoretical Issues: Report on February Meeting in Paris. *Administrative Science Quarterly*, 21 (3), pp. 511–513.

Weber, M. (1963). Objectivity in Social Science and Science Policy. In: M. Nathanson, ed., *Philosophy of the Social Sciences*. New York: Random House, pp. 355–418.

Weick, K.E. (1979). Cognitive Processes in Organizations. *Research in Organizational Behavior*, 1 (1), pp. 41–74.

Weick, K.E. (1996). Drop Your Tools: An Allegory for Organizational Studies. *Administrative Science Quarterly*, 41, pp. 301–313.

Whisler, T.L. (1974). The Business Organization of the Future. In: H. Leavitt, L. Pinfield and E. Webb, eds., *Organizations of the Future: Interaction with the External Environment*. New York: Praeger Publishers, pp. 176–188.

Willmott, H. (1981). The Structuring of Organizational Structure: A Note. *Administrative Science Quarterly*, 26, pp. 470–474.

Willmott, H. (2011). Journal List Fetishism and the Perversion of Scholarship: Reactivity and the ABS List. *Organization*, 18 (4), pp. 429–442.

Zald, M.N. (1993). Organization Studies as a Scientific and Humanistic Enterprise: Toward a Reconceptualization of the Foundations of the Field. *Organization Science*, 4 (4), pp. 513–528.

Zald, M.N. (1996). More Fragmentation? Unfinished Business in Linking the Social Sciences and the Humanities. *Administrative Science Quarterly*, 41 (2), pp. 251–261.

7 Science versus scientificity

Introduction[1]

When seeking explanations for the type of knowledge produced in mainstream representations, particularly in journal articles, of Burns and Stalker's book, one of the unexpected findings was the difference in interpretation by researchers of the same scholarship published in the *Administrative Science Quarterly* (*ASQ*). Some felt that papers accepted for publication in that journal were confined to those that were objectivist, scientific or positivist; others that the scholarship was more pluralist. There were similar differences of opinion about the direction that scholarship was taking. And there were naturally differences about which type of scholarship was desirable and legitimate.

Certain issues underpinning these differences and the debates around them became evident. It had been suggested that there were ambiguities in what the original editors wanted (Palmer 2006). The role and status of structural contingency theory, used by many as a benchmark for all contingency theories and for organisation/management studies in general, had been regarded by some as major, and by others as increasingly marginal, aside from their differences in opinion as to whether contingency theory was from the outset objectivist or more sociological in approach.

This difference of opinion in respect of what has constituted valid scholarship, and the lack of clarity about the scholarship actually produced, may have been the result of a confusion in the definitions of key concepts. Terms that may have been instrumental in the evolution of different interpretations of what has been judged to be legitimate knowledge include 'scientific' and 'positivist'. These concepts have been interpreted by mainstream scholars and others who have had the power to influence the direction of scholarship as being measurable, quantitative and neutral, uninfluenced by human consciousness and agency, and with subjectivist, interpretive approaches invalidated and absented.

Definitions of what counts as science and positivism are explored and alternative views of science, scientific method and positivism outlined. The terms scientific and positivist are then linked to constructs of commensurability and incommensurability between approaches in the social sciences and more specifically in the organisation/management field. One question that then arises is the extent to which there has been an unnecessary curtailing of the content and approaches of scholarship in organisation/management over the last fifty and more years through the upholding of incommensurability between different paradigms and the types of knowledge produced in each.

Objectivist knowledge

Amongst the fiercest proponents of objectivist approaches have been positivist philosophers (Reiter and Williams 2002). They have advocated knowledge that is value free, and descriptions of the world with no reference to normative value judgements. An extreme version of positivism, which became common currency in much social science research, is logical positivism. This was the 'Vienna Circle', a school of thought developed in the 1920s and 1930s by a group of philosophers, mathematicians and scientists. True knowledge for them was properly scientific, attained through a radical empiricism which recognised only observable elements acquired through sense data, and a formal, mathematically formulated logic. The mainstay of this was a methodology which involved sampling, scaling and statistical analysis. Other information was cognitively insignificant and nonsensical. Science was value free and there was no place for theory or the logic of deduction (Turner 2001).

Neurath, an eminent philosopher of science and one of the leading members of the Vienna Circle, was of the view that sociology, in order to be accepted as a science, needed to engage in such methods of inquiry to establish regularities between observables and eventually to connect all logically compatible laws into a unified science. Social forces had no place in this approach, nor did metaphysics or mental thought processes. Sociological methods based on these ideas were continued long into the twentieth and into the twenty-first centuries despite the fact that from the middle of the twentieth century logical positivism had begun to come under sustained attack from the Frankfurt school, and because of internal contradictions, from its own supporters (Halfpenny 2001).

Subjectivist knowledge

Interpretive approaches (an umbrella concept for various subjectivist approaches such as phenomenology, hermeneutics, symbolic interactionism and ethnomethodology) were developed as rebuttals to logical positivism (Hatch and Yanow 2003). The idea that the social world could be understood and studied in the same way as the natural and physical worlds was refuted. As mentioned in the chapter on paradigms, central to studies about people was the idea that knowledge could only be acquired through an understanding of the human subjects involved – an understanding of the shared meanings and interpretive frameworks through which people made sense of, and acted upon, their situations (Halfpenny 2001). Bourdieu describes these approaches as 'constructivist', whose tenets are that objects are identified only through an act of construction on the part of people, unlike an empiricist theory which holds that knowledge is produced through studying external realities (Bourdieu 1993:54).

This difference in what counts as legitimate knowledge affects what are considered to be valid research methods. Instead of the study of objective social processes outside the consciousness and opinions of human subjects, interpretive methodologies are about documenting actors' own understandings of their situations and the meanings they give to them. They are about interpreting sense perceptions rather than an 'uninterpreted grasping of them' (Hatch and Yanow 2003:67).

Reality may be construed differently by different people in a world of potentially varied interpretations of multiple realities. Because of their own situatedness (Sarbin and Kitsuse 1994), researchers can also influence the research process and the knowledge produced. Rather than being a neutral and impartial observer, the researcher is subject to the same 'meaning-making' as are her respondents. This necessitates the additional requirement of reflexivity by the researcher as to how her research results have been arrived at (Hatch and Yanow 2003:67).

The notion of multiple meanings is strengthened by Wittgenstein's idea that language serves multiple functions and creates several realities rather than reflecting an external, objective world. This has encouraged research methods such as participant observation and in-depth interviews. These are ideographic, seeking in-depth knowledge about the meanings continually being constructed by people about their *milieux* and their activities (Halfpenny 2001). Hatch and Yanow conclude that 'all knowledge is interpretive, and interpretation (of acts, language and objects) is the only method appropriate to the human, social world' (Hatch and Yanow 2003:71).

Scientific knowledge

What science is and what counts as scientific method has involved a complex and longstanding debate among scholars in both the natural and the social sciences. Definitions of what is scientific have varied from quantitative, empirical scholarship to approaches encompassing relationships in the social world. With positivism too, the definitions given above and held by many scholars are narrow compared with positivism's early founder-theorists. It is therefore important to unpack these definitions which have played such a large part in framing, delimiting and legitimating scholarship in the organisation/ management areas.

Kuhn (1970), Hanson (1972), Bourdieu (1990a) and Feyerabend (1993) have broader interpretations about what constitutes science and its practices. Kuhn, in his book on scientific revolutions, defined science as 'any field in which progress is marked'. Science was to do with solving problems about the 'behaviour of nature' (Kuhn 1970:162, 168). Both Kuhn and Feyerabend stated that science was *not* about steadily increasing the sum total of knowledge[2] through 'experiment and observation kept in order by lasting rational standards' or by 'strict and unchangeable rules' (Feyerabend 1993:xi, 11). Quite the opposite. Kuhn described the scientific revolutions he was writing about as 'non-cumulative developmental episodes' (Kuhn 1970:92). For Kuhn the transition to a new paradigm involved new questions, new solutions and new ways of handling data – a set of different relationships in a new framework – a process a historian had described as 'picking up the other end of the stick' (Kuhn 1970:85). Science needed people who were 'adaptable and inventive, not rigid imitators of "established" behavioural patterns' (Feyerabend 1993:159).

Kuhn disputed positivist views that the natural sciences were concerned with generalisations or universal laws. According to him scientific procedures were not uniform. A new paradigm produced new theoretical generalisations, new methods and applications. If existing scientific laws were followed using the same concepts and theories, this would impose a limitation on scientific progress – problems would be circumscribed in keeping with existing assumptions, as would acceptable solutions, thereby inhibiting scientific development (Kuhn 1970). Feyerabend echoed this (Green 2009). Procedures successful at one time could play 'havoc' at another (Feyerabend 1993:1).

One of the most common assumptions about science is that methods used in the natural sciences necessitate quantitative variables and statistical analysis. Yet no mention appears to have been made in Kuhn's work about the need for such methods. Kuhn did not see qualitative and quantitative scholarship as incommensurable. Quite the reverse. He gave Joule's experiments as an example of how the two were interdependent. Quantitative laws often emerged through paradigm articulation, which was qualitative. Kuhn asserted that

> so general and so close is the relation between qualitative paradigm and quantitative law that, since Galileo, such laws have often been correctly guessed with the aid of a paradigm years before apparatus could be designed for their experimental determination.
>
> (Kuhn 1970:29)

For Feyerabend quantification, even of scientific subjects, was not always successful. He gave an example of difficulties with this technique

> in one of the apparently most quantitative of all sciences, celestial mechanics ... [which] was replaced by qualitative (topological) considerations.
>
> (Feyerabend 1993:2)

Feyerabend claimed that all methodologies were limited and that pluralistic methods were needed. He suggested comparing theories with other theories and not with 'experience', 'data' and facts. Alternatives should be improved rather than discarded (Feyerabend 1993:33). This is relevant to questions of incommensurability discussed later.

The idea that science is value free, describing the world with no reference to normative value judgements and uninfluenced by human consciousness has also been challenged. Kuhn made great play of the importance of the scientific community and its consensus with respect to the activities of scientists within it. The group was important in deciding how science should be practised: the paradigm to be worked from, what counted as relevant and valid scientific problems to be investigated, which solutions were acceptable and what constituted scientific achievement (Kuhn 1970).

Neutrality by scientific researchers has been questioned too. According to Hanson, a philosopher of science, an observer, because of her own background knowledge and assumptions, could influence what was observed and therefore influence the results of an experiment. He gave as an example the astronomers Tycho Brahe and Kepler, who, when watching the dawn, would interpret it in different ways: the sun moving above the horizon or the earth rotating away to reveal the sun. These accounts of the dawn varied not because of differences in the data but because of '*ex post facto* interpretations of what is seen' (Hanson 1972:8).

Chia (1996) has supported this with his observation that the natural sciences had long abandoned the idea of neutral observation with the introduction of Einstein's theory of relativity, Heisenberg's principle of indeterminacy and Bohr's quantum postulate. This again raises the question as to whether it can be claimed that the kind of objectivist research referred to in relation to applications of Burns and Stalker's ideas is value free and neutral. This is addressed in the next chapter in connection with two research papers from *AOS*.

Positivism

Positivism was originally conceived as being more broadly based than its later interpretations and applications. Comte had advocated a positivist science based on 'empirical observations ... to generate and test abstract laws of human organization'. However, for Comte this did not mean 'raw empiricism' alone, with 'hard' methods and quantitative methodologies. Comte believed that facts were underpinned by theories, which were needed alongside empirical enquiry. Positivism could not be equated with empiricism. Positivism was, according to Comte, about discovering fundamental properties of human organisation and the abstract laws governing those properties (Turner 2001:31, 33).

Comte recognised observation, which required statistical and dynamic analyses of social forces, and experimentation regarding the interruptions to social organisms by social pathologies. This, significantly, required moral judgment as to what was and what was not normal. Comparison was one of the methodologies Comte advocated – a comparison between the structure and dynamics of different societies, social forms and past and present forms of social organisation. This was to establish the fundamental properties of human society. Historical analysis was required to examine structural arrangements across history in order to determine the laws of human organisation (Turner 2001).

This is different from later, narrower interpretations of positivism, which have been described as 'a gross distortion of what Comte intended' (Turner 2001:33). Separate strands in Comte's ideas had been selectively used. The narrow empiricism of the Vienna Circle had been rejected by Comte (Halfpenny (2001). But this narrower interpretation has had far-reaching implications for how research has been carried out in the social sciences and the kind of knowledge produced.

The social sciences

In 1937, Horkheimer, in what has been described as a 'seminal statement', rejected the idea that objective, value-free knowledge about social reality could be produced in the social sciences. All social processes took place within specific historical and cultural conditions as were the methods employed to analyse them (Scherer 2009:31). Such critiques are still made about the legitimacy of equating social science with the natural sciences, and the use of positivist methodologies which have served to decontextualise research (Habermas 1972). Claims of neutrality, which have sought to erase the influence on the production of knowledge of dominant societal structures, are also contested (Green 2005a, 2005b), as is the absenting of the latent power and significance of human agency (Green 2009, 2012).

In 1952, Mannheim raised questions about the categories or systematic conceptions used by different groups and how concepts were addressed differently according to different standpoints. Both he and Habermas (1972) approached this question through an attack on positivist approaches. For Mannheim there were advantages in positivism. It was relevant to contemporary society in that it shifted scholarship to the economic and social sphere away from speculative metaphysics. By the same token it focussed on empirical reality, another step in the right direction (Mannheim 1952).

But positivism was not only against speculative metaphysics. It was against metaphysics and theory of any kind, favouring the methodology of specialised research as an exclusive standard by which to judge and legitimate scholarship to the exclusion of ontology (Mannheim 1952). This was a particular view of empiricism, which contained the contradiction that the stating of certain methodologies as the only acceptable ones and that reality was about facts was a metaphysic in itself. It was phenomenologically false because what was perceived as meaningful involved interpretation and understanding. Facts were graspable only within a framework of meanings in a particular context. In fact knowledge should be questioned in order to find out precisely how far the empirical, scientific treatment of a problem is influenced by the philosophical, metaphysical standpoint of the investigator.

(Mannheim 1952:176)

He rather over-optimistically stated:

That carefree, self-assured epoch of positivism in which it was possible to assume that one could ascertain 'facts' without qualification is now over.

(Mannheim 1952:173)

According to Habermas this emphasis on methods which were about inquiry into the meaning of facts, meant that questions about the meaning of knowledge were replaced by these questions into the meaning of facts. Yet the frame of reference of an investigation had to be examined, as it was in the end arbitrary. Because positivist thinking precluded any approaches other than the methodological analysis of scientific procedures, and because a knowing subject was no longer the point of reference, this meant that epistemology was 'flattened out to methodology', losing sight of questions to do with the framing of research projects and the meaning of knowledge (Habermas 1972:68).

Bourdieu was particularly interested in the claim that methods in the social sciences were scientific. He had a much broader view of science than those frequently used techniques and models:

scientific practice never takes the form of an inevitable sequence of miraculous intellectual acts, except in methodology manuals ... [It requires] the long effort ... which little by little leads to the *conversion* of one's whole view of action and the social world that is presupposed by 'observation' of facts that are totally new because they were totally invisible to the previous view ...

(Bourdieu 1990a:16) (emphasis in the original)

Bourdieu's critique queried the validity of what he called 'scientificity' in the social sciences – sociology falling into epistemological errors the natural sciences were no longer prone to, and often adopting uncritically the most naïve signs of scientific legitimacy:

The mania for methodology or the thirst for the latest refinements of componential analysis ... assume the same ostentatious function as recourse to prestigious labels or fascinated attachment to the instruments – questionnaires or computers – most likely to symbolise the specificity of the craft and its scientific quality.

(Bourdieu et al. 1991:70–71)

Bourdieu concluded that so-called scientific research in the social sciences often fell into this category as it did not meet the criteria for what might be regarded as truly scientific. Much sociological positivist research was more to do with scientificity than with empirical rigour and scientific legitimacy (Green 2009). Scientificity was lacking in the painstaking 'construction of the object' whose 'real logic' was not in accordance with a 'socially sanctioned epistemology', but one which had to be continually corrected and reconstructed in its relational and spatial context, with presuppositions and relationships consciously examined. Bourdieu thought that the most important thing was 'constructing the object', which was not done once and for all at the beginning, but continued throughout the research 'through a multitude of small corrections' from different perspectives (Krais 1991:252, 253).

Implications

These definitions of scientific and positivist knowledge have consequences for claims about both the natural and the social sciences. Questions arise about what has standardly been claimed to be scientific and positivist; about what has counted as valid scholarship and about the dichotomies constructed between objectivist and subjectivist approaches. They challenge constructions of the boundaries, standards and objectivities of science, and of the lines drawn between scientific and other forms of scholarship. Broader views of science contest the values held by objectivist scholars that science is value free, neutral and underpinned by quantification. The natural sciences can be said to share more in common with broader views of the social sciences: subjectivist elements are not only seen as acceptable, but sometimes as necessary. Questions about incommensurability between different approaches then become germane to this debate.

Methodologies in the social sciences do not have to be confined to large-scale surveys or statistical data about factors apparently outside human subjectivity and agency, methodologies which, as demonstrated, many in the social sciences have tried to emulate and to claim are scientific. The implications for management scholarship are that it too need not be wedded to research based entirely on quantifiable data derived from structural and other factors which exclude subjectivist influences.

Incommensurability: the natural sciences

Maintaining the dialectic through a separation between objective/subjective, quantitative/qualitative and scientific/non-scientific approaches has reinforced the concept of their being incommensurable. The evidence has shown that this has had fundamental consequences for the framing, legitimation and transmission of scholarship. One of the earliest proponents of the concept 'incommensurability' is Kuhn, who in 1962 wrote that scientific advance was not a steady, incremental process filling in gaps in scientific knowledge; it often arose when researchers used unconventional methods and criteria of scientific inquiry incompatible with established knowledge. A new paradigm would be developed that conflicted with previous scholarship in terms of what would count as an 'admissible problem', the research methodologies used and a 'legitimate problem solution' (Kuhn 1970:6).

In his postscript to the 1970 edition of his book, Kuhn denied that he had said that proponents of incommensurable theories could not communicate. Incommensurability arose when people perceived the same situation differently while employing the same vocabulary. Each side proposing a theory incompatible with the other side's should communicate with and try to convert it, eventually leading to a concession by one or the other in the face of compelling proof. Because reasons for choosing one over another theory might be about values rather than accuracy, it was the scientific community, through persuasion, that could make effective decisions.

One solution would be to reconsider definitions and, in the case of science, the regrouping of objects. However this was insufficient, as there was no 'neutral' language that groups could resort to. Kuhn's suggestion for overcoming such incommensurabilities seems applicable also to the social sciences:

> what the participants in a communication breakdown can do is recognize each other as members of different language communities and then become translators ... to discover the terms and locutions that, used unproblematically within each community, are nevertheless the foci of trouble for inter-group discussions.
>
> (Kuhn 1970:202)

This might help address the problems raised as a result of the different definitions of science and positivism, and the connection between these and the separated, dichotomised scholarship in mainstream representations of Burns and Stalker's book, contingency theory and the subject area generally.

Incommensurability: the social sciences

The concept of incommensurability in the social sciences was stimulated by Burrell and Morgan's construction of their four sociological paradigms, which, they described as incommensurable on ontological, epistemological, methodological and 'human nature' criteria (Burrell and Morgan 1979:1). Their paradigms were based on

> different sets of metatheoretical assumptions about the nature of social science and the nature of society [and] ... founded upon mutually exclusive views of the social world.
>
> (Burrell and Morgan 1979:viii)

Their insistence on incommensurability has been disputed. Burrell, some 17 years later, pointed out that what their book may have succeeded in doing was in focussing on the conflict between the different paradigms, articulating, legitimating and protecting expression of the weaker, non-functionalist paradigms (Burrell 1996). This argument had also been put by Reed (1985), and was supported by Marsden (2005) and Tadajewski (2009), who all claimed that Burrell and Morgan's use of incommensurability was different from Kuhn's in that it served a political function. It is a similar idea to that put forward by Jackson and Carter (1991) in favour of incommensurability, discussed below.

Commensurability: the social sciences

The ideology of commensurability and against dichotomous frameworks has been supported by scholars from various traditions (Green 2009, 2012). One of the fundamental critiques of western philosophy by Derrida (2002b) was its bipolar thinking which looked at concepts and issues as irreconcilable opposites, instead of seeing them as interdependent and subject to each other's influence. Bourdieu (1990b) contested the positioning of epistemological and methodological approaches as incommensurable with each other, a problem he saw as pervading the social sciences. In the academy incommensurability in approaches based exclusively on objectivism or subjectivism were translatable into conceptual and methodological differences: objectivists or structuralists versus phenomenologists or interactionists. Where the first aimed at understanding 'objective relations that were independent of individual minds and wills', phenomenologists and other scholars in that camp were interested in 'what agents actually experienced of interactions and social contacts, and the contributions they made to the mental and practical construction of social realities' (Bourdieu 1990b:34).

Such divisions were invalid and dangerous. Neither approach could provide a sufficient explanation by itself, and these separate types of scholarship led to 'mutilations' in sociological analysis. Bourdieu called these the 'most ruinous' of all oppositions artificially dividing social science. In certain circumstances structural factors were central to what happened in organisational practice to the exclusion of human understanding and action; in others, people's perceptions, thoughts and actions played an important part in the social world. Bourdieu insisted that both were needed for adequate sociological analyses – objective structures could influence and constrain human actions, but people could equally well influence social events. Epistemological approaches in the subjectivist area might appear illusory from an objective standpoint, but they remained 'perfectly certain, *qua* experience' (Bourdieu 1990a:25).

Subjectivist knowledge alone was limited to descriptions of what characterised 'lived' experience of the social world. Objectivist features making the subjectivist experience possible would thereby be excluded. Conversely, objectivism, interested only in regularities independent of human consciousness and will, introduced a discontinuity between theory and practice.

Objectivism, by taking no account of primary experience which was 'both the condition and the product of its objectifying operations', caused a break between objective and experiential meaning and crucially was

> unable to analyse the conditions of the production and functioning of the feel for the social game that makes it possible to take for granted the meaning objectified in institutions.
>
> (Bourdieu 1990a:26, 27)

One had to have both approaches for valid scholarship (Bourdieu 1990a). Both types of knowledge were present in the social world: ontologies where there existed objective structures independent of human consciousness and action; and those dependent on human understanding and enactment, which in turn were dependent on their *habitus* – patterns of understanding and thought constitutive of people's background, world view, and experiences which Bourdieu called 'constructivism' (Bourdieu 1990b:123). This is similar to Bhaskar's critical realism with a dialectic in favour of a totalising and emancipatory scholarship which critiqued monovalent ontologies[3] because they omitted absences, particularly those to do with alterity (Bhaskar 2008).

Incommensurability: organisation/management studies

Scherer (1998), as guest editor of a special issue of *Organization* on incommensurability, defined the concept as needing the following conditions: two radically different systems of orientation in competition with one another concerning the use of language and action, so that definitions and solutions of problems did not allow for any coexistence of these different approaches; and the lack of an accepted system of reference for evaluating these competing perspectives. McKinley and Mone (1998:170) defined incommensurability similarly: 'logically or normatively incompatible systems of thought, and no consensually acknowledged reference system ... for deciding between them'.

There have been differences of opinion as to the desirability of incommensurability in organisation/management studies. Incommensurability has been treated as an epistemological and no less a political football in organisation/management, with arguments both for and against its practice, encompassing strange bedfellows. Incommensurability, as has been demonstrated, has been widespread in mainstream scholarship with respect to representations of *The Management of Innovation* and in the field as a whole. Strong arguments for incommensurability have, on the other hand, also been promoted to protect alternative paradigms from being swallowed up by dominant schools of thought.

Among the strongest proponents of incommensurability from this last perspective are Jackson and Carter, who wanted to maintain incommensurability between sociological paradigms as a defence against the social sciences being taken over by objectivist scholarship (Jackson and Carter

1991). Mindful of the dichotomous positioning of different types of knowledge, what was at risk in any attempt at seeking commensurability between the different paradigms was

> the re-establishment of the dichotomy between science and non-science, determined by a totalitarian scientism which claims the exclusive right to determine what is science.
>
> (Jackson and Carter 1991:111)

In principle, and in an ideal world, they were not against a genuinely unified body of knowledge, but given the strength of scientism, alternative approaches would be subject to the same problems as pluralism: the more powerful paradigm would subsume alternative paradigms (Jackson and Carter 1991). Upholding incommensurability would be emancipatory as it would protect the plurality of scholarship and allow for the development of 'genuine human understanding' (Jackson and Carter 1991:110–111).

This argument was supported by Burrell who warned against the tendency of functionalist orthodoxy to translate problems, concepts and approaches into its own paradigm, in its own terms. Burrell gave the example of 'alienation' as a concept divested of its meaning and political implications (Burrell 1996). Booth (1998:260) saw a move towards commensurability as leading to the 'enshrinement of currently dominant power and value structures'.

Commensurability: organisation/management studies

Commensurability has also been promoted from opposing points of view. Intrinsic factors such as the validity and development of knowledge, and extrinsic factors such as the strength of the discipline and the need to subsume the various approaches into one strong paradigm to be in a better position to acquire resources have been proposed in its support. Pfeffer (1993) and Donaldson (1998) have each been in favour of commensurability for different reasons. Donaldson supported commensurability precisely for the result feared by Jackson and Carter. He urged an integrationist approach with functionalism, of which he was a strong proponent. Commensurability was feasible as, while there might be differences in levels of analysis and methods between different approaches, there was no incommensurability in content. Others, such as Kuhn, could understand different paradigms and if he, 'why cannot the rest of us?' (Donaldson 1998:269).

His attack on those in favour of paradigm incommensurability contained arguments similar to Jackson and Carter's, but from an opposing stance. Incommensurability led to fragmentation in the field as well as to professional incompetence. Paradigm incommensurability was an attack on the foundations of functionalism and led to a dismissal by some of that whole body of work. Donaldson thought those views were political: they reflected permanent class conflict and were a 'continuation of radical critique by other means' (Donaldson 1998:268, 271).

Instead of leading to more tolerant views he saw the 'paradigm concept' as leading to 'narrowness, intolerance and the opposite of education' (Donaldson 1998:269). He urged that the idea of paradigm incommensurability be 'debunked' to allow for the reintegration of organisation theory and strategic management 'through open discussion, democratic decision-making and the assertion of the value of cumulation' (Donaldson 1998:271). This last phrase confirms that for Donaldson integration meant remaining with functionalist and positivist beliefs in the way knowledge was framed, acquired and increased. This is a very different view from other arguments for paradigm commensurability, and is a justification of Jackson and Carter's fears.

Pfeffer was against the concept of incommensurability largely for pragmatic reasons – the strength of the field in academe and particularly its resources risked being lost to other paradigmatically stronger disciplines. Unlike Donaldson, he was not arguing for a particular paradigm, but for the organisation field to strive towards the development of a single, consensual paradigm. Pfeffer had in fact written favourably about the 'large tent' of theoretical perspectives in organisation studies, but saw this as detrimental to the intrinsic development of the discipline and especially to the possibility of gaining extrinsic benefits (Pfeffer 1993:615). His argument differed from Jackson and Carter's in that he saw the threat from another field and not from within the field.

Others from alternative, non-functionalist perspectives supported commensurability for reasons more to do with scholarship than politics. Weaver and Gioia (1994) disputed Burrell and Morgan's and others' claims that meaningful communication was not possible across paradigms. Incommensurability did not necessarily mean incomparability – it depended on the goals. Contradiction was no reason for accepting an impasse in communication across different paradigms. Quite the reverse: contradiction enabled meaningful communication. They gave the example of 'it's a dog' and 'it's not a dog' as statements that could be argued about, unlike two statements where in one case dog meant 'canine' and in the other it meant 'despicable'. Here there was no possibility of contradiction and no possibility of meaningful communication. If paradigms could be seen as contradictory, they were comparable. People's different assumptions and beliefs did not preclude their being able to understand and evaluate them. These authors wanted a consensual form of knowledge, able to be arrived at only if other perspectives were embraced (Weaver and Gioia 1994).

Scherer, while acknowledging Jackson and Carter's position that incommensurability might be necessary to counter the dominance of the functionalist paradigm, nevertheless preferred a continuing dialogue between paradigms. In his view it was not about establishing an external, neutral frame of reference, but about engagement between different participants in conflict (Scherer 1998). Kagan and Phillips suggested that incommensurability should be countered not by a unified paradigm, but through a continual process of activity by 'heterogeneous communities with distinct specialized languages, methods and representational genres' as was typical of scientific communities. They used the metaphor of the Tower of Babel from their interpretation of Pieter Brueghel's painting of it – as an ongoing project, a 'locus of collective activity', rather than it signifying the destruction of a common language (Kagan and Phillips 1998:192).

Echoing Kuhn (1970), they claimed that knowledge and the methods used to produce it were to do with 'communities of discourse and practice embedded within a larger set of social relationships, practices, and belief systems' which could 'usefully be studied and compared with other communities of discourse and practice' (Kagan and Phillips 1998:196). But this is no guarantee that Jackson and Carter's fears would not be realised. Moves to broaden the debate between different paradigms could still result in the overpowering of other paradigms by the dominant functionalist approach, a criticism long made of pluralism (Fox 1971).

For Tourish the social sciences, instead of adhering purely to the positivist and functionalist paradigm, should use a wide range of research methods. Both qualitative and quantitative approaches had their limitations as well as their strengths, and if 'properly utilized', could achieve the furtherance of knowledge. He made the interesting point that the goal of social science should be to provide 'plausible' explanations rather than the definitive hypotheses about causal relationship derived from purely quantitative research (Tourish 2012:185).

Ittner (2014) took this further, stating that causal inferences in the social sciences could never be proved conclusively because of many unverifiable assumptions. The inclusion of qualitative methods could provide rich institutional knowledge and thereby enhance the internal validity of positivist research and its causal connections. Qualitative research in advance of statistical tests could ensure more appropriate selections of statistical methods, improve such models, strengthen their validity, help explain unexpected or insignificant results and be in a better position to suggest further analyses and refinements.

This has been supported by management scholars. Willmott stated that:

> an adequate understanding of the 'compelling' force of structure requires an adequate theory of the dynamics of human agency.
>
> (Willmott 1993:696) (emphasis in the original)

Kakkuri-Knuutila, Lukka and Kuorikoski agreed:

> any adequate theoretical understanding of the society necessarily requires an integration of the subjectivist and objectivist accounts of it.
>
> (Kakkuri-Knuutila et al. 2008:286)

Some management accountants have defended commensurability on the grounds of better scholarship. Luft and Shields (2014) pointed to difficulties in separating objectivist from subjectivist research: objectivist research was linked with sub-jectivist factors in that, as far as accounting was concerned, many phenomena were socially constructed. Moreover, the objective/subjective distinction was a con-tinuum and not a dichotomy, with different degrees of agreement about criteria for evaluating assertions and individual judgements.

Brown and Brignall felt that critical realism might bridge the gap between quantitative and qualitative methods and between their respective theoretical underpinnings: positivism and interpretivism. This was necessary in order better to understand both objective realities and their subjective interpretations (Brown and Brignall 2007). They were however among those who pointed to difficulties in combining different paradigmatic approaches in research. Three possibilities for a unified body of knowledge were that different approaches 'complemented each other; challenged each other; or "talked past" each other', rooted as they were in different philosophical and ontological positions (Brown and Brignall 2007:32).

They were however optimistic about such obstacles being overcome with researchers' self-awareness and reflexivity. Their experience prompted some down-to-earth advice: success for a dual-methodology project meant recognis-ing that the roles of the researcher differed according to whether the research was quantitative or interpretive, and there had to be a balance of power in negotiations between the different research teams with respect to the impor-tance accorded their respective methodologies, irrespective of the status of the institutions they hailed from (Brown and Brignall 2007).

Bromwich and Scapens (2016) in their review article of 25 years of the journal *Management Accounting Research* (*MAR*) described scholarship as divided, each into an

> island of research ... somewhat isolated from the other islands, and tourists from other islands are not warmly welcomed. ... more integration would be desirable ... we could consider how qualitative and quantitative work can support each other.
>
> (Bromwich and Scapens 2016:5)

They recognised the difficulties of such integration from papers in that journal, and suggested exploring multiple research methods and combining knowledge from different subfields in management accounting and from outside disci-plines. Different types of research would encourage the development of more practical knowledge, without needing to compromise the high-quality research required by journal editors (Bromwich and Scapens 2016).

The Management of Innovation is an example of the combination of objectivist and subjectivist factors in content and objects of inquiry (though not in methodology). Burns and Stalker had raised issues concerning formal structures alongside organisational processes and the workings of informal structures often interleaved with the formally constituted ones. While acknowledging the argument made by Carter and Jackson, it is suggested here that commensur-ability would enrich objectivist scholarship. Mainstream scholarship would be more robust in the knowledge produced about organisational processes and problems. Representations of Burns and Stalker's book would provide more knowledge of organisational practices and solutions if they included the more subjectivist elements addressed by Burns and Stalker and other authors. This would be more useful to managers and other practitioners. It would also allow for the possibility of countering the absences in mainstream scholarship of the influence of human agency, and of issues of alterity in the form of employee action, resistance and its influence on managerial strategies and organisational outcomes.

Conclusion

There has been a longstanding and widespread dialectic constructed through dichotomous ontologies, epistemologies and methodologies between objectivist and subjectivist approaches. What has been considered to be scientific has been laid open to more inclusive approaches not necessarily quantitatively based. Arguments by Kuhn (1970), Hanson (1972), Feyerabend (1993) and Bourdieu (1990a, 1990b) suggest that approaches in the natural sciences do not accord with methods traditionally considered scientific. All these weaken the dialectical oppositions constructed between objectivist and subjectivist scholarship.

In the management field, statements in support of objectivist knowledge underpinned by 'scientific' approaches have been challenged. Its methodology has been inadequately modelled on techniques adopted in the natural sciences. The strength and validity of objectivism standing apart from subjectivist factors and methods has been shown to be limited. Subjectivist approaches alone have likewise been viewed as inadequate. The implications for scholarship and practice are discussed in the next chapter through examples of research where different approaches were adopted.

Notes

1 This chapter is based on a paper by Green (2009) (Emerald) and a book chapter (2017) (Edward Elgar). The author would like to thank Emerald and Edward Elgar for copyright permission.
2 Extreme functionalist, particularly positivist views held that knowledge was cumulative and acquired through scientific methods which would add to the total knowledge about the external world (Feyerabend 1993).
3 Monovalent ontologies were the presentation of one set of facts to the exclusion or absenting of others, or the 'sequestration of *existential* questions' (Bhaskar 1993:234) (emphasis in the original).

References

Bhaskar, R. (2008). *Dialectic: The Pulse of Freedom*. London: Routledge.
Booth, C. (1998). Beyond Incommensurability in Strategic Management: A Commentary and an Application. *Organization*, 5 (2), pp. 257–265.

Bourdieu, P. (1990a). *The Logic of Practice*. Trans. R. Nice. Stanford: Stanford University Press.

Bourdieu, P. (1990b). *In Other Words: Essays Towards a Reflexive Sociology*. Trans P. M. Adamson. Cambridge: Polity Press.

Bourdieu, P. (1993). *Sociology in Question*. Trans. R. Nice. London: Sage.

Bourdieu, P., Chamboredon, J.-C. and Passeron, J.-C. (1991). *The Craft of Sociology: Epistemological Preliminaries*. B. Krais, ed., Trans. R. Nice. Berlin: Walter de Gruyter.

Bromwich, M. and Scapens, R. (2016). Management Accounting Research: 25 Years On. *Management Accounting Resesarch*, 31, pp. 1–9.

Brown, R. and Brignall, S. (2007). Reflections on the Use of a Dual-Methodology Research Design to Evaluate Accounting and Management Practice in UK University Central Administrative Services. *Management Accounting Research*, 18 (1), pp. 32–48.

Burrell, G. (1996). Normal Science, Paradigms, Metaphors, Discourses and Genealogies of Analysis. In: S.R. Clegg, C. Hardy and W.R. Nord, eds., *Handbook of Organization Studies*. London: Sage, pp. 642–658.

Burrell, G. and Morgan, G. (1979). *Sociological Paradigms and Organisational Analysis: Elements of the Sociology of Corporate Life*. Aldershot: Ashgate.

Chia, R. (1996). *Organizational Analysis as Deconstructive Practice*. Berlin: Walter de Gruyter.

Derrida, J. (2002b). Semiology and Grammatology: Interview with Julia Kristeva. In: J. Derrida, ed., *Positions*. Trans. A. Bass. 2nd ed. London: Continuum, pp. 17–36.

Donaldson, L. (1998). The Myth of Paradigm Incommensurability in Management Studies: Comments by an Integrationist. *Organization*, 5 (2), pp. 267–272.

Feyerabend, P. (1993). *Against Method*. 3rd ed. London: Verso.

Fox, A. (1971). *A Sociology of Work in Industry*. London: Collier Macmillan.

Green, M. (2005a). Are Management Texts Produced by Authors or by Readers? Representations of a Contingency Theory. *Philosophy of Management*, 5 (1), pp. 85–96.

Green, M. (2005b). The Representation of a Contingency Theory in Organization and Management Studies: Knowledge Management in the Academy. *The Icfaian Journal of Management Research*, 4 (1), pp. 62–73.

Green, M. (2009). The Embedding of Knowledge in the Academy: "Tolerance", Irresponsibility or Other Imperatives? *Social Responsibility Journal*, 5 (2), pp. 165–177.

Green, M. (2012). Objectivism in Organization/Management Knowledge: An Example of Bourdieu's "Mutilation"? *Social Responsibility Journal*, 8 (4), pp. 495–510.

Green, M. (2017). Research Methods in Organization, Management and Management Accounting: An Evaluation of Quantitative and Qualitative Approaches. In: D. Crowther and L.M. Lauesen, eds., *Handbook of Research Methods in Corporate Social Responsibility*. Cheltenham, UK: Edward Elgar Publishing Limited.

Habermas, J. (1972). *Knowledge and Human Interests*. Trans. J.J. Shapiro. London: Heinemann.

Halfpenny, P. (2001). Positivism in the Twentieth Century. In: G. Ritzer and B. Smart, eds., *Handbook of Social Theory*. London: Sage, pp. 371–385.

Hanson, N.R. (1972). *Patterns of Discovery: An Inquiry into the Conceptual Foundations of Science*. Cambridge: At The University Press.

Hatch, M.J. and Yanow, D. (2003). Organization Theory as Interpretive Science. In: H. Tsoukas and C. Knudsen, eds., *The Oxford Handbook of Organization Theory*. Oxford: Oxford University Press, pp. 63–87.

Horkheimer, M. (1937). *Critical Theory*. New York: Herder and Herder.

Ittner, C.D. (2014). Strengthening Causal Inferences in Positivist Field Studies. *Accounting, Organizations and Society*, 39 (7), pp. 545–549.

Jackson, N. and Carter, P. (1991). In Defence of Paradigm Incommensurability. *Organization Studies*, 12 (1), pp. 109–127.

Kagan, W. and Phillips, N. (1998). Building the Tower of Babel: Communities of Practice and Paradigmatic Pluralism in Organization Studies. *Organization*, 5 (2), pp. 191–215.

Kakkuri-Knuuttila, M.-L., Lukka, K. and Kuorikoski, J. (2008). Straddling between paradigms: A naturalistic philosophical case study on interpretive research in management accounting. *Accounting, Organizations and Society*, 33 (2/3), pp. 267–291.

Krais, B. (1991). Meanwhile, I Have Come to Know All the Diseases of Sociological Understanding: An Interview with Pierre Bourdieu (1988). In: P. Bourdieu, J.-C. Chamboredon and J.-C. Passeron, eds., *The Craft of Sociology: Epistemological Preliminaries*. B. Krais, ed. Trans. R. Nice. Berlin: Walter de Gruyter, pp. 247–259.

Kuhn, T.S. (1970). *The Structure of Scientific Revolutions*. 2nd ed. Chicago, IL: Chicago University Press.

Luft, J. and Shields, M.D. (2014). Subjectivity in Developing and Validating Causal Explanations in Positivist Accounting Research. *Accounting, Organizations and Society*, 39 (7), pp. 550–558.

Mannheim, K. (1952). *Essays on the Sociology of Knowledge*. London: Routledge and Kegan Paul Ltd.

Marsden, R. (2005). The Politics of Organizational Analysis. In: C. Grey and H. Willmott, eds., *Critical Management Studies: A Reader*. Oxford: Oxford University Press, pp. 132–164.

McKinley, W. and Mone, M.A. (1998). The Reconstruction of Organization Studies: Wrestling with Incommensurability. *Organization*, 5 (2), pp. 169–189.

Palmer, D. (2006). Taking Stock of the Criteria We Use to Evaluate One Another's Work: *ASQ* 50 Years Out. *Administrative Science Quarterly*, 51 (4), pp. 535–559.

Pfeffer, J. (1993). Barriers to the Advance of Organizational Science: Paradigm Development as a Dependent Variable. *Academy of Management Review*, 18 (4), pp. 599–620.

Reed, M. (1985). *Redirections in Organizational Analysis*. London: Tavistock Publications.

Reiter, S.A. and Williams, P.F. (2002). The Structure and Progressivity of Accounting: The Crisis in the Academy Revisited. *Accounting, Organizations and Society*, 27 (6), pp. 575–607.

Sarbin, T.R. and Kitsuse, J.I. (1994). A Prologue to Constructing the Social. In: T.R. Sarbin and J.I. Kitsuse, eds., *Constructing the Social*. London: Sage, pp. 1–18.

Scherer, A.G. (1998). Pluralism and Incommensurability in Strategic Management and Organization Theory: A Problem in Search of a Solution. *Organization*, 5 (2), pp. 147–168.

Scherer, A.G. (2009). Critical Theory and Its Contribution to Critical Management Studies. In: M. Alvesson, T. Bridgman and H. Willmott, eds., *The Oxford Handbook of Critical Management Studies*. Oxford: Oxford University Press, pp. 29–51.

Tadajewski, M. (2009). The Debate that Won't Die? Incommensurability, Antagonism and Theory Choice. *Organization*, 16 (4), pp. 467–485.

Tourish, D. (2012). 'Evidence Based Management', or 'Evidence Oriented Organizing'? A Critical Realist Perspective. *Organization*, 20 (2), pp. 173–192.

Turner, J.H. (2001). The Origins of Positivism: The Contributions of Auguste Comte and Herbert Spencer. In: G. Ritzer and B. Smart, eds., *Handbook of Social Theory*. London: Sage, pp. 30–42.

Weaver, G.R. and Gioia, D.A. (1994). Paradigms Lost: Incommensurability vs Structurationist Inquiry. *Organization Studies*, 15 (4), pp. 565–590.

Willmott, H. (1993). Breaking the Paradigm Mentality. *Organization Studies*, 14 (5), pp. 681–719.

8 Dialectical oppositions

Introduction[1]

Examples of management accounting research using both objectivist and more diverse methods are examined in more detail, including the knowledge gained from objectivist as compared with more subjectivist approaches, the scientific nature of the research, its objectivity, the neutrality of the researchers and the commensurability or otherwise of the different paradigmatic approaches. Examples of objectivist research in *Accounting, Organizations and Society* (*AOS*) are analysed for the knowledge both presented and absented. These are compared with a more broadly based research paper in terms of the knowledge produced with regard to the implementation of change strategies, also published in *AOS*.

One might have expected objectivist claims to be weaker in research in the social sciences. Yet, as the evidence has shown, this is not the case. There has been a push for scientific credibility through the use of subject matter and research methodologies considered to be scientific and outside the purview of individual subjectivities, both respondents' and researchers'. Donaldson, a prolific and respected writer on contingency theory, contrasted organisational structure with organisational members' consciousness. He asserted that 'the key to the explanation of organizational structure does not lie in the consciousness of the organizational inhabitants'. They did not have freedom of choice in what they did; it was up to managers to choose an appropriate structure based on contingencies such as organisational size, technology and environmental stability. Some employees would not even be in a position to make such decisions as they 'may even be quite unable to comprehend the exact nature of the present organizational structure' (Donaldson 1996:172).

In 2003 Donaldson affirmed that although he did not preclude the decisions of social actors from having an effect, these had little relevance, as what would override their ideas was the 'logic of functionalism'. Decisions would be made according to effectiveness and functionality (Donaldson 2003:44). Such a dichotomy cuts to the heart of theoretical divisions in organisation theory. These differences are thought to have led to a separation of disciplines between organisation and management studies, a distinction some might think ironic, seeing managers no less than organisation theorists need to know about the roles and influence of social actors in organisations and organisational change processes – unless, of course, Donaldson's ideas that social actors have no relevance are upheld. The examples below are taken from management accounting research in *AOS*, as it was in that journal that many writers used Burns and Stalker's ideas as a basis for their research. The research discussed first is by researchers whose approach was to engage in objectivist research and scientific methods, seeking regularities between selected variables.

Simons (1987)

This example of objectivist research based on Burns and Stalker's ideas has already been given. Here Simon's (1987) paper is analysed in more detail. His work has been seen as among

> important research efforts which mobilized contingency principles in the examination of the use of managerial accounting systems and information in a strategic manner.
>
> (Covaleski et al. 1996:7)

Simons, using Burns and Stalker's claim that different organisation structures were appropriate for different environmental conditions, set out to examine the relationship between strategies in firms dealing with environmental contingencies and their control systems in Canada. What Simons did was to identify those companies which were in stable environments and those in more volatile ones. Following various researchers including Snow and Hambrick (1980), Simons used Miles and Snow's (1978) typology of different strategies practised in companies, ranging from those in fairly stable situations (defenders), to those in unstable environments (prospectors). Simons wanted to test Khandwalla's (1972) and Miller and Friesen's (1982) findings from an accounting point of view about the relationship between organisational control systems and strategy. He hypothesised that there would be correlations between control system and strategy, with defenders adopting more formal, mechanistic procedures, and prospector organisations more flexible, organic systems (Simons 1987).

Simons' approach was in line with the objectivist approaches outlined earlier as he investigated accounting control systems and their relationships with organisation strategies in environments of stability and change. Simons examined control systems through the organisations' formal structures. He did not include informal structures in his research, acknowledging that 'excluded (somewhat arbitrarily) from this analysis are informal control mechanisms such as social and cultural control' (Simons 1987:358) (brackets in the original).

Simons' research supports what has been considered to be a scientific methodology. He carried out lengthy semi-structured interviews with senior general managers in order to confirm the strategy classification of the firms, to get ideas for his questionnaire design and to identify differences in the use of controls between prospector and defender firms. Questions were developed after consulting the existing literature in similar areas and after they fitted with the interview data supplied by the senior managers about the control characteristics they considered important. Further checks were carried out for ambiguity and applicability. The questionnaire consisted of 33 questions based on a seven-point Likert-type scale concerning control system rigidities or flexibilities. It was completed by senior managers from 76 firms, and then subjected to a detailed statistical analysis, with supporting arguments for his choice of quantitative techniques from several authors, including Gordon and Miller (1976), Govindarajan and Gupta (1985) and Govindarajan (1984) (Simons 1987).

Such research is in keeping with Chua's (1986) and Panozzo's (1997) descriptions of what has been categorised as scientific research: large scale surveys; empirical evidence through the collection of quantitative data; the testing of generalisable connections; and the use of statistical methods of analysis. The emphasis on organisation systems as the focus of inquiry strengthens objectivist claims that these were matters outside the reach of human agency and subjectivities.

Abernethy and Brownell (1999)

Abernethy and Brownell's (1999) paper is another example of objectivist research. They did not use Burns and Stalker's ideas, but their research, also involving a comparison between organisation systems and outcomes, is relevant to discussions on objectivist research in management accounting scholarship and is an example of popular research which was extensively cited and also published in *AOS*. Their research question, using Simons' (1990) definition of 'interactive', was whether change processes were more successful with interactive uses of budgets. Interactive processes involved a 'continual exchange' between top management and lower levels in the organisation, participation between superiors and subordinates and an ongoing dialogue between organisation members. The authors claimed that the research was important because of problems with change processes, as managers might have to make complex and unpredictable decisions, and employees might find themselves in a situation of uncertainty and ambiguity (Abernethy and Brownell 1999:191).

Their paper was similar to Simons' in their choice of senior managers exclusively as respondents. Abernethy and Brownell's methodology consisted of written questionnaires sent to the chief executive officers and financial and medical directors of the large Australian public hospitals they were studying. The respondents were asked to indicate the extent of their agreement with four statements relating to budget behaviour on a seven-point Likert-type scale. This was followed by their identifying whether their organisations used an interactive or a diagnostic style of budget in their organisations by choosing between two vignettes describing these different systems of budgeting. To supplement this data Abernethy and Brownell conducted eight semi-structured interviews with CEOs in the field (Abernethy and Brownell 1999).

Like Simons they were careful to justify their research methodology. Their criteria included the homogeneity of their hospital selection; the uniformity in the structures of governance in these hospitals; the triangulation of their data from financial and medical directors; a targeted follow-up of non-respondents; and a comparison between early and late respondents. They too used Miles and Snow's (1978) strategic typology of the continuum from defender to prospector organisations. And like Simons, they took care to assess the validity of the appropriateness of this measure for the hospitals they were researching (Abernethy and Brownell 1999).

Simons' research: implications

Simons had set out to examine whether there was a link between firms in different environmental conditions and different control systems. He carried out statistical analyses on the data from these organisations' control systems. Despite its objectivist framework, the research conforms in some aspects to subjectivist criteria, probably unavoidable in any research. Subjectivist influences are evident in the object of inquiry – the decision to limit the research to formal structures; the choice of senior managers as respondents; the omission of employees at lower levels as sources of data; and the content of the questions asked. These affected the type and range of knowledge produced.

Luft and Shields have supported the view that positivist research methods, including the validation of causal explanations, is 'often dependent on subjective judgements and decisions', as are the choices made with respect to theoretical perspectives; which alternatives to include; which questions to ask; which assumptions to make; which explanations to choose and which limitations to report. They, along with the historians of science discussed in the previous chapter, asserted that empirical inquiry in the natural sciences was subjective. A theory was legitimated provisionally until a better theory came along. Such legitimation was based partly on tradition and partly on intuition (Luft and Shields 2014:550). Bourdieu, too, thought that there was no such thing as a neutral question, particularly if the researcher did not subject her own questioning to sociological scrutiny (Bourdieu et al. 1991). Luft and Shields describe how researchers' judgements are made subjective through the elimination of alternatives:

> by developing their preferred causal explanations in such a way as to limit the number of alternatives against which evidence needs to be provided.
>
> (Luft and Shields 2014:550)

Simons was scrupulous on many counts to do with his selection and identification of suitable organisations and the research methods and statistical techniques employed. He also made clear what the limitations of his study were in terms of the questions asked, his sources of information and the aims of his research. One must accept that his findings, according to his own criteria, were legitimate, valuable and useful particularly to managers contemplating change in changing environments. However, one might query his choice of respondents, or at least suggest that it was a subjective choice, and that his restricted sample might preclude knowledge about organisational issues emphasised by more applied management theorists.

What Simons gained from interviewing and questioning senior managers was likely to be limited to their perceptions about their organisations' control systems. This knowledge may have differed in important respects from the views of others in these organisations.[2] If we assume that Simons' respondents were giving accurate information about what they thought their organisations' control systems were (that is if they were telling the truth – in itself potentially problematic) we still cannot rely on the control systems being just as described in the interviews and survey responses. The restriction of interviewees to those in senior manager roles was likely to lack precise or adequate information at the very least about subordinates' attitudes to, and potential influence on, these control systems. To get a fuller and possibly more accurate picture, Simons would have had to interview subordinates at different levels of the organisations he investigated.

Research has been done showing differences between what senior management assumes is the organisation system present throughout the organisation and what is in fact the case. Preston's (1986) paper (also published in *AOS*) is one such example. He found a lack of information–processing between the managing director and production manager on the one hand, and the more subordinate factory managers who had developed their own informal communication systems on the other. This led to possibilities for conflicting information and inaccuracies, and different constructions of a situation. Preston claimed that there were many examples in the literature of limitations in communication through formal systems, and that organisations might be better served if informal systems were also taken into account. More relevant and useful knowledge would be produced if the influence of informal groups was included in mainstream scholarship about organisations, not least in relation to the management of change.

It is also problematic if a small number or only one manager is interviewed from each organisation. According to Van der Stede et al. (2005), if surveys focussing on organisation–level issues used very few respondents from each organisation this weakened the strength of the scholarship, as one individual could not represent everyone. Exclusive reliance on unverified self-reports might be vulnerable to bias:

> subjective measures of performance are likely to be less reliable as measures of higher-level performance ... especially when they are obtained from only one respondent who is ... far removed from it.
>
> (Van der Stede et al. 2005:676)

Otley, in his survey of contingency-based research, raised a similar problem – that of relying on managers for both information about the system which they themselves may have designed, and for information about its effectiveness (Otley 2016).[3]

The information obtained by Simons was limited in that the questions themselves were general and could not elicit specific information about the organisations investigated. Respondents were required to identify to what extent each control mechanism suggested by Simons was relevant to them on a scale of one to seven. As an example, one of the questions required respondents to estimate to what extent 'Internal audit groups in checking financial information systems and reports' were used in their organisation (Simons 1987:373). As with questions in many surveys, this meant that respondents' understandings of their organisations had to fit into pre-determined questions. Although Simons had conducted semi-structured interviews to help design his questionnaire, there may have been factors individual to these organisations which would not have been picked up by those questions. This is an example of the researcher forming, framing and delimiting knowledge (Chia 1996).

Establishing causal relationships through empirical surveys had limitations. In contrast to natural phenomena, organisations were 'human creations headed by people (managers, say) with the *capacity and authority to make changes*' (Van der Stede (2013:568) (emphasis in the original). There are people at every level in organisations who may have the intention and capability if not the authority, to facilitate, modify or obstruct managerial policies. The difficulties in implementing managerial change strategies have been well documented. One need only go to Burns and Stalker's book to see this. But Simons had acknowledged that his research was not designed to find out what happened in practice. As mentioned, he stated in a footnote that he had assumed that when certain organisational attributes were beneficial to the success of companies, the use of these attributes would be more prevalent. His research was not aimed at seeing 'potential differences between reported control systems and those actually in use' (Simons 1987:398, fn.2).

Abernethy and Brownell's research: implications

Abernethy and Brownell's (1999) methodology, like Simons', can be said to be subjective in their choice of respondents. Abernethy and Brownell had set out to examine whether interactive use of budgets enhanced performance. The interactions were between senior management and employees at different levels of the organisation. Yet their research was based on information solely from the perceptions of the CEOs, and similar (and possibly more critical) questions arise as with Simons' choice of respondents. The authors acknowledged problems raised in the literature about objectivity resulting from respondents' self-ratings, but they justified their choice on the grounds that the CEO was the 'key agent of strategic change' and that therefore the 'relevant theoretical construct for the style of budget use is that style, or role for budgets, intended by the CEO' (Abernethy and Brownell 1999:195). They felt confident to judge whether budgeting had been used interactively and the performance of the organisation enhanced.

In Abernethy and Brownell's research, as in Simons', the questions asked were general and the answers were also mapped on a seven-point scale. Their research was designed to collect data estimating the performance of organisations ranging from 'below average' relative to other hospitals of a similar size, to 'above average' (Abernethy and Brownell 1999:197). The first of the four questions was, 'I often use budgeting information as a means of questioning and debating the ongoing decisions and actions of department/clinical managers.' Respondents had to indicate on the scale the extent of their agreement (Abernethy and Brownell 1999:202).

Their methods, like Simons', were unlikely to achieve an in-depth analysis of the organisations studied, as detailed information about individual organisations and their strategies and practices could not be obtained through these research methods. The use of two short case studies representing diagnostic and interactive uses of budgeting, between which respondents were asked to choose in order to identify their organisations' preferred systems, also could not provide much actual information about those organisations.

In the section on limitations and directions for future research, Abernethy and Brownell suggest a more complex model incorporating the antecedent conditions of clarity of the objectives and knowledge of the means/end relationship. The role of non-accounting controls in strategic change might also be studied in future. Other methodological improvements concerned measurement (Abernethy and Brownell 1999). However, as in Simons' 1987 and 1990 papers, there was no suggestion of the need to interview people at diverse and lower levels of organisations. Evaluating the success of an interactive approach, however, might well be enhanced by examining the success of the interactivity from the standpoint of those more subordinate participating in the project.

Just as Simons' 1987 and 1995 papers have been cited extensively, so too has Abernethy and Brownell's, principally because of their research into interactive systems, for which Simons (1995) had developed a typology (Davila et al. 2009). Abernethy and Brownell's 1999 paper has been cited many times in *AOS*, for example by Marginson and Ogden (2005), Naranjo-Gil and Hartmann (2007), Cadez and Guilding (2008), Chapman and Kihn (2009) (who included in their research method the questions developed by Abernethy and Brownell on interactive budgeting, with a similar target sample of senior managers), Davila et al. (2009), Adler and Chen (2011) and Fauré and Rouleau (2011).

Dissenting voices: organisation/management

As already shown, there have been critiques of objectivist methods and not least implicitly through examples of subjectivist, multi-paradigmatic research relating to actual organisational processes in organisations in the UK and the US. In the 1970s, organisation theorists influenced by sociologists at the University of Chicago, stated that

one cannot fully comprehend organizational dynamics unless one under-
stands the importance of local interpretive structures and ritualized
practices.

(Barley et al. 1988:31)

A few years later Van de Ven and Poole (1988), in a chapter in a book edited by
Quinn and Cameron on change in organisation and management, advocated the
interrelationship of social structure with individual action (Berlinger 1990).

Stern and Barley (1996), echoing Bourdieu's et al. (1991:75) concept of
scientificity, had harsh criticisms of the scientific methodologies used in
organisation studies. They advocated a broader concept of the scientific
method, closer to the *ASQ* editors, Litchfield and Thompson's (1956) notions.
Current scientific approaches to organisation theory had taken a narrower
focus even than what had been done in the natural sciences. Where they might
have used observational or descriptive models as was done in geology,
astronomy or organismic biology, instead statistical models rooted in experimentation were used (Stern and Barley 1996).

Chia questioned analyses of organisations which assumed that their ontological status was static, structured, discrete and concrete, as opposed to being
about actions, interactions and relationships. Making an organisation the object
of analysis while ignoring processes of organising, implied a 'forgetting'. This
forgetting was achieved first by speculating about how the world might be;
using this to project a particular 'object', then taken up as the legitimate focus
for research. This object was then constructed as an object independent of our
ideas about it. The processes by which the object was identified in the first
place were forgotten and a fallacious logic was created whereby scholars
assumed their objects of analysis to be existing 'out there' independent of any
construction they might have created (Chia 1997:692).

The type of research carried out by more applied scholars such as those
included in *Harvard Business Review Must Reads on Change* was largely lacking.
Although Hemp and Stewart (2011) one of the pairs of authors selected for
that publication also interviewed only the chief executive of IBM, Sam
Palmisano, the questions they asked were wide-ranging and educative regarding change management. These contained questions about the translation of
mission statements into operational strategies; cultural values; the effects of
change on employees; the main points of conflict; the seeking of employee
opinion and how this was acted upon. The information obtained, though less
'academic' in terms of theory and methodology, was probably of more
practical value with respect to actual issues and problems.

Examples of more pluralistic methods such as the research techniques in
Dickson's et al. study were inclusive of employees at different levels in their
organisations. They used a method of case study research which included
semi-structured interviews at different levels of the firms. This served 'to
highlight both the consistencies and inconsistencies between the various
actors, and so provide a richer and more realistic story' (Dickson et al.

2013:143). Another example of a wide-ranging methodology was research done by Hendry et al. (2013), who studied ten companies' strategies in skills acquisition. They conducted an average of 40 interviews; spent periods of 'real-time' observation; and looked at company documents and reports. They conducted fewer interviews in another ten firms, but with employees across the board – from directors, training managers to shop stewards and shop floor employees (Hendry et al. 2013).

Dissenting voices: management accounting

Criticisms by management accounting scholars levelled at research methods in contingency studies have continued. Otley more recently with Merchant pointed to the insufficiencies of purely 'positivist' contingency theory research. They were not convinced that contingency research would ever be able to provide 'positivistic prescriptions that are stable across time and national and organizational culture' (Merchant and Otley 2007:788). It was not surprising that former studies involving people might be difficult to replicate. These, far more than natural matter, were individual, unpredictable, with potentially different understandings of their situations and, depending on their degree of power, often self-directing (Merchant and Otley 2007). Otley recommended a combination with qualitative research which could define and interpret problems analysed quantitatively by researchers (Bromwich and Scapens 2016).

One editor of the influential US journal *The Accounting Review* had as early as the 1960s been keen for accountants to use approaches from other disciplines. He was eclectic in that he advocated the 'more sophisticated techniques of mathematical analysis' used for business problems to enable accountants to improve their performance. But he also wanted accountants to take into account the behavioural effects of the use of models. He was interested in historical analysis, as an academic journal should take 'the long view' so as to put 'many contemporary problems in a more understandable light' (Vance 1966:49).

With regard specifically to Simons' later research and Abernethy and Brownell's 1999 paper, Wouters and Wilderom advocated complementary research to these authors', for example through the use of employees at lower levels of the organisation together with more idiographic methods such as semi-structured interviews or observation methods. These might enrich the research, and bring it closer to an understanding of specific employee responses and organisational processes in the organisations studied (Wouters and Wilderom 2008).

They cited Abernethy and Brownell (1999) along with Simons (1990, 1991, 1994, 1995) as among researchers who had studied performance-measurement systems from the perspective of top management. Wouters and Wilderom pointed out that there had been little research on middle and lower-level employees' perceptions of performance management systems:

> These well-intentioned, standardized methods carry the danger of insufficiently reflecting the local organizational contexts or the available

experience and unique expertise of employees ... Typically, expert-led
approaches initiated by top-management, are not likely to expend the
effort necessary to build an in-depth understanding of locally-developed
existing reporting practices

(Wouters and Wilderom 2008:494)

There has been some movement in this direction. Hopwood, the founder editor
of *AOS*, claimed that research traditions already established provided a good basis
for accounting to go beyond abstract schemes for organisational change towards
an exploration of actual organisational functioning (Hopwood 2009). Vollmer, in
a review article of a book on management accounting change by Wickramasinghe
and Alawattage (2007), affirmed that management accounting had become a social
science transcending narrower technical and economic aspects of accounting
practice, and defined by a plurality of paradigmatic approaches (Vollmer 2009).

There are examples of research in the management accounting field intended
to bridge the dialectical oppositions traditionally constructed between objectivist
and subjectivist research, as mentioned previously.[4] In a survey of management
accounting research over the last 25 years, Wouters and Wilderom's own work
on performance-measurement systems is an example of action research. It was
both qualitative and quantitative, with the use of mixed methods for a single
organisation, and included interviews, action research, participation in meetings
and archival research over a period of time (Malmi 2016).

Brown and Brignall (2007:39) had also recommended 'complementary'
approaches with respect to accounting issues, encompassing mathematical
techniques for accounting relationships and qualitative research for human
and organisational aspects. Their research employed a triangulated methodology through a dual-method, mixed paradigm approach. Modell (2009) supported mixed methods research, and pointed to a long history of management
accounting research combining quantitative and qualitative methods. Davila
et al. (2009) (cited above) wanted to produce rich research through a cross-
sectional, multi-method, multi-case research design.

Chenhall and Euske (2007)

A paper by Chenhall and Euske (2007) in *AOS* is given here as a more
detailed example of qualitative research that investigated how people perceived
and acted in situations of organisational change. They researched two military
establishments undergoing a change to more managerially oriented cultures,
and used Huy's (2001) schema for different kinds of planned change at
different stages. The context – external pressures, organisational or local
initiatives, the level of structural autonomy of the unit and employees' attitudes
to the changes – were all taken into account. They investigated the implementation of an Activity-Based Cost Management system in these two military
establishments as they changed from military to commercial cultures.

Their research methodology included a diachronic study over a relatively long period of time – from 1993 for one organisation and from 1995 for the second, both continued to 2004. They engaged in direct observation at formal and informal meetings; studied administrative processes; carried out an archival study; engaged in semi-structured interviews; and held discussions with key participants about their research findings and the progress of the change processes. Their aim lay in

> integrating the technical approach to MCS [management control systems] with a behavioral approach that focuses on how individual users respond to MCS facilitated change.
>
> (Chenhall and Euske 2007:608)

Chenhall and Euske adopted a rich approach. In order to understand the technical aspects of change they had to understand the extent to which there was integration between change initiatives and their social context; the relationship between the organisation and changes in its environment; the issues involved in changing the organisation's culture; why certain interventions might be more successful than others; and the actual organisational processes in play (Chenhall and Euske 2007:635, *passim*).

Their research showed that several factors influenced the change process and that different issues arose at different stages of that process. Prominent were social factors: the extent of the listening, discussion and socialising between senior managers, operational managers and junior officers; the engagement or otherwise of the potential users of the new systems; and whether or not there were close, trusting working relationships. Linked to these were attitudes to this culture change. If the people in the field did not see the changes as beneficial, they would implement them only through coercion. Support from senior management was crucial to the success of these changes (Chenhall and Euske 2007).

They studied structural relationships between the central and local levels in the organisations. At certain stages the change process worked better when more autonomy and power was given to people at local levels; at others, close supervision from the centre was more successful. The degree of co-ordination between the different systems in the organisations, including external consultants and in-house managers, was crucial, as was the degree of co-operation between the different actors. Non-standardised work processes complicated matters. So too did people who had been involved in the change process and then moved to other positions. At all times and through all the stages of the change process the timing and pacing of the changes needed to be compatible with the different types of intervention used (Chenhall and Euske 2007).

Chenhall and Euske's research: implications

The knowledge acquired through Chenhall and Euske's research offers an insight into how people at different levels in the organisations they studied understood, responded to and enacted the change initiatives proposed; what the successes and failures were and the reasons for them. The roles played by organisational systems and processes were made visible. Research which combined what Chenhall and Euske called the technical aspects with behavioural ones go some way to meeting Panozzo's criticisms that positive accounting scholars produced knowledge irrelevant for policy makers and practitioners (Panozzo 1997).

Chenhall and Euske's approach in adopting richer research methods provided a picture of structures actually in use and processes by which people negotiated those structures to their own and their organisations' advantage or disadvantage – an outcome Simons did not intend and did not achieve. Their data was more informative about actual social processes and human subjectivities determining the successes and failures of organisational changes in the two establishments.

Their research was soft – there were no surveys and no statistical analyses. This may have constituted a weakness. Where Simons (1987) and Abernethy and Brownell (1999) had surveyed scores of organisations 76 and 63 respectively, Chenhall and Euske researched only two. Chenhall and Euske's research might have been complemented by adding the quantitative-based research analysed above and able to be used for many more organisations. More diverse, multi-paradigmatic research methods might have resulted in a more holistic, more satisfying and more relevant approach epistemologically and for practice.

Conclusion

There is a case for complementary research. The feasibility of a rich methodology in conjunction with a wider survey raises possibilities for commensurability between different research methodologies, and for more inclusive scholarship. Commensurability between different ideologies and approaches might be achieved through problems being framed differently. The rejection of assumptions about employee passivity with predictable and uniform reactions to managerial initiatives could result in developing research questions that are more informative about human agency and its effect on actual organisation processes. Qualitative data acquired regarding these issues, for example from interviews, might then be used to develop a questionnaire, with richer questions put to a more diverse set of respondents at different levels in the organisations studied, possibly at different stages of the change process as did Chenhall and Euske. This could produce more comprehensive knowledge about organisational change and at the same time reach many more organisations, as did Simons' and Abernethy and Brownell's research.

Research into structural change would be more informative if seen not only as the development of new structures implicitly or explicitly by managers, but also as an analysis of the reactions, agency and potential resistance of employees and their effects on organisational outcomes. The argument is not against research into structural issues. Structural aspects are important. For Bourdieu (1990) it was essential to understand the structural aspects of organisations as potential influences and constraints on human agency. A dialectical synthesis between the structural approaches to research such as Simons' and Abernethy and Brownell's and the more subjectivist aspects of Chenhall and Euske's study might overcome criticisms about management research being unrelated and irrelevant to real issues and actual practice on the one hand, and overly subjective on the other.

Notes

1 This chapter is based on chapters by Green (2016) (Emerald), (2017a) (Routledge), (2017b) (Edward Elgar). The author would like to thank Emerald, Routledge and Edward Elgar for copyright permission.
2 Simons wrote a further paper in 1990. He adopted a more in-depth approach (Chapman 1997) in that he studied only two firms and described their control systems in more detail. He did in-depth interviewing, which, however, as in his 1987 paper was focussed on 'top managers' (Simons 1990:132). Thus the limitations identified using only these respondents, continue to apply to this later research.
3 This was contested by Ylinen and Gulkvist (2014). They carried out an empirical study on mechanistic and organic controls based on survey data, and claimed positive correlations between managers' subjective ratings for their subordinates, and objective measures of the latter's performance.
4 The previous chapter included claims by Hopper et al. (2001) that management accounting scholarship had largely veered away from objectivist approaches.

References

Abernethy, M. and Brownell, P. (1999). The Role of Budgets in Organizations Facing Strategic Change: An Exploratory Study. *Accounting, Organizations and Society*, 24 (3), pp. 189–204.

Adler, P.S. and Chen, C.X. (2011). Combining Creativity and Control: Understanding Individual Motivation in Large-Scale Collaborative Activity. *Accounting, Organizations and Society*, 36 (2), pp. 63–85.

Barley, S.R., Meyer, G.W., and Gash, D.C. (1988). Cultures of Culture: Academics, Practitioners and the Pragmatics of Normative Control. *Administrative Science Quarterly*, 33 (1), pp. 24–60.

Berlinger, L.R. (1990). Book Review of Paradox and Transformation: Toward a Theory of Change in Organization and Management by R.E. Quinn and K.S. Cameron. *Administrative Science Quarterly*, 35 (4), pp. 740–744.

Bourdieu, P. (1990). *The Logic of Practice*. Trans. R. Nice. Stanford, CA: Stanford University Press.

Bourdieu, P., Chamboredon, J.-C. and Passeron, J.-C. (1991). *The Craft of Sociology: Epistemological Preliminaries*. B. Krais, ed., Trans. R. Nice. Berlin: Walter de Gruyter.

Bromwich, M. and Scapens, R.W. (2016). Management Accounting Research: 25 Years On. *Management Accounting Research*, 31, pp. 1–9.

Brown, R. and Brignall, S. (2007). Reflections on the Use of a Dual-Methodology Research Design to Evaluate Accounting and Management Practice in UK University Central Administrative Services. *Management Accounting Research*, 18 (1), pp. 32–48.

Cadez, S. and Guilding, C. (2008). An Exploratory Investigation of an Integrated Contingency Model of Strategic Management Accounting. *Accounting, Organizations and Society*, 33 (7/8), pp. 836–863.

Chapman, C.S. (1997). Reflections on a Contingent View of Accounting. *Accounting, Organizations and Society*, 22 (2), pp. 189–205.

Chapman, C.S. and Kihn, L.-A. (2009). Information System Integration, Enabling Control and Performance. *Accounting, Organizations and Society*, 34 (2), pp. 151–169.

Chenhall, R.H. and Euske, K.J. (2007). The Role of Management Control Systems in Planned Organizational Change: An Analysis of Two Organizations. *Accounting, Organizations and Society*, 32 (7/8), pp. 601–637.

Chia, R. (1996). *Organizational Analysis as Deconstructive Practice*. Berlin: Walter de Gruyter.

Chia, R. (1997). *Essai*: Thirty Years On: From Organizational Structures to the Organization of Thought. *Organization Studies*, 18 (4), pp. 685–707.

Chua, W.F. (1986). Radical Developments in Accounting Thought. *The Accounting Review*, lxi (4), October, pp. 601–632.

Covaleski, M.A., Dirsmith, M.W., and Samuel, S. (1996). Managerial Accounting Research: The Contributions of Organizational and Sociological Theories. *Journal of Management Accounting Research*, 8), pp. 1–35.

Davila, A., Foster, G., and Li, M. (2009). Reasons for Management Control Systems Adoption: Insights from Product Development Systems Choice by Early-Stage Entrepreneurial Companies. *Accounting, Organizations and Society*, 34 (3/4), pp. 322–347.

Dickson, L.K., Smith, H. and Smith, S. (2013). Interfirm Collaboration and Innovation: Strategic Alliances or Reluctant Partnerships? In: R. Mansfield, ed., *Frontiers of Management: Research and Practice*. London: Routledge Revivals, pp. 140–160.

Donaldson, L. (1996). The Normal Science of Structural Contingency Theory. In: S.R. Clegg, C. Hardy and W.R. Nord, eds., *Handbook of Organization Studies*. London: Sage, pp. 57–76.

Donaldson, L. (2003). Organization Theory as Positive Science. In: H. Tsoukas and C. Knudsen, eds., *The Oxford Handbook of Organization Theory*. Oxford: Oxford University Press, pp. 39–62.

Fauré, B. and Rouleau, L. (2011). The Strategic Competence of Accountants and Middle Managers in Budget Making. *Accounting, Orgnanizations and Society*, 36 (3), pp. 167–182.

Gordon, L.A. and Miller, D.A. (1976). Contingency Framework for the Design of Accounting Information Systems. *Accounting, Organizations and Society*, 1 (1), pp. 59–69.

Govindarajan, V. (1984). Appropriateness of Accounting Data in Performance Evaluation: An Empirical Examina- Ation of Environmental Uncertainty as an Intervening Variable. *Accounting Organizations and Society*, 9 (2), pp. 125–136.

Govindarajan, V. and Gupta, A.K. (1985). Linking Control Systems to Business Unit Strategy: Impact on Performance. *Accounting Organizations and Society*, 10 (1), pp. 51–66.

Green, M. (2016). Organisational Governance and Accountability: Do We Have Anything to Learn from Studying African Traditional Societies? In: D. Crowther and L.M. Lauesen, eds., *Accountability and Social Responsibility: International Perspectives*. Developments in Corporate Governance and Responsibility, vol. 9. Bingley, UK: Emerald.

Green, M. (2017a). Behaviour in Academe: An Investigation into the Sustainability of Mainstream Scholarship in Management Studies. In: G. Aras and C. Ingley, eds.,

Corporate Behavior and Sustainability: Doing Well by Being Good. Finance, Governance and Sustainability: Challenges to Theory and Practice Series. London: Routledge.

Green, M. (2017b). Research Methods in Organization, Management and Management Accounting: An Evaluation of Quantitative and Qualitative Approaches. In: D. Crowther and L.M. Lauesen, eds., *Handbook of Research Methods in Corporate Social Responsibility*. Cheltenham, UK: Edward Elgar Publishing Limited.

Hemp, P. and Stewart, T.A. (2011). Leading Change When Business Is Good: An Interview with Samuel J. Palmisano. In: *HBR's 10 Must Reads: On Change Management*. Boston, MA: Business Review Press, pp. 35–57.

Hendry, C., Pettigrew, A. and Sparrow, P. (2013). Linking Strategic Change, Competitive Performance and Human Resource Management: Results of a UK Empirical Study. In: R. Mansfield, ed., *Frontiers of Management: Research and Practice*. London: Routledge Revivals, pp. 195–220.

Hopper, T., Otley, D., and Scapens, B. (2001). British Management Accounting Research: Whence and Whither: Opinions and Recollections. *British Accounting Review*, 33 (3), pp. 263–291.

Hopwood, A.G. (2009). Accounting and the Environment. *Accounting, Organizations and Society*, 34 (3/4), pp. 433–439.

Huy, Q.N. (2001). Time, Temporal Capability, and Planned Change. *Academy of Management Review*, 26 (4), pp. 601–623.

Khandwalla, P.N. (1972). The Effect of Different Types of Competition on the Use of Management Controls. *Journal of Accounting Research*, 10 (2), pp. 275–285.

Luft, J. and Shields, M.D. (2014). Subjectivity in Developing and Validating Causal Explanations in Positivist Accounting Research. *Accounting, Organizations and Society*, 39 (7), pp. 550–558.

Malmi, T. (2016). Managerialist Studies in Management Accounting: 19990-2014. *Management Accounting Research*, 31, pp. 31–44.

Marginson, D. and Ogden, S. (2005). Coping with Ambiguity through the Budget: The Positive Budgetary Targets on Managers' Budgeting Behaviours. *Accounting, Organizations and Society*, 30 (5), pp. 435–456.

Merchant, K.A. and Otley, D.T. (2007). A Review of the Literature on Control and Accountability. In: C.S. Chapman, A.G. Hopwood and M.D. Shields, (eds.), *Handbook of Management Accounting Research*. vol. 2. Amsterdam: Elsevier, pp. 785–802.

Miles, R.E. and Snow, C.C. (1978). *Organizational Strategy, Structure, and Process*. New York: McGraw-Hill.

Miller, D. and Friesen, P.H. (1982). Innovation in Conservative and Entrepreneurial Firms. *Strategic Management Journal*, 3 (1), pp. 1–27.

Modell, S. (2009). In Defence of Triangulation: A Critical Realist Approach to Mixed Methods Research in Management Accounting. *Management Accounting Research*, 20 (3), pp. 208–221.

Naranjo-Gil, D. and Hartmann, F. (2007). Management Accounting Systems, Top Management Team Heterogeneity and Strategic Change. *Accounting, Organizations and Society*, 32 (7/8), pp. 735–736.

Otley, D. (2016). The Contingency Theory of Management Accounting and Control: 1980–2014. *Management Accounting Research*, 31, pp. 45–62.

Panozzo, F. (1997). The Making of the Good Academic Accountant. *Accounting, Organizations and Society*, 22 (5), pp. 447–480.

Preston, A.M. (1986). Interactions and Arrangements in the Process of Informing. *Accounting, Organizations and Society*, 11 (6), pp. 521–540.

Simons, R. (1987). Accounting Control Systems and Business Strategy: An Empirical Analysis. *Accounting Organizations and Society*, 12 (4), pp. 357–374.

Simons, R. (1990). The Role of Management Control Systems in Creating Competitive Advantage: New Perspectives. *Accounting, Organizations and Society*, 15 (1/2), pp. 127–143.

Simons, R. (1991). Strategic Orientation and Top Management Attention to Control Systems. *Strategic Management Journal*, 12 (1), pp. 49–62.

Simons, R. (1994). How New Top Managers Use Control Systemsas Levers of Strategic Renewal. *Strategic Management Journal*, 15 (3), pp. 169–189.

Simons, R. (1995). Control in an Age of Empowerment. *Harvard Business Review*, 73 (2), pp. 80–88.

Snow, C.C. and Hambrick, D.C. (1980). Measuring Organizational Strategies: Some Theoretical and Methodological Problems. *Academy of Management Review*, 5 (4), pp. 527–538.

Stern, R.N. and Barley, S.R. (1996). Organizations and Social Systems: Organization Theory's Neglected Mandate. *Administrative Science Quarterly*, 41 (1), pp. 146–162.

Thompson, J.D. (1956). On Building an Administrative Science. *Administrative Science Quarterly*, 1, pp. 102–111.

Van de Ven, A.H. and Poole, M.S. (1988). Paradoxical Requirements for a Theory of Change. In: R.E. Quinn and K.S. Cameron, eds., *Paradox and Transformation: Toward a Theory of Change in Organization and Management*. Cambridge, MA: Ballinger Publishing Company, pp. 19–64.

Van der Stede, W.A. (2013). A Manipulationist View of Causality in Cross-Sectional Survey Research. *Accounting, Organizations and Society*, 39 (7), pp. 567–574.

Van der Stede, W.A., Young, S.M., and Chen, C.X. (2005). Assessing the Quality of Evidence in Empirical Management Accounting Research: The Case of Survey Studies. *Accounting, Organizations and Society*, 30 (7), pp. 655–684.

Vance, L.L. (1966). What the Editor of an Academic Journal Expects from Authors. *The Accounting Review*, 41 (1), pp. 48–51.

Vollmer, H. (2009). Management Accounting as Normal Social Science. *Accounting, Organizations and Society*, 34 (1), pp. 141–150.

Wickramasinghe, D. and Alawattage, C. (2007). *Management Accounting Change: Approaches and Perspectives*. London: Routledge.

Wouters, M. and Wilderom, C. (2008). Developing Performance-Measurement Systems as Enabling Formalization: A Longitudinal Field Study of a Logistics Department. *Accounting, Organizations and Society*, 33 (4/5), pp. 488–516.

Ylinen, M. and Gulkvist, B. (2014). The Effects of Organic and Mechanistic Control in Exploratory and Exploitative Innovations. *Management Accounting Research*, 25 (1), pp. 93–112.

9   Conclusions

Purpose of this study

The purpose of this book was to examine what has counted as legitimate knowledge in the organisation/management area, to define and establish epistemological criteria for the knowledge produced and for the knowledge absented. Comparisons between Burns and Stalker's *The Management of Innovation*, an influential book in the management and management accounting fields and its representations were used as benchmarks against which the types of knowledge produced were evaluated. The extent of the similarities and differences between Burns and Stalker's original text and mainstream representations was investigated in order to see whether there was sufficient reason for this to be an issue about the type of knowledge produced in the organisation/management and management accounting fields.

Three popular and widely used textbooks in business schools were adopted as exemplars for the type of knowledge derived from *The Management of Innovation*. The academic paper most referred to, the paper by Simons (1987), was used as an example of orthodox research based on Burns and Stalker's ideas. Discrepancies between the original text and its mainstream representations were highlighted, as were their implications for the knowledge produced for the academy and for practice.

Similarities and differences

Issues to do with establishing meanings in texts were investigated, to support yet another mediated interpretation of Burns and Stalker's book. Examples were given of discrepancies in interpretations of texts by other writers, principally Kurt Lewin, Adam Smith, Karl Popper and Ludwig Wittgenstein. Various problems with establishing meanings raised by Barthes (1977), Derrida (2002a, 2002b, 2002c) and Eco (1992a, 1992b) were presented. Derrida's solution, which was to go to the text itself and undertake a minute 'explication de texte', was followed (Miller 1976:336).

Eco's (1992b) priority, given to *intentio operis* (the intention of the text rather than that of the author or reader), was adopted in textual analyses of *The*

Management of Innovation and its representations in textbooks and journal articles. Another of Eco's injunctions – the need for an interpretation of the text to be coherent with all the meanings attributed to it - was also useful as a way into the meanings of these various texts.

The problems with representation were, as outlined in Chapter 3, the validity of the data and the researcher's background, context and pressures under which she was working (Sarbin and Kitsuse 1994; Bourdieu 1998). Comparisons were made between journal articles in the organisation/management and management accounting fields with Burns and Stalker's work.

Detailed textual analyses were made of *The Management of Innovation* and some of its textbook representations. Further comparisons were made using Fairclough and Hardy's (1997) critical discourse analysis, Derrida's (1973, 1995, 2002c) concept of binary opposites and Eco's (1992a, 1992b) criteria for representation. A further analysis of the approaches in these two types of text was made using Burrell and Morgan's (1979) construct of sociological paradigms to examine the paradigmatic boundaries of these different texts.

Findings

The main finding and central argument of this book is that mainstream representations of Burns and Stalker's study exemplify objectivist approaches typical of the dominant scholarship in the organisation/management and management accounting fields. The discourse in Burns and Stalker's original text in contrast to the exclusive focus on formal structure and control systems was wider: in terms of the issues raised, the methods by which they were researched, and the concern with political and practical problems facing managers – experienced and acted on by staff at different levels in their organisations as a result of the implementation of managerial change strategies.

Burns and Stalker had identified three independent variables: structural fit with environmental contingency; employee commitment to organisational change; and the capabilities of the chief executive in evaluating and implementing appropriate policies. Mainstream representations had largely focussed on the first variable – structure in relation to environment. The absences in these representations of the human factors addressed by Burns and Stalker through their second and third variables set up a dialectical opposition between these and the structural factors. Epistemologically these were significant omissions in comparison with the fuller and richer knowledge that might have been produced. Practically it probably provided less helpful guidance for managers and other practitioners faced with implementing organisational change. And it ignored the potential power and influence that could be and was wielded by employees in the organisations investigated by Burns and Stalker. Research based on Burns and Stalker's ideas also differed methodologically. The research was in the main objectivist and quantitatively oriented as opposed to the interpretive, qualitative, idiographic work carried out by Burns and Stalker.

Comparisons between the two sets of texts based on the paradigmatic approaches and boundaries in Burrell and Morgan's (1979) construct of sociological paradigms, was additional confirmation of significant differences between them. Where mainstream representations, because of their objectivist approaches were located wholly in the functionalist paradigm, the more interpretive and qualitative analyses in Burns and Stalker's text straddled both the functionalist and the interpretive paradigms, with their location shown to lie largely in the latter. Resistance to critiques of this mainstream research, often by scholars writing in the same journals, encouraged investigation into explanations for the persistence of these differences in representations of Burns and Stalker's book and in management scholarship more widely.

Explanations

Problems raised about representation were about the assumptions and pressures under which researchers were working – their political and social contexts (Bourdieu 1990a, 1990b; Alvesson and Skoldberg 2000), their 'situatedness' (Sarbin and Kitsuse 1994) and *habitus* (Bourdieu 1998). It was therefore decided to investigate the social and political contexts in which mainstream scholars were working, as these might explain why they were producing that particular kind of knowledge. The second part of the book offers explanations for the differences between the original text and these representations. Influences on orthodox scholarship from different sources and at different levels of analysis were examined including more fundamental underpinnings to this scholarship.

The academy

An investigation was first directed to the academy. Several scholars had made the point that journal editors in high-ranking journals such as the *Administrative Science Quarterly* (*ASQ*) required objectivist scholarship with empiricist methodologies, and that this explained contingency theorists and other researchers channelling their research into formats that would meet those requirements (Burrell and Morgan 1979). It was found that the content of what had been written in the *ASQ* was more complex, in that objectivist scholarship coexisted with other, more eclectic subject matter and methodologies, including Marxist analyses and qualitative, interpretive approaches.

Nevertheless claims were made by Palmer (2006), editor of the *ASQ* at the time, that academic journals and the requirements of their journal editors were for positivist and scientific scholarship. It was found that such requirements were strengthened by additional pressures arising from the all-important journal rankings which, it had been claimed, encouraged the homogeneity of mainstream approaches. These, it was suggested, had an impact on representations of Burns and Stalker's ideas, and on scholarship more generally in the organisation/management fields.

Further investigation showed that there were other pressures on scholars to engage in objectivist scholarship in order to fulfil their career ambitions. Departmental heads, particularly in the US, could strengthen their department or acquire more resources by having a strong mono-paradigmatic approach, which usually was functionalist and objectivist. Another major influence for fostering objectivist scholarship was classical economics, considered to be the dominant discipline in the social sciences (Marsden 2005).

But the question had only been partially addressed. Further answers were needed as to why pressures from the academy directed scholars to choose that particular approach, particularly when it had been a subject of serious critique over several decades. There were examples of alternative richer scholarship which was broader epistemologically, of more practical relevance and could have complemented mainstream objectivist approaches.

Interestingly, inconsistencies and contradictions among scholars had spread in the *ASQ* to their conclusions about which approaches were deemed desirable, which scholarship actually found favour with editors in this and other high-status journals, and what the trends were for both objectivist and more pluralist scholarship. This demonstrated the fragility, shifting and contingent nature of interpretations and evaluations in academic journals in these fields. Such differences attracted further investigation into why there were these opposing views, and whether these had any bearing on representations of Burns and Stalker's book. From the 1950s there were pressures on departments from wider afield. Influential bodies including governments wanted scholars to engage in more quantitatively based scholarship in the face of technological competition from the Soviet Union (Maher 2001; Willmott 2011).

Definitions of science

It was suggested that deeper reasons for the dominance of objectivist knowledge were to do with definitions of key terms which legitimated knowledge in the social sciences – the most important being science and scientific method. There was strong support for the application of scientific methods to the social sciences, including to management scholarship. The criteria for scientific work followed the logical positivist cannon that legitimate knowledge had to be objectivist (Reiter and Williams 2002). Thus what was regarded as valid and exclusively legitimate knowledge had been underpinned by a particular definition of science and scientific method.

This claim had been called into question at least from as early as the 1960s. Interpretations of science passionately advocated by Kuhn (1970), Hanson (1972) and Feyerabend (1993) went against logical positivist ideas. Their definitions of science rejected the view that science and scientific method had to be exclusively objectivist, empiricist and quantitatively based. They attributed many features to science that were characteristic of subjectivist approaches, such as the necessity for using qualitative methods in certain circumstances, the openness of scientists to pluralist ideas and to overturning established methods and ways of thinking, the influence of the communities in which scientists worked and the subjective interpretation of their data. It was suggested, therefore, that the appellation 'objectivist', so important to scholarship in the management field, was open to question, given the subjectivist characteristics ascribed to science, and already present in the methods in management research claimed to be objectivist, as discussed in the previous chapter.

Commensurability and incommensurability

Differences in paradigmatic approaches have been played out in management scholarship through concepts of commensurability and incommensurability. Could different approaches be made to work together to achieve complementary knowledge, or was this not possible for epistemological, practical, political or ideological reasons? One of the claims made in this book is that the oppositional dialectic between objectivist and subjectivist knowledge is weakened by the broader definitions of science. This is relevant to the choices made in respect of representations of Burns and Stalker's book, and the general direction of management scholarship and social science research.

Contingency theory as a model and benchmark

Contingency theory has been a benchmark for evaluating scholarship in the organisation/management and management accounting fields more widely over the decades. Those who saw contingency theories as objectivist and dominant were of the opinion that objectivism was still strong in the organisation/management literature (e.g. Drazin and Van de Ven 1985). Those who saw contingency theories as objectivist but as losing their importance extended this more generally to scholarship in the field, concluding that the subject area was becoming more eclectic (e.g. Hopper et al. 2001). The importance and role accorded to structuralist contingency theory in management studies in general – the fact it was the template for contingency theory among many scholars in the UK as well as the US – is potentially a further explanation for objectivist representations of Burns and Stalker's ideas.

The fact that even scholars like Hopper and Powell (1985) who were critical of objectivist approaches were of the view that Burns and Stalker's work was objectivist, was probably the result of this model largely being used for representations of all contingency theories. The generalisation of structuralist contingency theory to all contingency theories may serve as an explanation for an interesting discrepancy in *Accounting, Organizations and Society*. The journal was founded to include pluralist approaches in the interface between organisation processes and management accounting (Hopwood 1976). But when it came to research applications of contingency theory, including Burns and Stalker's work, objectivist scholarship was predominant in that journal too.

Significance for practice

The advantages and limitations of mainstream objectivist scholarship have been considered in relation to practice. Management accounting scholars have claimed that despite the growth in research over recent decades, there has in the main been little interest in, understanding of or influence over practice (Moizer 2009; Baldvinsdottir et al. 2010; Bromwich and Scapens 2016). The requirements for publication in high-ranking journals have played a part in influencing management accounting researchers to choose to work in areas favoured by journal editors, but not necessarily of value to practitioners (Moizer 2009; Baldvinsdottir et al. 2010; Van Helden et al. 2010; Bromwich and Scapens 2016). Yet it has been recognised through research assessment exercises that research to do with solving practical problems and published in professional rather than academic journals can equal or surpass the quality of research published in academic journals (RAE 2008; cited in Van Helden et al. 2010).

Empirically-based management accounting research has often been viewed as stemming from existing research literature rather than originating from practical problems (Baldvinsdottir et al. 2010). Academic research, even when directly about practice, may still not provide clear and practical solutions to problems and therefore not be sufficiently useful for practice (Van Helden et al. 2010). Because of the requirements of the academic discipline, research is in the main produced more for other academic researchers than for practitioners, with the result, as pointed out by Baldvinsdottir et al., and previously by Pfeffer and Sutton (1999), that the research loop is confined to the academic community, with a knowledge gap between 'theories of knowing and knowing what action needs to be taken' (Baldvinsdottir et al. 2010:81).

Argyris reveals what might be an unlikely attitude among some management researchers – their not thinking it important for their work to have practical value. He reported one scholar as saying: 'I really don't worry about implementality' and another as admitting: 'I think if I were honest I would say I am proud that the ideas are not applicable'. Both scholars, when questioned, did in fact acknowledge that it was important for knowledge to have practical relevance. Argyris tries to explain, not defend such attitudes, by pointing out that although it was important for scholars to have the freedom to pursue their interests, they should be accountable when their work 'can be shown to retard the production of knowledge'. To colleagues who maintained that as the present system worked, 'why try to change it', Argyris' response was that while the present system might have some advantages, it would be improved with more effective research. It should also be subject to public testing and to criteria of falsifiability (Argyris 2013:18).

This lack of interest in practical value is evident from the way Burns and Stalker's book was theorised in terms of structure, with the other problems they presented, ignored. Baldvinsdottir et al. (2010) have suggested questions to guide scholars engaged with contingency theory:

Can it assist in identifying potential practical strengths and weaknesses? How can research in management accounting change help practitioners who face the challenge of changing their systems? Can it lead to good predictions of how staff will react to changes? Can it suggest actions that can be taken to improve the likelihood of change being successful?

(Baldvinsdottir et al. 2010:81)

These implied strictures confirm suggestions that much management and management accounting research has been perceived by managers as irrelevant or indifferent to their concerns. It has encouraged an interest by practitioners in popular texts and their fads, which have very little credibility in terms of research rigour (Tourish 2012; Bromwich and Scapens 2016).

Even where research has been more practically oriented, the accessibility of scholarly research to practitioners and its acceptance by them can be problematic. Hopper and Bui (2016) have pointed to consultants' limited knowledge of research and of access to international research journals. Senior managers might shy away from academic ideas which they might see as threatening their interests, or alternatively adopt such ideas without fully understanding their implications (Seal 2010; Tourish 2012). The much more limited time frames of professional managers and their need for immediate and saleable solutions make it even more unlikely that they would prefer more theoretical academic research over their own more directed, experiential and tacit knowledge (Van Helden et al. 2010; Hopper and Bui 2016).

This has been seen as a problem of different epistemic cultures with scientific detachment as against practical involvement, the general and abstract over the particular and contextual, and quantitative over qualitative approaches:

to improve the practical relevance of academic management research ... scholars need to identify and problematize the subtle yet profound cultural differences in epistemic practice that may not only complicate interaction and communication with business practitioners but also hinder collaborative learning in the development of management tools.

(Moisander and Stenfors 2009:240)

One of the cultural differences is the contextual situation of managers needing to deal with 'the unusual, the ad hoc, and the unplanned, where problem boundaries are typically hazy and unstable' and where there is a high risk of uncertainty and ambiguity and the potential for miscalculation, instead of the abstract, idealised research which has so often been the hallmark of management scholarship (Hall 2010:303).

Cynical views about consultants include their dealing more in expert persuasion or rhetoric (Sturdy et al. 2009); following fads from popular texts rather than academic texts (Tourish 2012); engaging with and manipulating ideas for their own interests, taking advantage of new income generated from such ideas without actually incorporating them into the substance of their advice as consultants; and resisting ideas inconsistent with their interests (Whittle 2008).

The general lack of connection between theory and practice potentially has a deleterious effect on practice as well as on mainstream management scholarship. Many scholars, including management accountants have underlined the need for the relevance to practice of organisational research (see e.g. Van der Stede 2014). It has also been acknowledged that practitioners' experience arising from their outsider status can be of value in contributing to organisational knowledge (Sturdy et al. 2009) – an issue outside the scope of this study.

One interpretation

It must be emphasised that this is only one interpretation of representations of *The Management of Innovation* and of what has counted as knowledge in the organisation, management and management accounting fields. It is acknowledged that different interpretations are possible and that different conclusions might be reached. However, the evidence given is considered to provide support for the position adopted. Detailed research showing differences in the texts, the links made with more general theoretical issues in the organisation/ management fields, and particularly with the embeddedness and reconciliation of constructed ontological, epistemological and methodological oppositions constitute the bases for the analysis in this book.

Limitations of the book

One limitation of the book is that wider societal explanations and implications have not been explored. The furthest this analysis has been taken is to demonstrate pressures on the academy from corporations particularly in the US, and from the US government in the face of Soviet technological competition. In the UK, the government's hostility to sociology in the 1980s was shown to have had the unintended consequence of sociologists moving to business and accounting departments and influencing the scholarship produced there. An analysis of the relationship between mainstream scholarship and the concepts and imperatives of broader issues in society, extending to links with capitalism itself, is outside the parameters of this book.

Questions of the relationship between knowledge and power have been limited to an exploration of the dominant knowledge produced in the organisation/management fields, the pressures in the academy, the epistemological preferences for structural factors and data from senior management sources and the consequences of this for the construction of power in organisations and for the knowledge that is passed on. The ideology has been unremittingly managerialist in terms of the organisational knowledge accorded to senior managers, the recourse to them alone by researchers seeking to understand organisational change and the exclusive prerogative given them to design and implement organisational change strategies. The latent power of organisational employees in more subordinate positions has been touched on through comments by scholars and researchers, and particularly by Burns and Stalker themselves. Attention has been given to the fact that such power and its consequences for the success or otherwise of managerial strategies has been largely absented from mainstream knowledge.

Another possible limitation is that only two journals were used as the main sources for the data – *Accounting, Organizations and Society* (*AOS*) and the *Administrative Science Quarterly* (*ASQ*). This has been discussed and a rationale emphasising the importance and relevance of these journals, given. The advantage of making a more in-depth study of fewer journals was that the different scholarly approaches within them could be compared more easily, and the degrees of interaction between scholars employing similar and different approaches more easily seen, including the extent to which critiques were taken up and debated between authors writing in the same journals. Trends in the knowledge produced were also more readily apparent.

It is possible that the picture might have been somewhat different had other journals been investigated, such as *Management Accounting Research* (*MAR*), which, it has been claimed, is more eclectic, multi-disciplinary and multi-paradigmatic. But that journal too had similar limitations on analyses of power and politics, with managerialist and corporate problems favoured over public and employee concerns (Hopper and Bui 2016). In 2010 the editors of *MAR* stated that their aim was to accept research that was different, multi-paradigmatic, which questioned mainstream scholarship and employed mixed methods. This was to buck the trend as they saw it of the 'homogenisation and narrowness which is claimed to be an increasing feature of mainstream accounting research'. They concluded however that the majority of papers published in that journal also probably fitted into the category of dominant management accounting research (Scapens and Bromwich 2010:284).

Scope for further research

There is much scope for further research. There is the need for other texts in these fields and their representations to be examined in detail. Although there have been articles published on this theme, and comparisons drawn with other textbook and journal articles, it is important to compare in detail representations of other influential texts with the originals. If substantially different, as the evidence has shown to be the case in this study, it should encourage a revision of accepted interpretations of such texts in the interests of a fuller and epistemologically more satisfactory and sustainable scholarship. It might even have an influence on what should be considered to be legitimate and desirable scholarship in the future.

Conclusion

Far more than scholarly judgment and practical competence are at issue. The evidence has shown that knowledge is intimately connected with broader societal social, economic and political imperatives in an academic establishment itself governed by personal, career, paradigmatic, discipline and institutional rivalries. What counts as knowledge has been shown to be fragile, and based on a variety of non-scholarly criteria as well as on scholarly ones.

Objectivist scholarship and the construction of an oppositional subjectivist dialectic is contested. Social theorists and philosophers, particularly Derrida and Bourdieu have been cited for their objections to the dialectical oppositions in western thought and in social science scholarship. One of the problems with objectivism, was that it 'introduced a radical discontinuity between theoretical and practical knowledge' (Bourdieu 1990a:26). Both objectivist and subjectivist aspects were essential for knowledge, and the opposition constructed between the two was the most 'fundamental' and the most 'ruinous' (Bourdieu 1990a:25).

Derrida criticised western scholarship for the centrality of binary oppositions, which he called violent hierarchies and which, through his concepts of deconstruction and supplementarity he recommended be overturned in order to bring 'low what was high', disorganise the inherited order and arrive at a new concept (Derrida 2002c:41–42). Bhaskar's work on critical realism contained the argument that the absences created by dialectical oppositions in dominant scholarship were de-emancipatory. A major emphasis in his work was about the 'absenting of absences', and towards a totalising scholarship in which the interdependence of objectivist and subjectivist approaches would be recognised, and appropriate methodologies adopted so that a stronger and emancipatory scholarship could be achieved (Bhaskar 1993:83).

In this book objectivist scholarship is discussed in terms of its ontological, epistemological and methodological implications most specifically in the context of the knowledge produced about change management but generally applicable to the field as a whole. Its political ramifications were discussed in terms of issues of alterity particularly in relation to questions of managerialism, politics, control and resistance.[1] The power of managers through the sometimes implicit assumption that they had the exclusive knowledge, prerogative and capability to plan and effect change has been legitimated in textbooks, academic research and business schools, particularly in the US, and has overridden epistemological and political problems such as the absences in the scholarship of employee voice and agency, and the risks of managerial strategies being modified, resisted, rendered dysfunctional and failing – issues which Burns and Stalker had discussed time and again.

The question arises as to future trends in management scholarship. Tourish (2012) among others is pessimistic about the likelihood of its becoming more inclusive and more critical. He sees the political, institutional and social context and the growth of managerial control leading to an intensification of objectivist research, continuing to give managers' voices priority over others' and reflecting their interests over others'. The recent proliferation of journals including those on open-access were still conforming to current norms in order to gain legitimacy and submissions from researchers (Starbuck 2016). The editors of *MAR*, Scapens and Bromwich, point to the increasing use of journal rankings in a greater number of countries – which, in their opinion, did not bode well for a more open, creative and diverse scholarship (Scapens and Bromwich 2010).

It is interesting to speculate what it would take for the academy to be willing and able to overcome those institutional, political and ideological pressures acting on scholars individually and collectively, and to resolve the dialectical oppositions constructed between objectivist and subjectivist knowledge so embedded in mainstream academic scholarship. Should one envisage management scholarship becoming more inclusive, sustainable and emancipatory only when, or more pessimistically, if, there is deeper and more comprehensive political, social and ideological change on a societal scale?

Note

1 See also Green (2009, 2012, 2017) for further discussions on managerialism.

References

Alvesson, M. and Skoldberg, K. (2000). *Reflexive Methodology: New Vistas for Qualitative Research*. London: Sage.

Argyris, C. (2013). The Discipline of Management and Academic Defensive Routines. In: R. Mansfield, ed., *Frontiers of Management: Research and Practice*. London: Routledge Revivals, pp. 8–20.

Baldvinsdottir, G., Mitchell, R., and Nørreklit, H. (2010). Issues in the Relationship between Theory and Practice in Management Accounting. *Management Accounting Research*, 21 (2), pp. 79–82.

Barthes, R. (1977). *Image Music Text*. Trans S. Heath. London: HarperCollins.

Bhaskar, R. (1993). *Dialectic: The Pulse of Freedom*. London: Verso.

Bourdieu, P. (1990a). *The Logic of Practice*. Trans. R. Nice. Stanford, CA: Stanford University Press.

Bourdieu, P. (1990b). *In Other Words: Essays Towards a Reflexive Sociology*. Trans. M. Adamson. Cambridge: Polity Press.

Bourdieu, P. (1998). *Practical Reason: On the Theory of Action*. Cambridge: Polity Press.

Bromwich, M. and Scapens, R.W. (2016). Management Accounting Research: 25 Years On. *Management Accounting Research*, 31, pp. 1–9.

Burrell, G. and Morgan, G. (1979). *Sociological Paradigms and Organisational Analysis: Elements of the Sociology of Corporate Life*. Aldershot: Ashgate.

Derrida, J. (1973). *Speech and Phenomena*. Trans. D.B. Allison. Evanston, IL: Northwestern University Press.

Derrida, J. (1995). There Is No *One* Narcissism. In: E. Weber, ed., *Points . . . Interviews 1974–1994*. Trans. P. Kamuf, et al.. Stanford, CA: Stanford University Press, pp. 196–215.

Derrida, J. (2002a). Implications: Interview with Henri Ronse. In: J. Derrida, ed., *Positions*. Trans. A. Bass. 2nd ed. London: Continuum, pp. 1–14.

Derrida, J. (2002b). Semiology and Grammatology: Interview with Julia Kristeva. In: J. Derrida, ed., *Positions*. Trans. A. Bass. 2nd ed. London: Continuum, pp. 17–36.

Derrida, J. (2002c). Positions: Interview with Jean-Louis Houdebine and Guy Scarpetta. In: J. Derrida, ed., *Positions*. Trans. A. Bass. 2nd ed. London: Continuum, pp. 37–96.

Drazin, R. and Van de Ven, A.H. (1985). Alternative Forms of Fit in Contingency Theory. *Administrative Science Quarterly*, 30 (4), pp. 514–539.

Eco, U. (1992a). Interpretation and History. In: S. Collini, ed., *Interpretation and Over-interpretation: Umberto Eco with Richard Rorty, Jonathan Culler and Christine Brooke-Rose*. Cambridge: Cambridge University Press, pp. 23–44.

Eco, U. (1992b). Overinterpreting Texts. In: S. Collini, ed., *Interpretation and Over-interpretation: Umberto Eco with Richard Rorty, Jonathan Culler and Christine Brooke-Rose*. Cambridge: Cambridge University Press, pp. 45–66.

Fairclough, N. and Hardy, G. (1997). Management Learning as Discourse. In: J. Burgoyne and M. Reynolds, eds., *Management Learning: Integrating Perspectives in Theory and Practice*. London: Sage, pp. 144–160.

Feyerabend, P. (1993). *Against Method*. 3rd ed. London: Verso.

Green, M. (2009). The Embedding of Knowledge in the Academy: 'Tolerance', Irresponsibility or Other Imperatives? *Social Responsibility Journal*, 5 (2), pp. 165–177.

Green, M. (2012). Objectivism in Organization/Management Knowledge: An Example of Bourdieu's "Mutilation"? *Social Responsibility Journal*, 8 (4), pp. 495–510.

Green, M. (2017). Behaviour in Academe: An Investigation into the Sustainability of Mainstream Scholarship in Management Studies. In: G. Aras and C. Ingley, eds., *Corporate Behavior and Sustainability: Doing Well by Being Good*. Finance, Governance and Sustainability: Challenges to Theory and Practice Series. London: Routledge.

Hall, M. (2010). Accounting and Managerial Work. *Accounting, Organizations and Society*, 35 (3), pp. 301–315.

Hanson, N.R. (1972). *Patterns of Discovery: An Inquiry into the Conceptual Foundations of Science*. Cambridge: At the University Press.

Hopper, T. and Bui, B. (2016). Has Management Accounting Research Been Critical? *Management Accounting Research*, 31, pp. 10–30.

Hopper, T, Otley, D., and Scapens, B. (2001). British Management Accounting Research: Whence and Whither: Opinions and Recollections. *British Accounting Review*, 33 (3), pp. 263–291.

Hopper, T. and Powell, A. (1985). Making Sense of Research into the Organizational and Social Aspects of Management Accounting: A Review of Its Underlying Assumptions. *Journal of Management Studies*, 22 (5), September, pp. 429–465.

Hopwood, A.G. (1976). Editorial: The Path Ahead. *Accounting, Organizations and Society*, 1 (1), pp. 1–4.

Kuhn, T.S. (1970). *The Structure of Scientific Revolutions*. 2nd ed. Chicago, IL: Chicago University Press.

Maher, M.W. (2001). The Evolution of Management Accounting Research in the United States. *British Accounting Review*, 33 (3), pp. 293–305.

Marsden, R. (2005). The Politics of Organizational Analysis. In: C. Grey and H. Willmott, eds., *Critical Management Studies: A Reader*. Oxford: Oxford University Press, pp. 132–164.

Miller, J. H. (1976). Stevens' Rock and Criticism as Cure II. *Georgia Review*, 30 (2), pp. 330–348.

Moisander, J. and Stenfors, S. (2009). Exploring the Edges of Theory-Practice Gap: Epistemic Cultures in Strategy-Tool Development and Use. *Organization*, 16 (2), pp. 227–247.

Moizer, P. (2009). Publishing in Accounting Journals: A Fair Game? *Accounting, Organizations and Society*, 34 (2), pp. 285–304.

Palmer, D. (2006). Taking Stock of the Criteria We Use to Evaluate One Another's Work: *ASQ* 50 Years Out. *Administrative Science Quarterly*, 51 (4), pp. 535–559.

Pfeffer, J. and Sutton, R.I. (1999). Knowing What to Do Is Not Enough: Turning Knowledge into Action. *California Management Review*, 42 (1), pp. 83–108.

RAE (Research Assessment Exercise), (2008). UOA 35, Accounting and Finance.

Reiter, S.A. and Williams, P.F. (2002). The Structure and Progressivity of Accounting Research: The Crisis in the Academy Revisited. *Accounting, Organizations and Society*, 27 (6), pp. 575–607.

Sarbin, T.R. and Kitsuse, J.I. (1994). A Prologue to Constructing the Social. In: T.R. Sarbin and J.I. Kitsuse, eds., *Constructing the Social*. London: Sage, pp. 1–18.

Scapens, R. and Bromwich, M. (2010). Editorial Report: Management Accounting Research: 20 Years On. *Management Accounting Research*, 21 (4), pp. 278–284.

Seal, W. (2010). Managerial Discourse and the Link between Theory and Practice: From ROI to Value-Based Management. *Management Accounting Research*, 21 (2), pp. 95–109.

Simons, R. (1987). Accounting Control Systems and Business Strategy: An Empirical Analysis. *Accounting Organizations and Society*, 12 (4), pp. 357–374.

Starbuck, W.H. (2016). 60th Anniversary Essay: How Journals Could Improve Research Practices in Social Science. *Administrative Science Quarterly*, 61 (2), pp. 165–183.

Sturdy, A.J., Clark, T., Fincham, R., and Handley, K. (2009). Between Innovation and Legitimation-Boundaries and Knowledge Flow in Management Consultancy. *Organization*, 16 (5), pp. 627–653.

Tourish, D. (2012). 'Evidence Based Management' or 'Evidence Oriented Organizing'? A Critical Realist Perspective. *Organization*, 20 (2), pp. 173–192.

Van der Stede, W.A. (2014). A Manipulationist View of Causality in Cross-Sectional Survey Research. *Accounting, Organizations and Society*, 39 (7), pp. 567–574.

Van Helden, G.J., Aardema, H., Ter Bogt, H., and Groot, T.L.C.M. (2010). Knowledge Creation for Practice in Public Sector Management Accounting by Consultants and Academics: Preliminary Findings and Directions for Future Research. *Management Accounting Research*, 21 (2), pp. 83–94.

Whittle, A. (2008). From Flexibility to Work-Life Balance: Exploring the Changing Discourses of Management Consultants. *Organization*, 15 (4), pp. 513–534.

Willmott, H. (2011). Journal List Fetishism and the Perversion of Scholarship: Reactivity and the ABS List. *Organization*, 18 (4), pp. 429–442.

Index

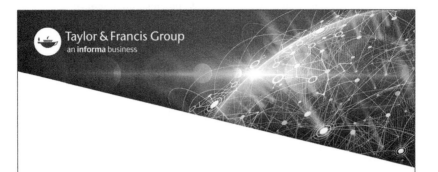

For Product Safety Concerns and Information please contact our EU
representative GPSR@taylorandfrancis.com Taylor & Francis Verlag GmbH,
Kaufingerstraße 24, 80331 München, Germany

Printed and bound by CPI Group (UK) Ltd, Croydon, CR0 4YY
01/05/2025
01858422-0004